CONTENTS

Acknowledgements 5

Clinical contributors 6

Foreword 8

Introduction 10

Principle recommendations 12

1   THE QUALITY OF CARE AND THE
    CAUSATION OF DEATH 15

2   THE CONTRIBUTION OF POSTMORTEM
    EXAMINATIONS TO AUDIT OF
    POSTOPERATIVE DEATHS 21

3   THE REQUIREMENT FOR IMPROVED
    INFORMATION SYSTEMS 23

4   DATA QUALITY AUDIT 25

    Introduction 25

    Method 26

    Results 28

        General remarks 28

        Ability to retrieve notes 28

        Number of notes reviewed 28

        Quality of notes in general
        (CRABEL scores) 28

        Data quality analysis of
        anaesthetic records 29

        Data quality analysis of
        surgical records 30

    Comment 31

5   GENERAL DATA 33

    Introduction 33

    Data collection 34

    General data analysis 35

    Sample data analysis 38

        Reasons for non-return of
        questionnaires 40

        Lost medical records 42

6   GENERAL INFORMATION ABOUT
    ANAESTHESIA AND SURGERY 45

    Introduction 45

    Completion of questionnaires 46

    Hospital and facilities 46

        Critical care facilities 46

    Patient profile 49

        Age and sex 49

        Preoperative status 49

    Admission and operation 50

        Admission category 50

        Admission route 51

        Operation 51

        Delays to operation 52

        Consent for the operation 52

    Staffing 53

        Surgeons 53

        Anaesthetists 54

        Operations by a SHO surgeon or
        anaesthetist 54

    Operative monitoring 56

    Postoperative care 58

        ICU and HDU care 58

    Postoperative complications 59

    Postmortem 59

    Audit 60

6A GENERAL ANAESTHESIA WITH
    REGIONAL ANALGESIA 62

    Type of anaesthesia 62

        General and regional anaesthesia in
        association with dehydration or sepsis 62

        General and regional anaesthesia
        in association with other medical
        disorders 64

CONTENTS

6B AORTIC STENOSIS 66

Aortic stenosis and operative risk 66

Preoperative assessment 67

Operative and postoperative care 68

6C THE ORGANISATION OF PERIOPERATIVE CARE AND THE INVOLVEMENT OF CRITICAL CARE TEAMS 70

Preoperative care 70

Preoperative assessment 70

Preoperative ward based resuscitation 71

The preoperative involvement of critical care teams 72

    Resuscitation 72

    Combined specialty decision-making 73

Postoperative ward based care 73

    The responsibilities of ward based doctors in training 73

    Ward based central venous pressure monitoring 74

7 SURGERY IN GENERAL (excluding malignancy) 77

Introduction 77

Quality of questionnaires 79

Procedures performed 79

Delays 79

Transfer 79

Clinical considerations 79

    Perioperative care and fluid management 79

    Radiological support for an acute surgical unit 80

    Perforated peptic ulceration 81

    Inappropriate operations in surgery 82

    Pancreatitis 82

    Diverticular disease 82

    Upper GI haemorrhage 83

    Use of staples in the presence of intestinal obstruction 83

    Shared care in orthopaedic and urological surgery 84

8 VASCULAR SURGERY 84

Quality of questionnaires 84

Procedures 84

Transfer of patients, delays and cancellations 86

Inappropriate operation 86

    Ruptured aneurysms 86

    Elective aortic surgery 86

    Patients not fit for operation? 87

Lack of supervision 88

Preoperative investigation 88

Infection and MRSA 88

Retroperitoneal haematoma from superficial femoral angioplasty 88

Ruptured abdominal aortic aneurysm 89

    Specialty of surgeon 89

    General surgeons seeking help from vascular surgeons 89

    Ischaemic leg 89

    Coagulopathy, platelets and packing 90

9 MANAGEMENT OF MALIGNANCY 91

Introduction 91

Overview of cancer services 93

    Questionnaire completion 93

    Admission category 93

    Basic cancer data 94

    Multidisciplinary teams 94

    Cancer status of hospital 95

    Guidelines for GPs 95

    Continuing professional development 95

    Nursing 95

    Questionnaire deficiency 95

    Aims of treatment 95

Patients undergoing surgery with palliative intent 96

    Bowel obstruction 96

    Orthopaedic surgery 101

Patients undergoing surgery with curative intent 102

    Distribution of cancers 102

CONTENTS

Rectal and rectosigmoid carcinoma 102

Colon...103

Upper gastrointestinal cancer 105

Gynaecology 106

Urology 107

Head and neck 108

Cardiothoracic surgery 109

Neurosurgery 109

Paediatric surgery 109

Orthopaedic and plastic surgery..............109

Patients undergoing surgery for diagnosis.......110

Patients undergoing surgery where the
aim stated was "Not sure"............................111

Intention of procedure not stated 112

Conclusion...112

9A REVIEW OF HISTOLOGY REPORTS....113

Introduction...113

Type of specimen and anatomic site 113

Tumour origin, size, cell type and
histological grade 114

Adequacy of tumour excision 114

Adequacy of reports...115

Conclusion...115

10 PATHOLOGY 117

Postmortem rate..117

Clinical history...118

Description of external appearances 118

Gross description of internal organs
and operation sites...118

Postmortem histology 119

Summary of lesions, clinicopathological
correlation and ONS cause of death 119

Overall score for postmortem examinations ..120

Attendance of the surgical team at
the postmortem examination 120

Communication of the postmortem result
to the surgical team 121

Comment...121

REFERENCES **123**

APPENDICES **127**

A   Reported deaths by Trust/Hospital Group......127

B   Glossary..137

C   Abbreviations 139

D   NCEPOD corporate structure 140

E   Data collection and review methods..............142

F   Local Reporters..144

G   Participants (anaesthetists) 154

H   Participants (surgeons and gynaecologists) 161

I   NCEPOD exclusions 169

J   Case studies 172

ACKNOWLEDGEMENTS

This is the thirteenth report published by the National Confidential Enquiry into Perioperative Deaths and, as in previous years, could not have been achieved without the support and cooperation of a wide range of individuals and organisations. Our particular thanks go to the following:

● The Local Reporters, whose names are listed in Appendix F, and those who assist them in providing initial data on perioperative deaths.

● All those surgeons and anaesthetists, whose names are listed in Appendices G and H, who contributed to the Enquiry by completing questionnaires.

● The Advisors whose names are listed overleaf.

● Those bodies, whose names are listed in Appendix D, who provide the funding to cover the cost of the Enquiry.

The Steering Group, Clinical Coordinators and Chief Executive would also like to record their appreciation of the hard work of the NCEPOD administrative staff: Peter Allison, Fatima Chowdhury, Paul Coote, Sheree Cornwall, Jennifer Drummond and Dolores Jarman.

The views expressed in this publication are those of NCEPOD and not necessarily those of the National Institute for Clinical Excellence, or any other funding body.

The National Institute for Clinical Excellence is associated with the National Confidential Enquiry into Perioperative Deaths through a funding contract. The Institute considers the work of this organisation to be of value to the NHS in England and Wales and recommends that it be used to inform decisions on service, organisation and delivery.

CLINICAL CONTRIBUTORS

NCEPOD COORDINATORS

K G Callum	Clinical Coordinator, NCEPOD and Consultant General and Vascular Surgeon, Southern Derbyshire Acute Hospitals NHS Trust
A J G Gray	Clinical Coordinator, NCEPOD and Consultant Anaesthetist, Norfolk and Norwich University Hospital NHS Trust
R W Hoile	Principal Clinical Coordinator, NCEPOD and Consultant General Surgeon, Medway NHS Trust
G S Ingram	Principal Clinical Coordinator, NCEPOD and Consultant Anaesthetist, University College London Hospitals NHS Trust
I C Martin	Clinical Coordinator, NCEPOD and Consultant Oral and Maxillofacial Surgeon, City Hospitals Sunderland NHS Trust
K M Sherry	Clinical Coordinator, NCEPOD and Consultant Anaesthetist, Sheffield Teaching Hospitals NHS Trust

SPECIALTY ADVISORS

Anaesthesia

N Barham	South Tees Acute Hospitals NHS Trust
A Dennis	Sheffield Teaching Hospitals NHS Trust
B J M Ferguson	Bro Morgannwg NHS Trust
P Laurie	Oxford Radcliffe Hospitals NHS Trust
K R Milligan	Belfast City Hospital Health & Social Services Trust
J Rickford	East and North Hertfordshire NHS Trust
A C Timmins	Essex Rivers Healthcare NHS Trust
J H Tomlinson	Royal Wolverhampton Hospitals NHS Trust
S M Underwood	United Bristol Healthcare NHS Trust

Surgery

Cardiothoracic surgery

M Jones	South Manchester University Hospitals NHS Trust
S Livesey	Southampton University Hospitals NHS Trust
S A M Nashef	Papworth Hospital NHS Trust

General surgery

A Kingsnorth	Plymouth Hospitals NHS Trust
M Lansdown	Leeds Teaching Hospitals NHS Trust
A Senapati	Portsmouth Hospitals NHS Trust
H G Sturzaker	James Paget Healthcare NHS Trust
H Sweetland	Cardiff and Vale NHS Trust
R W Talbot	Poole Hospital NHS Trust

Gynaecology

J A Latimer	Addenbrooke's NHS Trust
J B Murdoch	United Bristol Healthcare NHS Trust
K S Metcalf	Southampton University Hospitals NHS Trust

Neurosurgery

A J Kellerman	Barking, Havering and Redbridge Hospitals NHS Trust
F Nath	South Tees Acute Hospitals NHS Trust

Ophthalmology

D Verma	Hull and East Yorkshire Hospitals NHS Trust

Oral and maxillofacial surgery

A Stewart	South West London Community Hospital NHS Trust

Orthopaedic surgery

S R Carter	Royal Orthopaedic Hospital NHS Trust
W M Harper	University Hospitals of Leicester NHS Trust
P Hirst	Central Manchester/Manchester Children's University Hospital NHS Trust
C Marx	Ipswich Hospital NHS Trust
A D Patel	Norfolk & Norwich University Hospital NHS Trust
B E Scammell	Queen's Medical Centre Nottingham University Hospital NHS Trust

Otorhinolaryngology

J G Buckley (deceased)	Leeds Teaching Hospitals NHS Trust

Paediatric surgery

D C G Crabbe	Leeds Teaching Hospitals NHS Trust
D Drake	Great Ormond Street Hospital for Children NHS Trust

Plastic surgery

D J Ward	University Hospitals of Leicester NHS Trust

Urology

N W Clarke	Salford Royal Hospitals NHS Trust and Christie Hospital NHS Trust
R D Pocock	Royal Devon & Exeter Healthcare NHS Trust
J E Whiteway	South Tees Acute Hospitals NHS Trust

Vascular surgery

C P Gibbons	Swansea NHS Trust
A R Naylor	University Hospitals of Leicester NHS Trust
S D Parvin	Royal Bournemouth & Christchurch Hospitals NHS Trust
D A Ratliff	Northampton General Hospital NHS Trust

Pathology

M Burke	Royal Brompton & Harefield NHS Trust
N J Carr	Southampton University Hospitals NHS Trust
K P McCarthy	East Gloucestershire NHS Trust
V Suarez	Mid Staffordshire General Hospitals NHS Trust

Oncology and Palliative Care

N G Burnet	Addenbrooke's NHS Trust
A E Champion	Conwy & Denbighshire NHS Trust
R J Hart	St Margaret's Somerset Hospice
J Taylor	Burton Hospitals NHS Trust

FOREWORD

This latest report provides a stark comparison of the changing medical scene over the past decade. It demonstrates that patients being subjected to emergency surgery are both older and sicker than they were ten years ago. In turn, this has a profound impact on the service provision necessary to deal with these clinical problems.

NCEPOD has repeatedly emphasised the need for both Intensive Care and High Dependency facilities to deal satisfactorily with many of the surgical problems of severely ill patients. In 'Extremes of Age'[1] we pointed out the best practice of providing multidisciplinary critical care teams to deal successfully with both the preoperative resuscitation and postoperative care of the elderly surgical emergency. This report not only re-emphasises that point, but also exposes a wider issue of providing an enlarged cadre of both doctors and nurses capable of dealing with the increased demand for management of the severely ill.

It is not only at the ICU/HDU level that provision is needed, but equally on the general wards since these patients will spend but a short time within the higher dependency facilities before being relocated to the main ward areas. The nationwide lack of nurses has had a long term effect on the recruitment of staff trained, particularly in ICU/HDU skills, with patients needing

higher levels of care generally on the one hand, or day stay facilities on the other. The net consequence for most wards is a deficiency in the nursing staff complement to look after these increasingly aged and sick patients. Unfortunately, there is an inevitable disincentive to recruitment of staff to overly busy wards.

Critical care courses developed by the Royal Colleges are over-subscribed with a lack of resources, both human and fiscal, to provide sufficient training programmes to satisfy demand. This swing in the pattern of disease over the last ten years must call into question the balance of bed distribution and the associated staffing, when so frequently higher dependency facilities are needed to provide a successful outcome to surgical interventions. This is further illustrated in the section on management of malignancy, where the volume of emergency admissions is outstripping the Calman-Hine recommendations due to the inadequacy of resources on the ground.

The recent Shipman enquiry demonstrated problems with medical records. There is good evidence in this report to suggest that medical record keeping is falling below acceptable standards, an example being that a third of the patients undergoing laparotomy for non-malignant disease did not apparently have any operation note to accompany the procedure. NCEPOD has been concerned, not only about the apparent paucity of good record keeping, but also about communications generally. Instances where communication failures within surgical and anaesthetic teams have led to inappropriate actions are exposed, as are failures of communication between primary and secondary care practitioners. NCEPOD has long sought means whereby the deaths of patients in the community following discharge after surgery could be recorded. The HES data does not provide a sufficiently robust method for such analysis and there is, therefore, a continuing need for communication and record keeping at all levels to be improved. It is fundamentally a clinical governance issue and should be addressed accordingly. Unfortunately, poor record keeping will inevitably lead to poor completion of NCEPOD questionnaires, which must call into question the validity of some of the data in the Enquiry.

Finally, the continuing low level of postmortem examination rates has to be mentioned, particularly in the light of both the Bristol Royal Infirmary[2] and Royal Liverpool Children's Hospital[3] enquiries. The need for an analysis of patients who should have had such an examination but did not, must form part of a future NCEPOD enquiry.

We are all well aware of the clinical standards which should be achieved, but this report does provide a salutory reminder that achieving those goals demands much greater awareness of the issues at hand and a desire to satisfy the Quality Agenda set out in the NHS Plan.

John Ll Williams
Chairman

INTRODUCTION

NCEPOD has been publishing reports for over eleven years, during which time the emphasis has changed. The perspective of the main report has always been viewed from the position of a patient's death; that, after all, is the basis of our protocol. The main thread that has run through all the reports is perhaps best summed up by Professor Blandy's words in the foreword to a previous report[4] *"Modern surgery and anaesthesia are so safe that when an operation is followed by death, the reason is nearly always because the underlying condition is fatal. The purpose of The National Confidential Enquiry into Perioperative Deaths is to identify remediable factors in anaesthesia and surgery, such as the provision of better facilities or different skills. The enquiry calls for the active co-operation and effort of busy surgeons, anaesthetists and gynaecologists".* Whereas initially the tone of the reports was very critical of anaesthetists and surgeons, this has now changed and the focus is much more on the resourcing, provision and management of services. Sadly, many issues re-occur and, in particular, inappropriate surgery still remains a concern. Whilst clinicians have changed their practice in the light of the findings of this and other enquiries, provision within our health services has often lagged behind. Of course errors will not disappear and it is inevitable that incidents will happen, some of which will result

in death. Often these incidents are the result of errors in system management, inadequate facilities, the pressure of the workload and the need to meet impossible targets. There are examples of all these situations throughout this report.

The report contains several specific sections, which are focused on the following issues: the quality of our data, the management of patients with malignant disease, the role and provision of critical care services, the influence of variations in quality of care on the causation of death and the difficulties faced by NCEPOD as a result of poor hospital information systems. There is also a section on pathology. NCEPOD considers the postmortem examination to be of great value in assisting both the clinician to arrive at an understanding of the cause of death, and the relatives to come to terms with their loss. The role and quality of postmortem examinations is considered in some depth.

There are several interlinked issues concerning the quality of our data. We need to be assured that the data is accurate and that the returns faithfully reflect the contents of the notes and the clinical events. To investigate this, we conducted a limited data quality audit at selected hospitals. There is also a section on the general methodology of NCEPOD and the collection of data. Both these sections raise questions about the impact of medical records systems on clinical care. Our audit suggests that some clinicians are not doing what is expected of them in terms of returning accurate data. This behaviour could result in questions being raised about the validity of our conclusions and recommendations and we would urge these clinicians to be more diligent when returning data. The organisation of medical records and the recording of information within them are one of the building blocks of our medical system. There is clear evidence that the clinicians' job (and ability to comply with an increasing demand for audit data) is being made more difficult by the poor organisation of medical records, difficulties with the retrieval of information and the lack of nationally compatible record systems. Problems with medical records have a considerable impact on clinical care and education. Information may well be recorded but, if this information about patient care is not readily accessible, clinicians will experience time consuming difficulties in the retrieval and application of the information.

Recent years have seen the introduction of proposals for the organisation and provision of services for patients suffering with malignancy. We have analysed answers to specific questions concerning the management of such patients. In the year of the study (1999-2000) there appeared to be a lack of uniformity of provision of care.

Critical care services are pivotal to the survival of many patients with life-threatening illnesses and the influence of the availability (or otherwise) of these services is again explored in this year's report. Despite assurances to the contrary, there remains concern amongst clinicians that there is still a deficiency in the provision of critical care services[5, 6].

The causes underlying the death of a patient following anaesthesia and surgery are multifactorial. The past few years have been marked by frenzied criticism of medical professionals and an intense focus on adverse events. These criticisms, whether from the media, politicians, health service managers or fellow clinicians, have often implied that there was wilful negligence by clinicians. But the practice of medicine (with anaesthesia and surgery particularly in mind) is not an exact science, it involves humans and humans err[7]. There needs to be an acceptance that doctors and nurses are not infallible and that they do make mistakes. We have attempted to tease out the various factors that contribute to managing a successful outcome for the patient. When things go wrong it is then possible to ask the question 'Who is to blame?' However this question is based on a culture which we should be leaving behind. The answer will rarely be simple and is likely to be multifactorial. Given the focus on

doctors and their mistakes referred to above, clinicians should find this reassuring.

An adverse event may be defined as 'an unintended injury or complication which results in disability, death or prolongation of hospital stay, and is caused by health care management rather than the patient's disease[8]. From our viewpoint, there will be few deaths that fall into this definition. A recently published study from two London hospitals has also shown a low incidence of death after an adverse event[9]. However, there are a few cases where we feel that care falls below accepted practice i.e. below a 'current level of expected performance for the average practitioner or system that manages the condition in question[7]. The key words here are 'unintended' and 'system'. It must be remembered that clinicians do not set out to deliberately do harm and that the primary disease process and comorbidities are often too severe and advanced to allow for a successful outcome. Similarly, if the system within which the clinician works is defective then adverse events are inevitable. We believe that NCEPOD, supported by clinicians, has an established credibility and that the lessons learnt from the analysis of perioperative deaths should be applied to help prevent future incidents. Part of the remedy is in changing systems of practice and creating safeguards wherever possible. The remedy is in design[10, 11, 12]. The comprehensive application of recommendations emanating from NCEPOD publications over the years would contribute greatly to preventing errors of management due to failure to follow accepted practice, whether this is at an individual or system/organisational level.

Rather than asking 'Who is to blame?' we should focus on the remedial actions needed to produce a major improvement in the quality of care and ask 'Whose problem is it?' The reader may find pointers to the answer within this report.

Ron Hoile and Stuart Ingram
Principal Clinical Coordinators

PRINCIPAL RECOMMENDATIONS 2001

- Surgeons and anaesthetists should partake in **multidisciplinary audit,** specialists meeting together to discuss improvements in care. These meetings should concentrate less on asking 'Who is to blame?' and more on changing systems of practice to safeguard patients wherever possible (page 61).

- All Trusts in the NHS should use **information systems** with a nationally agreed specification. This should apply to case notes, patient information systems etc. Such uniform systems would facilitate the retrieval of standardised information and ease the introduction of the Electronic Patient Record (page 23).

- There is a gap in the levels of medical and nursing expertise between ICU/HDU services and ward based care. In particular, there is a need to increase the skills of nurses and doctors on the wards in **central venous**

pressure (CVP) management and interpretation. This deficiency should be addressed. There ought to be sufficient ward equipment with transducer pressure monitoring facilities to allow accurate and continuous CVP monitoring. More national and local training programmes are required to provide education in the appropriate skills required to apply these techniques in ward areas (page 75).

● The service provision for **cancer patients**, presenting either as an emergency or urgently, requires review. The current system is failing patients, despite the best efforts of clinical staff. Most patients with cancer who die within 30 days of an operation are admitted as an emergency or urgently and many are not referred either to a surgeon with a sub-specialised oncology interest, a multidisciplinary team, medical oncologist or specialist cancer nurse when it is indicated. Clinical networks and local guidelines should be constructed in order to ensure that all patients with cancer receive an early and appropriate referral to specialists (page 112).

● **Clinicians, pathologists and coroners** should review their working relations and means of communication. The aim must be to improve the quality and timeliness of information provided, in order to inform the understanding of events surrounding a perioperative death (page 121).

● There needs to be an education programme to re-establish public confidence in pathology services and the **postmortem examination** as a vital tool with which to investigate a postoperative death (page 121).

THE QUALITY OF CARE AND THE CAUSATION OF DEATH

Death taking place in hospital within 30 days of a surgical operation is generally the consequence of a number of interrelated factors. This is very clearly seen by NCEPOD coordinators and advisors as they examine the questionnaires and other information for the many hundreds of deaths that make up each year's sample. Within these interrelated factors that contributed to the death of a patient will be some that are avoidable and some that are unavoidable. It is the responsibility of NCEPOD to identify the avoidable or remediable factors and then make recommendations as to how they might be eliminated. With quantifiable issues, for example organisational arrangements or the provision of facilities such as critical care beds, this is relatively straightforward but when it is an issue that is subject to judgement, for example the actions and behaviour of medical staff, then those judgements need to be carefully considered. NCEPOD only examines those patients who died and does not consider those who did well. In addition, we have the advantage of hindsight, and both these factors can cause bias unless we guard carefully against them. Yet much of the recent criticism of doctors has come from those outside of the profession who also have the advantage of hindsight and are invariably looking at aspects of care that did not go well for the patient. Often the judgements made appear simplistic to those who have a fuller understanding of all the factors that were involved.

Collected here are a number of cases from the current NCEPOD sample that in some way illustrate the interlinking of factors that contribute to death and the arbitrary way in which blame can sometimes fall on a single individual who may themselves be unaware of the consequences of their actions. If there is a conclusion to be drawn then it must be that only through examining the issues relating to individual cases can we begin to understand the relative importance of the many factors involved. For surgeons and anaesthetists this should be through multidisciplinary audit; specialists meeting together to improve care, recognising and wishing to overcome one's own shortcomings and limitations and not just blaming others. For patients, relatives and the public in general, it is the development of an understanding of modern healthcare, and particularly surgery and anaesthesia, based on the realities and not the fictional dramas of the mass media.

Case Study 1

An elderly man was admitted with a fractured neck of femur following a fall. He was a Jehovah's Witness and made clear that he would not accept a blood transfusion, signing forms to this effect. The consultant anaesthetist responsible for his care completed a detailed free text entry in the questionnaire returned to NCEPOD. This together with the postoperative notes from the intensive care unit gives a very clear description of the patient's medical management.

The anaesthetist and the theatre staff were concerned about the competence of the designated orthopaedic surgeon - a long term locum staff grade doctor - to undertake the operation on this patient. The theatre sister contacted two consultant orthopaedic surgeons to express these concerns prior to the operation, but they did not apparently feel the need to intervene.

The operation lasted nearly two hours and the measured blood loss was 1500 ml. The patient was moved to recovery and initially awoke and was orientated with stable vital signs. However, he then began to deteriorate with significant bleeding from the wound. He was transferred to the ICU where his haemoglobin which had been 12.5 gm/dl prior to the operation, was now measured as 4.9 gm/dl. The patient continued to develop progressive hypotension despite ventilation, fluids and adrenaline. He eventually died ten-and-a-half-hours after the end of the operation. At autopsy, the left anterior descending coronary artery was 70% stenosed by atheroma and the right coronary artery showed 50% stenosis by atheroma. The pathologist gave the disease or condition leading to death as congestive cardiac failure due to or as a consequence of coronary artery atheroma. Anaemia secondary to osteoporotic fractured neck of femur (operated) was listed as a significant condition contributing to the death but not related to the condition causing it.

The orthopaedic surgeons did not return the questionnaire sent to them by NCEPOD.

Can we take the pathologist as the final arbiter and accept that the coronary artery atheroma was the primary cause of this patient's death? Alternatively, should we read between the lines of the anaesthetist's comments and accept that this death was avoidable if a more competent surgeon had carried out the operation? Or is the death the consequence of the patient's own choice in being a Jehovah's Witness, refusing blood transfusion and then suffering a significant traumatic injury?

Case Study 2

An 86-year-old woman was admitted in the late evening from the A&E Department under the care of a locum consultant surgeon. The admission note records that she had had a lump in the left groin for a year and during the previous three weeks she had been unwell with vomiting. However, her general health was good and she lived independently. On examination she was severely dehydrated, she had abdominal pain with vomiting and a long-standing uterine prolapse. Although the presumptive diagnosis was an incarcerated left femoral hernia, no decision was made to operate but further investigations were requested. It was stated that the patient needed an HDU bed. However, for some reason she stayed for resuscitation on the general ward.

At 01.00 the ICU SpR visited the patient and examined her. The note made at the time recommends hourly CVP and urine output measurement but it was felt that she did not warrant ICU admission at that time. At the ward round the following morning it was recorded that the patient had had no urine output since admission but no medical staff had been made aware by the ward staff of her overnight anuria. At 10.00 the patient was transferred to the ICU but despite aggressive

resuscitation with fluids she continued to deteriorate and required intubation and ventilation. A review at 12.30 notes that she was now on adrenaline and dopamine, peripherally shut down with a distended abdomen and a base deficit of -16.5 mmol/l. Following discussion, it was agreed that although the prognosis was very poor, it was necessary to proceed to an emergency laparotomy. At the operation, which was carried out by another consultant, the peritoneal cavity was found to be full of faecal fluid and that a large part of the bowel was ischaemic. The wound was closed. She was returned to the ICU and made comfortable. She died at 17.48.

Would the findings at operation have been different if she had gone to theatre soon after admission rather than 14 hours later? Would the resuscitation have been more effective if she had gone to ICU overnight rather than being on a ward where her continued anuria was ignored? Or was the patient's apparent stoicism, which resulted in her not reaching hospital until her malaise and vomiting had lasted for three weeks, the ultimate cause of her own demise? Her son and daughter lived close to her and their involvement with the decisions relating to her hospital care are carefully recorded; could they have done more prior to her admission? Certainly once she developed extensive bowel ischaemia her death was inevitable, but at what time was this point of no return reached?

Case Study 3

A 57-year-old arteriopath died three days after a below knee amputation. The cause of death given at the post-mortem was 1a) acute left ventricular failure 1b) myocardial ischaemia 1c) coronary artery atheroma. Fifteen years earlier, at the age of 42, he had undergone an aorto-femoral by-pass and later a false aneurysm developed at the distal end of the graft. A second operation to repair this had been followed by ischaemia which had necessitated the amputation.

The patient admitted to smoking 70 cigarettes a week, but the anaesthetist recorded the consumption as up to 50 per day. The report of the carefully conducted postmortem makes no reference to this history of cigarette consumption nor is smoking listed anywhere as the cause of death.

This is a gross example of the contribution that patients can make to their own death. In many other cases there are less obvious, but none the less important contributory factors, that relate to the patient's lifestyle and general health, excess weight being the most obvious. In assessing the causation of death there is a curious reluctance to state openly the patient's own contribution. Perhaps this is because we can all, including doctors and other health professionals, be patients. It is however still remarkable that in a case such as this, the officially recorded cause of death makes no reference to this self-inflicted factor.

Case Study 4

Four days before Christmas, a man aged 63 went to theatre for a right hemicolectomy. He suffered from hypertension and was receiving treatment with atenolol and nifedipine but he was of normal weight and was graded as ASA 2. The anaesthetist inserted a radial arterial line, a triple lumen CVP through the right internal jugular and sited an epidural at L2/3. The surgery lasted 90 minutes and the patient was stable throughout, under a general anaesthetic together with the epidural. The operative blood loss was recorded as 850 ml and a litre of crystalloid followed by 2.5 litres of colloid was given in theatre. The anaesthetist noted that 'ideally the patient would have been managed in an HDU postoperatively so that the epidural could have been continued for analgesia'. As there was no HDU, the epidural catheter and arterial line were removed in the recovery suite and a PCA pump was set up for pain relief. The anaesthetist had left instructions that the patient was to be transfused if the haemoglobin fell below 7.0 gm/dl. A check on the blood gas machine in recovery showed it to be 8.4 gm/dl. After three-and-half-hours in recovery the patient was returned to the ward.

The postoperative information available is limited, because the surgical questionnaire was not returned. However the anaesthetist states that there was an initial fall in urine output on day one and it was unclear whether this was due to a blocked catheter or hypovolaemia. In any event, it is clear that the patient received 5500 ml of crystalloid and a further 2000 ml of colloid in what would appear to be four fluid challenges of 500 ml, during the first 24 hours following the operation. There was bleeding through the abdominal drain of 800 ml and the haemoglobin on the first post-operative day fell to 5.0 gm/dl. At this stage the patient received a 6-unit blood transfusion. On Christmas Day, day four, the patient who was continuing to receive pain relief

from the PCA and was requiring about 50 mg of morphine a day, suffered respiratory distress. There was consolidation in the right middle and lower lobe. This improved with physiotherapy and ICU transfer was considered but no bed was available. Following this, the patient's confusion increased and his oxygen saturation decreased. His arrest, at midday on Boxing Day, was noted as being unwitnessed by medical or nursing staff.

The anaesthetic questionnaire records that this anaesthetic department does not have morbidity/ mortality review meetings and that this case will not therefore be discussed.

The obvious response to this patient's demise is to say that all acute hospitals require HDU beds and this patient's management clearly suffered as a result of the lack of this essential resource. However, the failure to return a surgical questionnaire and the absence of essential medical audit in this hospital might suggest that the clinicians involved would benefit their patients if they examined the totality of the care they offered and developed a more coordinated cross disciplinary team ethos. Finally, although the information available on which to base conclusions is limited, there must be questions as to the quality of patient care on this ward during a long Bank Holiday period.

Case Study 5

An 81-year-old woman suffered a complicated intertrochanteric fracture of the femur. She had surgery the following day on a daytime trauma list. The surgeon was a locum registrar and there was no consultant in theatre. A consultant anaesthetist started the case. He advised the locum orthopaedic registrar to get senior help as the surgery was obviously going to be complicated and challenging. The registrar ignored this advice. The anaesthetist was called away and left the case with a staff grade doctor. There was considerable bleeding and eventually, when the operation was clearly not going well, the consultant orthopaedic surgeon was summoned. The operation took three-and-a- half-hours. The consultant anaesthetist specifically asked the locum registrar to review the patient postoperatively and consider blood transfusion if indicated. The anaesthetist reported that there was no documentation in the notes that this was ever done. The following day the patient developed a stroke. This was followed by a chest and wound infection. She died one week after surgery.

The locum orthopaedic registrar appears to lack insight. Faced with a difficult fracture and advice from a senior anaesthetic colleague to seek help, he ploughed on. The abortive attempts to reduce the fracture and subsequent difficulties resulted in excessive blood loss and an operation that took three times longer than expected (according to advice from our Advisors). To compound this patient's problems, the surgeon failed to review the patient in the immediate postoperative period and take appropriate steps to correct blood loss. However, not all the blame can be levelled at this registrar. We must ask what steps the consultant orthopaedic surgeon had taken to assess the locum's ability particularly when faced with a difficult fracture. Why was the consultant surgeon not present, at least at the start of the procedure? The consultant anaesthetist is critical of the locum registrar surgeon but was it reasonable given the concerns he or she expresses, to leave the anaesthetised patient with a staff-grade anaesthetist, and did not the anaesthetist also have a responsibility to visit the patient postoperatively to ensure all was well? Or are these various deficiencies in care irrelevant when the cause of the patient's death was the unfortunate postoperative stroke?

Case Study 6

An 80-year-old patient was admitted with a displaced intracapsular fracture of the femoral neck. She was known to have ischaemic heart disease, confusion and transient ischaemic attacks. Both the house surgeon and registrar were new and were not available to talk to the consultant anaesthetist when he visited the patient on the day prior to surgery. The anaesthetist noted that the patient had not had adequate fluid therapy and that the latest blood results were not available. The new orthopaedic registrar did a hemi-arthroplasty using cement. There was no surgical consultant in theatre. The patient suffered a cardiac arrest at 'cementation'. She was resuscitated but died in ICU 15 days later.

The consultant anaesthetist pointed out that the changeover of trainees at certain times of the year causes problems. These include inexperience, lack of knowledge of the patients and impaired continuity of care, poor communication and lack of awareness of local guidelines and surgical practice. In this case there were doubts about preoperative electrolyte imbalance, the preoperative biochemistry was not available and the surgical staff were not accessible in order to discuss the patient. Should we take these comments at face value or are they indicative of the anaesthetist shifting responsibility away from his/her failure to resuscitate the patient adequately prior to the operation?

Case Study 7

An 88-year-old man with senile dementia suffered an intertrochanteric femoral fracture. Five days were spent improving his general condition, as he had an established chest infection when admitted. With antibiotics and chest physiotherapy he improved and was deemed fit for anaesthesia albeit in a high-risk category. Surgery was done by an experienced registrar with a consultant assisting. He slowly declined and died in a community hospital six days later.

Fluid charts submitted with the questionnaires covered six days, from two days prior to surgery until the third postoperative day. Preoperatively these charts show no numerical entries in the 'Output' side other than comments such as 'wet bed', 'incontinent ++' and 'damp pads'. The totals for output are recorded as question marks. This situation clearly continued for two-and-a-half-days until the afternoon of surgery, during which the patient was catheterised. The catheter was removed on the third postoperative day and immediately the charts revert to recording output as '?' and 'wet bed'.

This patient was a high risk but a decision was made to embark on a programme of chest physiotherapy in the hope that successful surgery and subsequent mobilisation would relieve pain and help prevent further deterioration of respiratory function. Despite these positive decisions, he was allowed to lie in a wet bed for two-and-a-half-days, fluid charts were poorly completed and there can have been no satisfactory assessment of his state of hydration. There cannot be a sensible argument against catheterising such a patient and, even if the surgeons were reluctant to do so for fear of infection, there would have been some compelling nursing indications such as accurate fluid balance measurement and the prevention of pressure sores. The impression is one of neglect, poor nursing standards and the negation of the professed intention to achieve a successful outcome. The advisors identified many similar cases both in orthopaedic surgery and other specialties.

A mildly-obese woman (weight 86 kg: height 5' 6": BMI 31) aged 39 was admitted for an elective laparosopy to investigate abdominal pain that was thought to result from an ovarian cyst. She was otherwise well and was graded as ASA 1. The laparoscopy was carried out by an SpR 1/2 in gynaecology who had been seven months in the grade and who had carried out 45 similar procedures in the previous 12 months. The consultant was 'supervising but not scrubbed'. The ovaries were found to be normal but there was old blood stained fluid within the adnexae and it was concluded that the pain was caused by a recurrence of the patient's endometriosis. Some adhesions were divided bluntly. The procedure lasted 20 minutes.

The patient recovered well and was seen four hours after the operation by the surgeon when she was eating, drinking and all appeared well. It was planned that she would go home the next morning but in the event she was unwell and could not do so. The consultant gynaecologist was engaged at peripheral clinics all day and did not see the patient. The note made by the SHO at the 09.00 ward round records that the patient complained of 'feeling terrible', had generalised abdominal pain and hot/cold sweats. On examination she was flushed with a temperature of 37.4°C, the pulse rate was 100 and the blood pressure 130/70 mmHg. Abdominal examination showed mild distension and it was noted that the patient 'doesn't allow the slightest touch'. The SHO's impression was that this might be the result of bleeding or the retention of laparoscopic gas. At 14.10 the patient was noted to have continuing lower abdominal pain and she had had diarrhoea and had been vomiting. She was examined and bowel sounds were heard. The lower abdomen was tender but there was no rebound or guarding. The impression recorded was that a bowel perforation was unlikely.

At 05.30 the following morning the patient pressed her buzzer as she wished to pass urine. The nursing note records that she was feeling dizzy and was breathing rapidly. As she sat on the edge of the bed she became 'quite clammy'. She was laid back in bed and her blood pressure was now 90/60 mmHg but was 'very faint'. The nurse could not measure her saturation as 'the machine would not work'. The gynaecology SHO was called but was unable to site an IV so the anaesthetic SHO who came to assist inserted

a 17G Venflon and started fluid resuscitation. Oxygen was given. The medical on-call SpR, the gynaecology SpR and the anaesthetic SpR from ICU were all called. The nursing note records that the ECG machine would not work and another had to be found. At 06.05 the anaesthetist states that the patient was 'severely unwell'. She was cold, clammy and peripherally shut down and was semi-conscious. Respiration was laboured and poor, an arterial blood gas showed the PCO$_2$ to be 10 kPa. It was decided to intubate the patient but it is recorded that no emergency drugs for intubation were immediately available nor was there any suction tubing. The patient was pre-oxygenated and given 10 mg etomidate and 100 mg suxamethonium. The initial intubation with cricoid pressure was into the oesophagus but this was immediately noted. However the patient was now pulseless with electro-mechanical dissociation on the ECG. After two further attempts intubation was successful and the patient was transferred to the ICU, but following various further interventions, she died just over an hour later.

At postmortem, well-established faecal peritonitis was noted and about 800 ml of thick faeculant fluid was drained. No bowel perforation could be identified despite a careful search. The pathologist in his report noted that

"Inadvertent traumatic perforation of the bowel is a well-recognised potential complication of laparoscopy, with reported incidence of 1.6 to 1.8 per 1000 procedures. Only about 60% of bowel injuries are detected at the time of the laparoscopy. Injuries to the bowel can be treacherous because they may not be recognised at the time of the procedure. Perforation, however small, leads to spillage of intestinal contents into the peritoneal cavity and hence peritonitis. Mortality is high once peritonitis has set in".

The consultant gynaecologist is critical of the nursing notes. The Anaesthetic Advisors at NCEPOD were critical of the consultant gynaecologist for not attending the postmortem because of 'other commitments' and because he 'did not know the time' of the procedure. They were also critical of the resuscitation arrangements on the ward. The Surgical Advisors were critical of the 'junior staff' for being 'unaware of the dangers of perforation and signs of perforation'.

When considering this unfortunate patient it is
difficult not to be influenced by her young age. A
death at the age of 39 years in such circumstances is
tragic, particularly when the patient was fit and the
procedure was essentially investigative. The case is
described in detail because individually, the actions
of the staff involved would appear to have been
satisfactory. Yet, as the criticisms made with the
advantage of hindsight by the Anaesthetic and
Surgical Advisors demonstrate, at some point this
must have been avoidable. But was it?

CONCLUSION

From time to time, NCEPOD has been condemned
for presenting vignettes that merely criticise
clinicians and afford no educational value. The cases
highlighted here might be seen as an example of this
tendency, particularly by those doctors who think
they can identify themselves from the amount of
information given. No clinician at NCEPOD would
be able to make such an identification due to the
anonymisation of the patient records. It is hoped
that those reading this section will, whilst
recognising the highly selected nature of the cases,
see that they represent the difficulties that are
experienced in everyday practice. Too often,
individuals or groups misunderstand the efforts of
others and so criticise their actions, whilst at the
same time they do not address their own failings.
This applies to patients as well as the medical staff
and those administering the provision of resources.

THE CONTRIBUTION OF POSTMORTEM EXAMINATIONS TO THE AUDIT OF POSTOPERATIVE DEATHS

The role of NCEPOD is to review the delivery of care to patients who die after anaesthesia and surgery and to make recommendations for improvement. Confirmation of the quality of delivery of care may rely on confirmation of the diagnosis by a postmortem examination. Good practice cannot be assumed and where available, the report of the postmortem report is a valuable aid. It is for this reason that NCEPOD reports have contained reviews of the quality and content of available postmortem examination reports. This year, as there is a section on the management of malignancy, we have also reviewed the quality of histology reports. It is worrying that a third of these reports were inadequate for the purposes of tumour staging.

If it is accepted that an accurate cause of death is central to the assessment of perioperative deaths, it is of concern that an autopsy was performed in only 31% of deaths this year. Last year's 'Then and Now'[13] Report, which compared 1990 with 1998/99, found that the overall postmortem rate had dropped from 41% to 30%. It was noted that the hospital (consented) postmortem rate in 1990 was only 9% of postoperative deaths. By 1996/97 the hospital postmortem rate had fallen to an unacceptably low figure of 8%[14]. Unfortunately this decline has continued, with hospital postmortem rates of 4% being noted in 1998/99 and of 5% noted in this year's report, covering 1999/00. What is now clear is that virtually all postmortems are done for coroners.

Why should we be concerned about the high proportion of coroner's postmortems? In contrast to hospital postmortems, retention of tissues and organs from coroner's postmortems beyond the time needed to determine the cause of death is limited by 'Coroner's Rule 9'. This states that *"the person performing a postmortem examination shall make provision, so far as possible, for the preservation of material which in his opinion bears upon the cause of death, for such period as the coroner sees fit"*[15]. As a result, the pathologist is not permitted to sample tissues and organs comprehensively unless the families give consent. If this consent is not forthcoming the pathologist will not be able to refine and validate the cause of death according to nationally accepted standards [16, 17] which, in turn, may limit the quality of the information made available for clinicians and families on the underlying disease and its treatment.

It is recognised that the postmortem examination can produce new and clinically valuable information. There have been many studies showing that autopsy findings differ greatly from the clinical impression in many cases, and there is no indication that there has been any decrease in the proportion of significant discrepancies despite the increasing sophistication of diagnostic procedures[18, 19, 20]. Our figures of a major discrepancy in 23% of cases this year are consistent with the data of other authors. However, clinicians should not see these revelations as criticism or a threat but rather as a confirmation of the surgical diagnosis and operative findings (in the majority of cases) and a valuable form of audit. The pathologist can and should be one of the surgeon's teachers.

Making a reliable postmortem diagnosis is important not only for clinicians but also for the relatives of the deceased[21], quite apart from any benefits to education and research[22]. As a result of the recent organ retention issues and the huge media attention there has been a collapse of public confidence in pathologists. There is, therefore, a risk that the number of autopsies may fall even lower. Furthermore, families may increasingly attempt to withhold their consent for retention of tissues or whole organs from coroner's or hospital (consented) postmortems without being fully aware of the benefits of appropriate retention of material, or they may consent to only limited autopsies. Another problem is that some coroners (fortunately only a few) are prohibiting any retention of tissue even if, in the pathologist's opinion, retention of tissues may have a bearing on clarifying the cause of death. In these circumstances pathologists should either refuse to conduct the postmortem examination or should state, in their report to the coroner, how this restriction has prevented the provision of a precise, reliable and auditable cause of death. We believe that it is time for some positive publicity for the autopsy. When properly performed, an autopsy is a crucial part of the investigation of a postoperative death[16, 21, 23, 24]. Appended to this editorial is a personal comment by Professor James Underwood, Vice-President of the Royal College of Pathologists.

Evidence-based comment and published recommendations will have no effect in producing change if they are ignored. In 1993 NCEPOD published a report into deaths which occurred during the years 1991/92[25] . Below is an abstract of some of the key issues from the review of postmortem examinations in that report:

- "The number of postmortems should be increased."

- "Better communication between pathologists and other clinicians is needed."

- "Although the overall quality of postmortem examination is good, more frequent use of clinical/pathological commentaries and greater precision in the statement of causes of death are desirable."

- "The Enquiry deplores the action of some coroners in refusing to supply the postmortem report to the surgical team."

The reader may notice many similarities with the key points from this year's report. Why has there been so little change in the performance of pathological services within our health services? One persisting issue is the lack of resources available to the coroner. There also needs to be a serious review of the persisting failures of communication and more teamwork between clinicians, pathologists[26] and coroners. This needs to be linked to improved support and provision from those agencies responsible for providing health care and concerted efforts to restore public confidence and understanding about the value of the autopsy.

POSTMORTEM EXAMINATIONS IN PERIOPERATIVE DEATHS

"Despite improvements in modern medicine and surgery, postmortem examinations continue to reveal that diagnoses made during life are incorrect or incomplete in about 30% of cases. Postmortem examinations therefore enable, first, bereaved families to have a more complete and reliable understanding of the reasons for their loss and, second, doctors to learn from autopsy findings for the benefit of future patients.

The climate of public opinion regarding postmortem examinations has recently deteriorated. The 'organ retention scandal' has resulted in an accelerated decline in the number of 'consent' cases and in fewer histological examinations of retained tissue for more reliably and precisely establishing the cause of death, particularly in postmortem examinations required by law. It has also exacerbated the consultant workforce crisis in histopathology, particularly in paediatric histopathology, by precipitating early retirements.

The Royal College of Pathologists is working actively with other agencies, including groups representing patients and bereaved families, to improve the public understanding of postmortem examinations. Much of the distress experienced by bereaved families is attributable not so much to the fact that tissues or organs were retained but that they were retained without the families' knowledge; at the time of burial or cremation, the body was assumed to be 'complete'.

Many families do recognise the value of postmortem examinations, to them and to future patients, and rightly wish to be actively involved, in partnership with doctors, in decisions about tissue and organ retention. In postmortem examinations required by law, it is essential that families have an opportunity, if they so wish, to seek justification for the examination and for the retention of tissue or organs which have a bearing on the cause of death.

Postmortem examinations may also be regarded by some families as an opportunity for altruism by allowing retention for teaching and research, thus enabling some good to accrue from their loss, in the same way that tissue and organ donation for transplantation has immediate benefits for the living."

James Underwood (Vice-President, The Royal College of Pathologists; Chairman, Royal College of Pathologists Working Group on Retention of Tissues and Organs at Postmortem Examination)

THE REQUIREMENT FOR IMPROVED INFORMATION SYSTEMS

A 'First Class Service'[27]- the 1998 document outlining how the government proposed to improve quality in the NHS contained this key statement: *"The new NHS will have quality at its heart. Without it there is unfairness. Every patient who is treated in the NHS wants to know that they can rely on receiving high quality care when they need it. Every part of the NHS, and everyone who works in it, should take responsibility for working to improve quality."*

NCEPOD has been participating in the improvement of the quality of care to patients for over a decade, yet still we see the same issues arising year after year. The clinical implications of our work are of paramount importance but without data our Enquiry could not continue. Whilst there are signs that some aspects of our data collection are improving, such as the response rates to detailed questionnaires, NCEPOD has increasing concerns with regard to the baseline data (deaths within 30 days of a surgical procedure) and the availability and accuracy of patient's case notes.

Whilst compiling 'Then & Now'[13] last year, it became apparent that there were significant discrepancies between the Hospital Episode Statistics (HES) data and the data reported to NCEPOD. Whilst the definitions of this information were marginally different, some Trusts showed many more deaths within the HES database than NCEPOD and some were vice versa. Some Trusts

had not reported any deaths to NCEPOD at all. During the preparation for this report NCEPOD and the Department of Health have been able to undertake a more accurate comparison and for the first time such information by Trust is detailed within the report.

The amount of money spent on information systems, within the NHS in particular, has increased tremendously over the last few years but the investment does not appear to have improved the quality of patient care. In some cases Trusts seem to be going backwards rather than improving the use of operational data. One Trust has already informed NCEPOD that data on deaths within 2000/01 will not be provided, as their new computer system cannot be interrogated to provide the required information. The system that has been replaced provided the information with no apparent difficulties. Has the time come for all Trusts to be made to use the same information system (case notes, Patient Administration System etc.) with a nationally agreed specification? Surely the move to the Electronic Patient Record (EPR) would then become much easier. It has always been understood that if a system is to be computerised successfully it is necessary to ensure that manual systems are well organised first. It is therefore with some trepidation that NCEPOD imagines how the EPR will progress if the problems with the content and retrieval of manual case notes are anything to go by.

"Case notes thrown into a room", and *"case notes sent to be archived with no record kept of what has been sent"*, are comments that NCEPOD have heard this year when pursuing non-returned questionnaires. Medical record departments have for many years been a 'Cinderella service' and the results speak for themselves. It is not necessary to undertake a cost/benefit analysis to see why many departments are failing to cope. Lack of suitably qualified and motivated staff due to poor remuneration, lack of sophisticated filing systems and adequate space, and the failure to invest in modern document imaging and retrieval systems all play a part in the problem. Clinicians need to ensure that Trust management are aware of the difficulties they face with regard to the loss of casenotes for all patients, whether alive or dead.

How can quality be improved if some of the basics aren't right? The dedication and keenness of staff within the health service cannot be overestimated and it is this that has enabled NCEPOD to deliver its reports over the past decade. It is now time to move into the twenty-first century and ensure that the information provided to NCEPOD amongst other audits and Enquiries is as accurate as possible in order that we can all play a full role in improving the quality of care to the patient.

DATA QUALITY AUDIT

INTRODUCTION

> ### Key points
>
> - There is no uniform case note system in the NHS.
>
> - Some hospitals were unable to retrieve the notes of deceased patients.
>
> - Clinicians are failing to send NCEPOD copies of clinical documents.
>
> - Completed questionnaires contain inaccuracies, which may lead to flawed judgements on clinical care.
>
> - Failure to submit complete and accurate data threatens the future maintenance of confidentiality.

Since the introduction of clinical governance there has been an increase in the percentage return of questionnaires to NCEPOD. In our 2000 Report 'Then & Now'[13] we noted a return rate of 83% for surgeons and 85% for anaesthetists; the highest return rates ever recorded by NCEPOD. We believe that the data contained in these questionnaires remains robust but this belief has been questioned[25]. It is possible that the questionnaires may be completed in a rather careless manner in order to achieve compliance with NCEPOD without regard to accuracy or completeness. An example of this was revealed during the analysis of the data for this report. There appeared to be too many deaths in elective day cases. Further painstaking review of the surgical questionnaires by NCEPOD coordinators showed that 42 cases had been incorrectly classified as day cases when they were mostly elective inpatient admissions. At least three-quarters of these particular questionnaires had either been completed by consultants or at least seen by them. If one small piece of information is incorrectly submitted, one has to question the thoroughness of questionnaire completion in other areas. So, we had to verify our overall impression that the data remained accurate and that clinicians were being accurate in their returns. An audit of the data was required in order to confirm or negate this impression.

To do this audit, which NCEPOD hoped would dispel any doubts about the veracity of our data, would mean a loss of anonymity for those clinicians/ hospitals whose case notes were reviewed. However the Clinical Coordinators are fully conversant with the requirements of confidentiality, and preliminary soundings through Advisors and a selection of

Medical Directors, suggested that this study would be welcomed and viewed as timely by clinicians and managers. A proposal to conduct the audit was therefore submitted to the NCEPOD Steering Group and subsequently approved.

METHOD

We devised a small pilot study, which involved comparing the clinical notes with certain verifiable entries in the questionnaires.

The six Clinical Coordinators visited hospitals within the geographic areas within which they work. Within these areas, the hospitals were chosen at random from amongst those from whom we had received questionnaires. We decided that the pilot study did not need to be comprehensive, in terms of covering the whole country, but a mixture of hospital types was desirable. Hospitals in the private sector indicated their willingness to participate but, as the number of questionnaires from this sector was very small, it was decided to exclude them from the initial study. Participation was voluntary and was confirmed with both the Chief Executives and Medical Directors of the chosen hospitals.

The participating hospitals and Trusts were:

- Airedale General Hospital (Airedale NHS Trust)

- Conquest Hospital (Hastings & Rother NHS Trust)

- Cumberland Infirmary (Carlisle Hospitals NHS Trust)

- Doncaster Royal Infirmary (Doncaster Royal Infirmary & Montagu Hospital NHS Trust)

- North Tees General Hospital (North Tees & Hartlepool NHS Trust)

- Hillingdon Hospital (Harrow & Hillingdon Healthcare NHS Trust)

- Middlesbrough General Hospital (South Tees Acute Hospitals NHS Trust)

- Maidstone Hospital (Maidstone & Tunbridge Wells NHS Trust)

- Kent & Sussex Hospital (Maidstone & Tunbridge Wells NHS Trust)

- Queen Elizabeth Hospital (King's Lynn & Wisbech Hospitals NHS Trust)

- Queen Elizabeth The Queen Mother Hospital (East Kent Hospitals NHS Trust)

- Royal Infirmary (North Staffordshire NHS Trust)

- Stepping Hill Hospital (Stockport NHS Trust)

- Leeds General Infirmary (Leeds Teaching Hospitals NHS Trust)

- Walsgrave Hospital (University Hospitals Coventry & Warwickshire NHS Trust)

- West Suffolk Hospital (West Suffolk Hospitals NHS Trust)

- Wexham Park Hospital (Heatherwood & Wexham Park Hospitals NHS Trust)

NCEPOD wish to express their gratitude for the warm welcome they received at all the participating hospitals and for the open and interested attitudes expressed towards the visits and data audit.

Three other hospitals or groups of hospitals were invited to participate but did not respond.

Each hospital was asked to provide the clinical notes, relating to the anaesthetic and surgical questionnaires held by NCEPOD, and a room where the visiting Clinical Coordinator could work in private. All the participating hospitals cooperated enthusiastically. The number of notes reviewed varied from hospital to hospital (see results below). The visiting Coordinators took with them a folder relating to each questionnaire. This contained a proforma, on which to enter the comparison of notes and questionnaires, and photocopied extracts from the questionnaire; these text extracts could then be compared with entries in the original notes. At no time did any of the original returned questionnaires leave the NCEPOD office. The proforma was designed to look at both accuracy and general style/attitude of completion of the NCEPOD questionnaire. Where requested documents, e.g. an operation note, had not been sent to NCEPOD, the Coordinators checked whether these were in the hospital notes. A small number of specific questions were asked, relating to information in the questionnaires, which we believed could be easily verified from the notes, e.g. 'Is the disclosure of the postoperative complications correct?'

The Coordinators also assessed the general quality and content of the notes relating to the questionnaires. The notes were compared with published guidelines[29] and scored using a recently published method, the CRABEL score[30] (CRABEL is an acronym of the author's names), thus allowing some comparison of performance within the sample.

An internal audit was also done to assess the thoroughness of questionnaire completion. Thus, if a question asked for certain information to be specified, we checked whether this information was provided.

An analysis of the results is given below. The full results are contained in the data set available separately from NCEPOD.

RESULTS

General remarks

The visits to most hospitals were very successful. The Coordinators were usually received enthusiastically, the appropriate notes were available and a suitable area was provided for the Coordinator to work. A member of the host hospital's Clinical Audit Department was often on hand to assist with queries or the identification of documents. In some hospitals the Medical Director or Chief Executive met the Coordinators and ensured that all was proceeding smoothly.

Ability to retrieve notes

Two hospitals were unable to provide any of the notes requested for the day of the visit, despite adequate notice. One hospital reported that the notes were not only stored off-site but in another city. There appeared to be no filing system and no simple method for retrieval of the notes relating to deceased patients. The visit to this hospital was cancelled and the Trust Chief Executive was informed of the problem. Subsequent correspondence from clinicians suggests that there is a widespread problem with retrieval of medical records at this hospital. This situation is discussed further in the section on General Data. The second hospital failed to provide the notes, claiming that the correspondence concerning the visit had been mislaid.

Number of notes reviewed

There was a potential total of 103 notes to review at the participating hospitals. Only 81 were reviewed. The reasons why 22 notes were not reviewed are given in Table 4.1.

Table 4.1	Reasons why notes not able to be reviewed
Reason	**Number**
Hospital unable to participate	9
Shortage of time for coordinator	7
Notes not found	3
Wrong notes obtained	1
No notes found for last admission/procedure	2
Total	**22**

This brief attempt to review the notes of deceased patients revealed a worrying situation in many hospitals. From a random sample of 103 sets of notes, 15% (15/103) either could not be retrieved on request or the hospital produced incorrect or inappropriate records. This has serious implications for researchers using retrospective data and for Trusts faced with litigation.

Quality of notes in general (CRABEL scores)

Many notes were immaculate, secure and clearly labelled. However, some were very scruffy with loose pages, no clear order for sections and these were very difficult to work through. Occasionally microfilmed reproductions were of poor quality and difficult to interpret. Coordinators reported difficulties in familiarising themselves with the individual format of the medical records at each hospital. The lack of a uniform note layout within the NHS was noted and deplored. All these general defects must also have implications for the ability of the service to retrieve information in the event of a complaint, inquiry or litigation (see also section on General Data).

The Coordinators found the CRABEL system of scoring easy to use although there were some anomalies. The system works by deducting points for omissions e.g. patient's name or a clinicians' signature, and then calculating a final score as a percentage. Perfect notes would score 100%. Limited notes, as a result of an early death, score highly as there will be few deductions. However, this system was useful and showed that there is a spectrum of quality within record keeping. Figure 4.1 shows the distribution of scores with a mean of 67%. Trusts could use such a system of note review to assess the standard of notes and to motivate attempts at improvement.

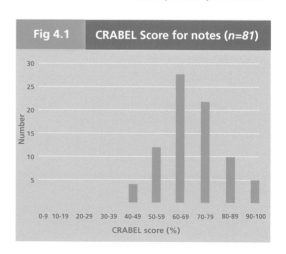

Fig 4.1 — CRABEL Score for notes (*n=81*)

Data quality analysis of anaesthetic records

When the 81 sets of notes were reviewed and compared against the anaesthetic questionnaires, the Coordinators identified nine cases where there was no return from an anaesthetist. However, some of these cases were identified as receiving a local anaesthetic and hence an anaesthetic questionnaire would not have been expected. Thus there were only 72 anaesthetic questionnaires to compare with the original notes.

The Coordinators first looked at the return of requested documents and the compliance of the clinicians with this request (Table 4.2).

Data concerning measures taken in theatre to maintain body temperature could not be verified from the clinical records in 28% (20/72) of the cases. Many anaesthetists will have answered this question from knowledge of their usual practice. We do want clinicians to provide information to the best of their ability and in the spirit of audit. We recognise that this is a limitation of this particular method of data evaluation and this data represents a 'softer' end point in our analysis.

An internal audit of the completed anaesthetic questionnaires was also done. This assessed whether the forms had been properly filled in where, for instance, an answer needed specific information to qualify a positive answer.

Table 4.2	Availability of anaesthetic information				
	Sent to NCEPOD	In the notes but not sent	Not in notes	Not applicable	Total
Preoperative anaesthetic record	62	6	3	1	72
Final anaesthetic record	66	4	2	0	72
Previous relevant anaesthetic record	10	3	52	7	72
Recovery room record	36	7	24	5	72
Fluid balance charts	39	18	13	2	72
Drug prescription charts	61	8	3	0	72
Pain assessment form	31	8	25	8	72

This is an interesting table, which demonstrates that information and the forms were in the notes, e.g. anaesthetic records and fluid charts, but they were not sent to NCEPOD as requested. This failure to send information was in the order of 10%. It is recognised that the information may not have been in the notes because it did not exist e.g. previous anaesthetic records if there has been no previous illness. It would seem that the system for the filing of recovery room and fluid balance charts is poor. Some hospitals do not retain fluid charts in patients' notes. That recovery charts for critically ill patients are not retained, on the scale suggested in this audit, is deplorable and a matter for Trusts to address.

Questions were then asked about the accurate disclosure of preoperative respiratory, cardiac and renal disorders. These were incorrect in 14% (10/72), 13% (9/72) and 17% (12/72) of cases respectively. Questions were also asked about the accurate disclosure of postoperative complications in the form of ventilatory, cardiac and renal disorders. These were found to be incorrect in 18% (13/72), 13% (9/72) and 15% (11/72) of cases respectively. These are facts that are verifiable from the clinical notes and as such represent 'strong' end points with which to judge the data.

This internal audit showed a high standard of completion (98-100%) and few omissions.

Table 4.3	Availability of surgical information				
	Sent to NCEPOD	In the notes but not sent	Not in notes	Not applicable	Total
Surgical operation notes	59	15	2	0	76
Discharge summary	35	20	16	5	76
Histology report(s)	18	5	44	9	76
Postmortem report	17	5	45	9	76

Data quality analysis of surgical records

Out of 81 cases, five surgical questionnaires were not returned and, therefore, could not be included in the study. This left 76 sets of notes for review. The Coordinators again looked at the return of requested documents and the compliance of the clinicians with this request (Table 4.3).

In 20% (15/76) of the cases the surgeon did not send the operation note as requested. Over a quarter of the discharge summaries were not sent and, where available, histology and postmortem examination reports were not sent in 22% (5/23) and 23% (5/22) of cases respectively. Some explanations are possible. In some hospitals formal discharge summaries are not produced for deceased patients. Histology and/or postmortem examination reports are not always pertinent to certain cases and there would be none in the notes. There is, however, no excuse for failing to forward an operation note when requested.

Evidence of a working diagnosis was sought and 89% (68/76) records contained a clear working diagnosis which agreed with that notified to the Enquiry. The notes were scrutinised for the accuracy of diagnosis and preoperative problems, as reported to NCEPOD by surgeons. There was a high level of accurate reporting with 80% of questionnaires containing accurate information. The reason for considering the remainder as incorrect was that often one of several comorbidities was omitted. The disclosure of postoperative complications was incorrect in 11% (8/76) of cases. In a similar manner to the anaesthetic data (see Table 4.2) this represents 'hard' evidence of compliance with requests for accurate data.

However, when evidence to corroborate statements about personnel present in theatre was sought, no evidence to support the statements could be found in 13% of the notes (10/76). This may be 'soft' information that is not recorded in the clinical records but which may be available from theatre information systems or record books.

There was no consent form filed in the notes in 18% (14/76) of the sample. This is a serious failing of the medical records system unless consent was irrelevant e.g. for a ruptured abdominal aortic aneurysm or other dire emergency. Where there was a consent form this was unacceptable or only partially acceptable in 23% (14/62) of cases. Eight consent forms were unacceptable because they were not legal, e.g. unsigned or consent given by relatives without legal powers to do so, and six were partially unacceptable because of omissions such as a lack of explanations of complications, illegible names or abbreviated procedures.

When referral to the coroner occurred, this could not be verified from the notes in 29% (15/51) of cases. In general, there was no documented evidence to support statements about the whole process of decision-making concerning postmortem examination in three-quarters of the notes examined.

The internal audit of completed surgical questionnaires showed a high degree of complete answers but questions about the qualifications of the operator and checking of the questionnaire by a consultant were less well answered with omissions of 36% (27/76) and 8% (6/76) respectively.

COMMENT

A pilot study such as this clearly has limitations and whilst there are many 'hard' end points with which to form opinions it must be admitted that there are also 'soft' data. The Clinical Coordinators are all experienced clinicians, used to navigating clinical notes, but it is possible that pieces of information were present in the notes but overlooked or not identified. Some questions within the questionnaires do rely on recall of the events, or other sources of information, and memory may be altered with time. However, there can be no excuse for leaving answers to questions totally blank.

The review of this small sample of notes has confirmed the existence of problems within the organisation of the NHS medical records service. It really is not acceptable for two hospitals to be unable to retrieve the notes of deceased patients. The quality of presentation and completion of medical records has also been found to vary considerably. If this small sample is an accurate reflection of the state of records within the NHS, then there is considerable scope for improvement.

NCEPOD bases conclusions and recommendations on the information received in the form of completed questionnaires and copies of documents from the patient's notes. This 'snapshot' of the original clinical notes raises serious concerns about omissions and accuracy of the data on which we found our comments. Clinicians fail to forward approximately 10-20% of important documents. These are in the hospital notes and there can be no excuse for failing to comply with the request from a National Confidential Enquiry.

Cooperation with an enquiry such as NCEPOD is now mandatory. However there is evidence here that participation is less than complete. Indeed there is a high level of inaccuracy.

A wider audit of data submitted to NCEPOD may be needed but the suspicion is that the data received is incomplete and inaccurate in more than 10% of instances. This is information on which the Coordinators and Advisors base their comments concerning clinical care. If a larger audit were to show inaccuracies in the data, a consequence might be the requirement to submit clinical records in their entirety, thus losing anonymity.

Recommendations

- There should be a uniform case note system in the NHS.

- Hospitals should review the procedures for the storage and retrieval of deceased patients' notes.

- A larger audit of data quality is needed.

GENERAL DATA

INTRODUCTION

Key points

- There are significant differences between the number of NCEPOD reported cases and Hospital Episde Statistics.

- The return rates for both surgeons and anaesthetists continue to improve at 87% and 90% respectively.

- Several Trusts are now involving clinical governance departments to assist clinicians in their participation of NCEPOD.

- All deaths are not reported and questionnaires on deaths remain unanswered.

- There is still no simple way of collecting details of deaths that occur in the community.

- In over 5% of the sampled cases it was not possible to identify the anaesthetist involved.

- A small minority of clinicians continue to question the policy of NCEPOD in terms of the relevance of the final procedure performed before death.

The data presented in this report relate to deaths occurring between 1 April 1999 and 31 March 2000. The period through which questionnaires were dispatched ran through until 31 August 2000 with the final deadline for return being 31 December 2000. It is unfortunate that the number of questionnaires returned late continues to increase despite a minimum of four months for completion. The protocol for data collection is detailed in Appendix E.

As NCEPOD reported last year[13], participation is now compulsory within NHS trusts. It is not yet mandatory for the independent sector although it is expected that this anomaly will be addressed as part of the proposed Care Standards Act due to be implemented in April 2002. Despite the guidance given in 'Clinical Governance: Quality in the new NHS'[31] which stated that "*NHS Trusts have a responsibility for ensuring that all hospital doctors take part in national clinical audits and confidential enquiries*", there are Trusts where the data looks incomplete. We also have evidence from a variety of sources that some high profile cases have not been reported. This can only lead to the conclusion that reporting is not complete across the NHS and that doctors have not learned the lessons of Bristol.

Whilst NCEPOD has put into place some mechanisms to improve this situation, such as quarterly reporting to Medical Directors, information systems within Trusts still need refinement to ensure that the correct base data is reported in order that NCEPOD can follow up individual cases.

The sample reviewed in detail during this period was, once again a random 10% of the total deaths reported. The selection of this group has enabled NCEPOD to make direct comparisons with data collected in 1990 and 1998/99 and reported in 2000[13] when a similarly randomised group was reviewed.

This year NCEPOD has asked additional questions about those patients in the sample who had a diagnosis of can-cer at the time of death regardless of the cause of death.

DATA COLLECTION

Data was requested from all hospitals in England, Wales, Northern Ireland, Guernsey, Jersey, Isle of Man and the Defence Secondary Care Agency. In addition, the majority of hospitals in the independent sector contributed data. Data was not collected from Scotland where the Scottish Audit of Surgical Mortality (SASM) performs a similar function.

Deaths occurring in hospital, between 1 April 1999 and 31 March 2000, and within 30 days of a surgical procedure were reported to NCEPOD by the designated Local Reporter for each hospital (Appendix F). A few reports of deaths occurring at home were also received. NCEPOD continues to pursue the possibility of collecting a more complete picture of this latter group of deaths but data collection remains extremely difficult. The simplest way of collecting this data would be to record on the death certificate if a surgical procedure had been performed in the preceding 30 days. NCEPOD will continue to pursue this issue.

GENERAL DATA ANALYSIS

Figure 5.1 shows that a total of 21 654 reports were received. Of these 1093 were excluded from further analysis: 858 were deemed inappropriate according to the NCEPOD protocol (Table 5.1 and Appendices E and I), 192 were received after the deadline of 31 August 2000 and 43 remained incomplete despite all efforts to identify missing information. It is interesting to note that although the total number of deaths reported in this period showed an increase of 401 over the previous year, the number of cases that could be included rose from 93.3% to 94.9% showing a small improvement in the quality and timeliness of the reports.

Fig 5.1	Total deaths reported

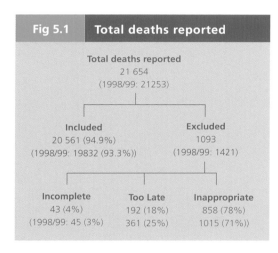

Table 5.1 shows that there have been further increases in the numbers of reported procedures performed by a non-surgeon from 221 in 1997/98 to 319 in 1999/00. The two special reports published by NCEPOD in 2000, Percutaneous Transluminal Coronary Angioplasty[32] and Interventional Vascular and Neurovascular Radiology[33], reviewed many of these procedures but by far the largest group of procedures performed which are not currently reviewed are endoscopies undertaken by physicians. These will form part of a future study by NCEPOD.

An area of improvement in the quality of data received from Trusts manifested itself in a reduction of duplicate reports received. One hundred and sixty one were received in 1999/00, a reduction from 485 in 1998/99. Whilst it is pleasing to report that reporting systems appear to be stabilising, NCEPOD still has considerable concerns that deaths are under reported, an issue discussed later in this section, and generally that information systems are not robust

Table 5.1	Inappropriate reports received and excluded		
Reason for exclusion	**1999/00**	**1998/99**	**1997/98**
Death occured more than 30 days after operation	265	230	220
Procedure not performed by a surgeon	319	235	221
Duplicate report	161	485	271
No surgical procedure performed or procedure excluded by NCEPOD criteria	110	59	106
Procedure performed in non-participating independent hospital	1	4	14
Procedure performed overseas	1	1	0
Patient still alive	1	0	2
Total	**858**	**1014**	**834**

A breakdown of the remaining 20 561 deaths, by region is shown in Table 5.2. Comparison with the figures for previous years is not possible due to the major regional boundary changes that occurred in April 1999. However, a comparison with the number of Finished Consultant Episodes (FCEs) from Hospital Episode Statistics (HES) has been given. The region with the highest difference is a good reporter of deaths to NCEPOD and this may act against them in this comparison. Appendix A gives more detail by reporting deaths by Trust.

Table 5.2	Deaths reported to NCEPOD by region		
Region	**1999/00**	**% of total deaths** (for England NHS)	**% of FCE's** (for England NHS)*
Eastern	1809	9.7	9.5
London	2558	13.7	12.3
North Western	2754	14.6	15.7
Northern & Yorkshire	3183	17.1	13.5
South Eastern	2531	13.6	14.6
South & West	1834	9.8	10.4
Trent	2104	11.3	11
West Midlands	1895	10.2	10.4
Wales	1217	-	-
Northern Ireland	360	-	-
Guernsey	14	-	-
Jersey	31	-	-
Isle of Man	22	-	-
Defence Secondary Care Agency	7	-	-
Independent Sector	242	-	-
Total	**20 561**		

*Over 250 000 FCE's could not be attributed to a region as place of residence was not recorded

Whilst NCEPOD has for several years suspected that not all deaths (within our criteria) are reported by hospitals, it now has actual evidence that this is the case. The following quote comes from a Medical Director following up on the non-return of questionnaires:

"My colleagues have been in difficulties with this particular case because as a result of the death of a patient a consultant.... in this Trust was suspended...., and an independent inquiry panel has been set up. I need hardly say that the case has been well and truly reviewed. I am not sure whether this information is of use to you. There are significant medical legal sensitivities around the death of this patient and this lies behind the reluctance of my colleagues to respond to your request for information."

Further high profile cases that have been reported in the national press are also missing from our database. It is a pity that all Trusts cannot benefit from the lessons to be learned from these cases.

Further support to our belief that numbers of deaths reported to NCEPOD are not accurate comes from the audit undertaken by Poloniecki and Roxburgh [34].

They found that less than 80% of deaths after cardiac surgery were recorded on either the departmental database or the hospital administration system.

Last year NCEPOD commented on the discrepancies that existed between the data submitted as HES to the Department of Health (DoH) and our data. The HES data is used by the DoH for a number of purposes including the calculation of NHS Performance Indicators. The DoH has provided a breakdown of deaths within Trusts that meet NCEPOD's criteria and the results are shown in Appendix A.

Both NCEPOD and the DoH are concerned at the results for some Trusts where there is a significant difference between the two figures. One might expect slightly fewer deaths to be reported to us as some Trusts rely on manual data collection for the data but what is difficult to explain is where NCEPOD reported deaths are higher than the HES data. As can be seen there are also Trusts that reported no deaths in 1999/00 despite a quarterly report to the Medical Director detailing the returns that had been made. We have already been notified by one Trust that they will not be returning details of deaths for 2000/01 because their newly acquired hospital information system cannot provide a report of this information. The specification for such a system should surely be examined. NCEPOD will be strengthening its links with the Commission for Health Improvement (CHI) to ensure that such problems are investigated during the four yearly clinical governance reviews.

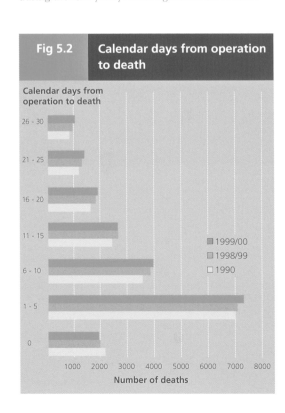

Fig 5.2	Calendar days from operation to death

Calendar days from operation to death

1999/00
1998/99
1990

Number of deaths

Figure 5.2 shows the distribution of the number of calendar days between operation (day 0) and death, with 44% (9132/20 561) of deaths occurring in the first six days compared to 48% in 1998/99 and 49% in 1990.

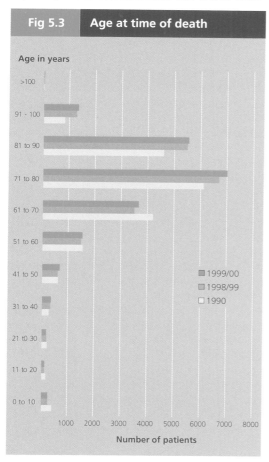

Fig 5.3   Age at time of death

Age in years

1999/00
1998/99
1990

Number of patients

There is a trend towards an increase in the age of patients that die after their operation (Figure 5.3). In 1999/00 68% of the patients were over 70 years, and this compares with 61% in 1990.

Using the HES data, the age of all patients who were operated on in 1999/00 (excluding certain non-NCEPOD operations - see Appendix I) were reviewed. This was compared with the age profile of deaths reported to NCEPOD and is shown graphically in Figure 5.4.

A recent study on assessment of operative risk, the Revised Cardiac Risk Index[35] failed to detect age as an operative risk factor. However, Figure 5.4 clearly demonstrates that it is. Most operations are on patients of between 15-59 years and most deaths are patients of 75 or older. The conclusions from the assessment of operative risk and the findings of this report differ because the profile of patients studied differed. Those in the risk assessment groups underwent non-emergency operations whilst most deaths reported to NCEPOD are after urgent or emergency operations. It would

appear then that age is a risk factor for death after an urgent or emergency operation.

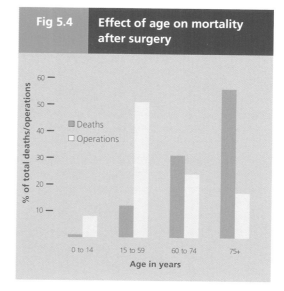

Fig 5.4   Effect of age on mortality after surgery

% of total deaths/operations

■ Deaths
□ Operations

Age in years

The distribution between the sexes is almost unchanged; in 1998/99 52% (10 277/19 832) were male compared to 51.4% in 1999/00 (10 572/20 561).

The number of days taken for Local Reporters to inform NCEPOD of deaths is shown in Table 5.3. Local Reporters are nominated by their Trust/hospital to collate this data and use a variety of different collection methods. Clinical audit and clinical governance departments are increasingly taking on this responsibility. It is of concern that the percentage of deaths being reported in less than 60 days has fallen slightly whilst those taking in excess of four months has risen. However Figure 5.1 shows that overall the number of notifications received too late is falling.

Table 5.3	Calendar days between deaths and receipt of report by NCEPOD					
Calendar days (i.e. not 24hr periods)	**Number of deaths reported**					
	1999/00		1998/99		1991/92	
1-29	4330	21%	4137	21%	9084	50%
30-59	4213	20%	4398	22%	3526	19%
60-89	3277	16%	3033	15%	1960	11%
90-119	2089	10%	2134	11%	1153	6%
120-149	1581	8%	1724	7%	747	4%
150-179	1179	6%	1099	6%	528	3%
180+	3892	19%	3307	17%	1134	6%
Total	**20 561**		**19 832**		**18 132**	

If there is a six-month delay before NCEPOD becomes aware of a death, then there is, of necessity, a considerable time lapse between death and receipt of a questionnaire by a clinician. This is particularly problematic for anaesthetists, since Local Reporters are often unable to provide the name of the relevant consultant. This then needs to be ascertained from correspondence with the local Anaesthetic College Tutor. The earlier questionnaires can be dispatched to clinicians, the more likely it is that the medical records will be available, the case clearly remembered and the relevant clinicians (especially junior staff) still working at the same hospital. In addition, it allows more time for questionnaires to be completed and returned by the annual deadline of 31 December.

In 1991/92 - the first year the data was analysed in this way over 50% of deaths were reported to NCEPOD within 29 days of death. As can be seen, this figure now stands at 21%. The investment in computerised information systems within the NHS over the last decade seems to have had a detrimental impact in this area of data collection. NCEPOD is reliant upon the efforts of Local Reporters to obtain this most basic of information on patients who have died and such information should be valuable throughout Trusts for local clinical governance and audit activities. It is unacceptable that Local Reporters are required to fulfil this now obligatory requirement without adequate resources in terms of time and information systems.

SAMPLE DATA ANALYSIS

The sample selected for review in 1999/00 was again a randomised 10% of the total deaths reported, with cases for inclusion being identified by the NCEPOD computer system on entering basic case details onto the main database. A randomised sample has the advantage of ensuring that no clinicians feel that they, or their speciality, are being unfairly burdened.

Questionnaires were sent to a total of 1359 different consultant surgeons and 1182 different consultant anaesthetists. Table 5.4 shows that the majority (70% of surgeons and 69% of anaesthetists) received only one questionnaire in the year.

It is important to stress that forms are sent to consultants, but relate to cases conducted not only by themselves but also by a range of non-consultant or locum staff. This is particularly the case for anaesthetists, where it is common for all forms relating to cases conducted by non-consultants to be sent to a single designated consultant who has taken the responsibility for the completion of NCEPOD returns. These figures do not, therefore, reflect poor practice.

Table 5.4	Number of questionnaires received by clinicians	
No of questionnaires received	Anaesthetists	Surgeons
1	820 (69%)	956 (70%)
2	265 (22%)	268 (20%)
3-5	92 (8%)	130 (9%)
6-8	4 (<1%)	5 (1%)
Over 9	1*	

* Local arrangement whereby one anaesthetist acts as receiving point in cases of non-identification of consultant

In relation to the 1999/00 sample, 11 surgical questionnaires were not sent as NCEPOD had already been notified that the consultant had left the Trust/hospital.

In the 277 (14%) cases where no anaesthetic questionnaire was sent, this was either because the procedure was performed without an anaesthetist present (142, 7%), the name of the appropriate consultant was unobtainable (109, 5%), the case was notified too late (21, 1%), or because NCEPOD had been notified that the appropriate consultant had left the Trust/hospital (5). The clinical governance implications of not knowing who the anaesthetist was are important but the legal ramifications are frightening. NCEPOD urges Trusts to review this situation to ensure that the names of all health professionals who have cared for a patient are recorded in the medical case notes.

One thousand seven hundred and eleven surgical questionnaires (1711/1967, 87%) and 1529 anaesthetic questionnaires (1529/1701, 90%) were returned (Figure 5.5). Clinicians should be commended for ensuring that the return rates continue to improve.

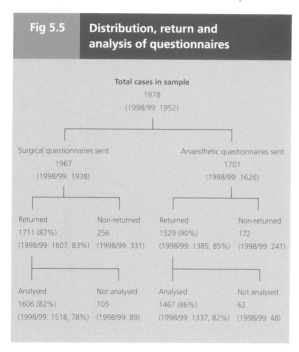

Fig 5.5	Distribution, return and analysis of questionnaires

Total cases in sample
1978
(1998/99: 1952)

Surgical questionnaires sent
1967
(1998/99: 1938)

Anaesthetic questionnaires sent
1701
(1998/99: 1626)

Returned
1711 (87%)
(1998/99: 1607, 83%)

Non-returned
256
(1998/99: 331)

Returned
1529 (90%)
(1998/99: 1385, 85%)

Non-returned
172
(1998/99: 241)

Analysed
1606 (82%)
(1998/99: 1518, 78%)

Not analysed
105
(1998/99: 89)

Analysed
1467 (86%)
(1998/99: 1337, 82%)

Not analysed
62
(1998/99: 48)

One hundred and five surgical questionnaires were excluded from analysis for the reasons given in Table 5.5. Similar exclusions occurred for 62 anaesthetic questionnaires (Table 5.6). For the first time, 2 questionnaires were completed for the wrong patient.

It remains a concern of NCEPOD that these questionnaires are unusable since they represent a significant investment of valuable time. It has been estimated that it can take a clinician up to a session to complete each questionnaire. This wasted time could therefore aggregate to over fifteen weeks work assuming 11 sessions a week (167 cases/11 sessions).

There continues to be a small number of clinicians who continually question NCEPOD's method because they seem to believe that NCEPOD is interested primarily in the cause of death. They therefore either refuse to complete a questionnaire for some patients where they do not believe that NCEPOD should be interested in a life-saving procedure or palliative procedure such as a tube oesophagostomy (as in the case below), or they insist on completing the

Table 5.5	Reasons for exclusion of surgical questionnaires from analysis	
Reasons for exclusion	**1999/00**	**1998/99**
Questionnaire completed for an earlier operation	57	54
Questionnaire received too late	40	32
Questionnaire incomplete	6	3
Questionnaire related to excluded procedure	2	0
Total	**105**	**89**

Table 5.6	Reasons for exclusion of anaesthetic questionnaires from analysis	
Reasons for exclusion	**1999/00**	**1998/99**
Questionnaire completed for an earlier operation	25	18
Questionnaire received too late	34	26
Questionnaire incomplete	0	4
Questionnaire related to excluded procedure	1	0
Questionnaire completed for wrong patient	2	0
Total	**62**	**48**

questionnaire for the more major procedure preceding death. The arrogance of a small minority of clinicians in regard to this issue is of great concern.

"I say to you without fear of contradiction that if I had to fill in one of these forms on every occasion that I performed a humanitarian procedure of this kind, my inclination to carry out the procedure would be greatly reduced to say the least. I have now reached the end of my surgical career and I feel that I should not leave without telling you that in this instance the form is totally inappropriate and you should in future take care to be a little bit more humane."

Fig 5.6 — **Response rates for questionnaires**

☐ Surgical questionnaire   ☐ Anaesthetic questionnaire

Table 5.7	Regional return rates	
Region	**Surgical questionnaire**	**Anaesthetic questionnaire**
Eastern	156/160	141/148
London	234/284	207/243
North Western	224/256	193/223
Northern & Yorkshire	244/292	241/255
South Eastern	195/227	155/178
South & West	168/185	143/153
Trent	166/195	160/179
West Midlands	154/176	151/164
Wales	115/128	90/102
Northern Ireland	26/31	25/28
Guernsey	No cases sampled	No cases sampled
Jersey	5/5	Anaesthetist unidentifiable
Isle of Man	6/6	6/6
Defence Secondary Care Agency	1/1	0/1
Independent Sector	17/21	17/21

Figure 5.6 and Table 5.7 show the return rate by region. It is not possible to show comparisons with the 1998/99 return rates as the regions changed in April 1999. A breakdown by Trust/independent group is shown in Appendix A.

Individual Trusts/hospitals are kept informed of their return rates on a quarterly basis so there is an opportunity to improve return rates where there are difficulties. NCEPOD is encouraged by the letters received throughout the year describing revised procedures to assist clinicians in completing their questionnaires.

"It is requested that all future requests for detailed reviews be directed to the Clinical Governance Support Centre (CGSC). The CGSC will take responsibility for validating the information provided, including the consultant in charge of the case at the time of death, and will arrange for the audit form and case notes to be made available to the relevant consultant. We anticipate that this new procedure will reduce the burden upon clinical staff and therefore improve our compliance with this important national review."

It is unfortunate that this is not the situation in all Trusts as this next letter from a surgeon illustrates.

"I recently received a second reminder from you about a CEPOD form I had not completed. I do not think it is at all appropriate for individual consultants to be named to their hospitals on clinical governance grounds as you suggest. To my knowledge, CEPOD has not provided any form of support whatsoever for the fairly arduous work involved in completing these forms, and the ever increasing pressure on consultants to complete reports for various bodies means that this type of activity is rapidly becoming unmanageable. Rather than taking your current approach, CEPOD should be supporting consultants by addressing their comments to the Chief Executives of hospitals, and demanding better support for consultants in their onerous administrative workload. You will gather that you have not persuaded me to give your request any priority. It will have to wait, like the other non-clinical duties that take up an increasing proportion of my time, until more urgent matters have been attended to."

The completed questionnaire was received three weeks after the closing date (27 weeks after it was sent).

Reasons for non-return of questionnaires

The figures for the last two years (Figures 5.7a, 5.7b, 5.8a and 5.8b) show little or no change in the high percentage of cases where no reason is offered for non-return of a questionnaire. Regular feedback to Trusts and hospitals indicating any valid reasons for non-return will, of course, highlight those cases where no contact has been made with NCEPOD to explain the inability to complete the questionnaire.

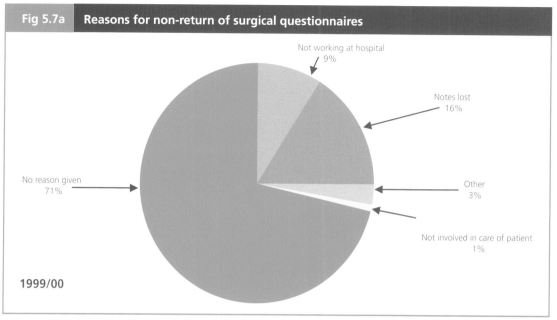

Fig 5.7a | **Reasons for non-return of surgical questionnaires**

Not working at hospital
9%

Notes lost
16%

No reason given
71%

Other
3%

Not involved in care of patient
1%

1999/00

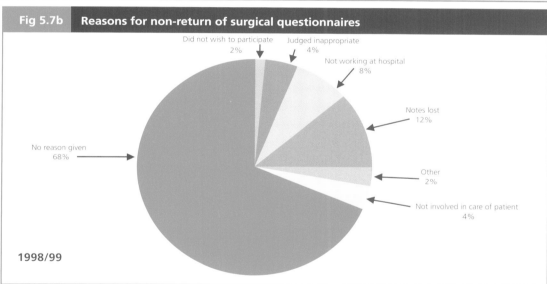

Fig 5.7b | **Reasons for non-return of surgical questionnaires**

Did not wish to participate
2%

Judged inappropriate
4%

Not working at hospital
8%

Notes lost
12%

No reason given
68%

Other
2%

Not involved in care of patient
4%

1998/99

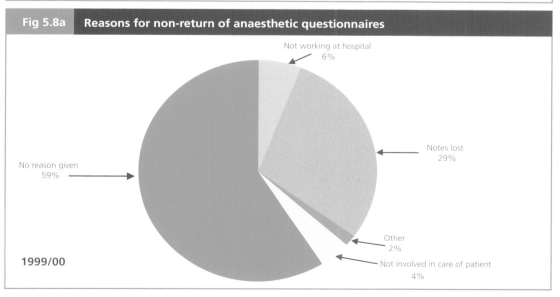

Fig 5.8a | **Reasons for non-return of anaesthetic questionnaires**

Not working at hospital
6%

Notes lost
29%

No reason given
59%

Other
2%

Not involved in care of patient
4%

1999/00

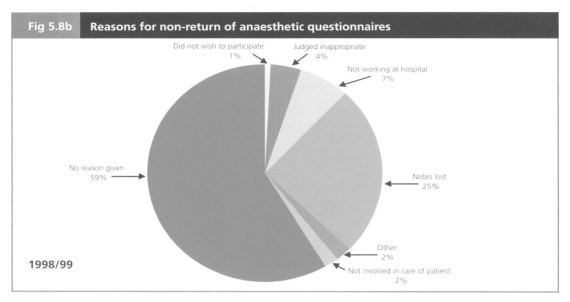

Fig 5.8b **Reasons for non-return of anaesthetic questionnaires**

Did not wish to participate 1%

Judged inappropriate 4%

Not working at hospital 7%

No reason given 59%

Notes lost 25%

Other 2%

Not involved in care of patient 2%

1998/99

There are mainly small percentage changes shown in these figures, which should disappear if hospitals take their clinical governance responsibilities seriously.

We would have hoped to see this group diminish as Medical Directors act on the feedback given and it is disappointing that this decrease is not yet in evidence.

Lost medical records

The final group needing particular attention is that where clinicians stated that they were unable to complete the questionnaire as the notes were incomplete, lost, or otherwise unobtainable. One of the Local Reporters has written a series of letters to the Medical Director, Chief Executive and Chairman of their Trust to bring their attention to the appalling way in which the notes of dead patients are stored.

"It is very disappointing for me to be writing to you on the above topic as yet again we are failing in our ability to complete NCEPOD forms due to a lack of clinical notes. This mandatory clinical governance issue should be of major concern to the Trust and should have resulted in some initiatives to correct the problems that I have highlighted during 1999, 2000 and now have to do again in 2001. I have a considerable file of correspondence with [the Medical Director] who assures me that "large initiatives" and "much effort" is being put into improvements in Medical Records. Initial impressions indicate this is not effective."

Another incident which indicated the difficulties of retrieving notes for deceased patients came to light during the data quality audit (see section 4), which was undertaken this year. The Chief Executive of the Trust had given permission for the audit to take place and asked NCEPOD to give seven days notice

in order that the notes could be pulled. In fact two months notice of the date the notes were needed was given. A week before the audit was due to take place, NCEPOD were advised that it would not be possible to retrieve the notes for at least another three weeks. The reason given was that the notes had been given to a document archiving company, they were possibly in Bristol (several hundred miles away from the hospital) but no details were kept of which notes had gone or their exact location.

"Further to your request for a CEPOD questionnaire to be filled in by myself on this gentleman, I write to inform you that the hospital have not been able to provide me with relevant notes to allow the said questionnaire to be completed. In fact in the notes provided to date, the only sign to indicate that he ever was under my care was a front sheet showing his date of admission and a sticker showing a Thompson's prosthesis. In the absence of appropriate notes you will understand that I cannot complete the questionnaire and I will request the hospital records department to find the notes for me, but in the meantime, I expect you to demonstrate patience and I hope that you will not harass me in the manner you have previously harassed me and my colleagues when we have had difficulty in filling in these questionnaires for you."

The harassment that NCEPOD was accused of comprised of a reminder 2 months after the questionnaire had been sent followed by another reminder 4 weeks later.

There has been an increase in the number of lost notes for both surgeons (1999/00:16%; 1998/99: 12%) and anaesthetists (1999/00: 29%; 1998/99 25%) which is disappointing given the improvement seen in the previous year. As commented on in 'Then and Now'[13] it would appear that in the majority of cases where anaesthetists state that notes are 'lost', they had in fact been retrieved by the operating surgeon.

Recommendations in last year's report[13] should have helped improve this situation. They cannot be improved on this year and so are repeated verbatim:

- *"Trusts/hospitals should establish systems to ensure that all 'NCEPOD case notes' are retrieved and passed from surgeon to anaesthetist."*
- *"If clinicians are informed by medical records departments that the notes are lost/missing, they should first enquire of their surgical/anaesthetic colleagues who may well have the records (this applies particularly to anaesthetists)."*
- *"Medical records departments should ensure that adequate tracer systems are in place in relation to the medical records of deceased patients."*

Health Service Circular 1999/053 'For the Record', gives guidance on the management of records including the best practice on the storage and retrieval of such records. NCEPOD would commend this to hospitals as the starting point in improving this 'Cinderella service'.

Recommendations

- There should be a standard way of collecting data on deaths occurring within 30 days of surgery but happening outside hospital.

- Trusts should ensure that all deaths (falling within the NCEPOD protocol) should be reported in a timely manner. Local Reporters should be given the necessary resources to ensure that this is possible.

- Trusts should review the discrepancies between HES data and NCEPOD data and ensure accurate data returns for both purposes.

- The names of anaesthetic personnel should be clearly recorded in the patient's casenotes.

- Medical Directors should ensure that all questionnaires are returned.

GENERAL INFORMATION ABOUT ANAESTHESIA & SURGERY

INTRODUCTION

Key points

- Eighty-three percent of surgical questionnaires and 64% of anaesthetic questionnaires were reviewed by a consultant involved with the case.

- One percent of patients who died were admitted for an elective day case operation. This small number compared to the total number of day case operations within the UK, suggests that overall there is appropriate patient selection and assessment for elective day case operations.

- A consultant or associate specialist surgeon was consulted before operation in 93% of cases. However, senior anaesthetic involvement was poor and a consultant or associate specialist anaesthetist was involved in some way in only 77% of cases.

- Some hospitals deny HDU facilities to selected patient groups.

- Six percent of patients had their operations delayed for non-medical reasons, mainly because of limited operating theatre availability or unavailability of an ICU or HDU bed.

- Where a pre-registration house officer obtained consent for the operation, 72% of the patients were ASA 3 or poorer.

- CVP monitoring was used in 44% of the patients. Peer review suggested that a further 13% might have benefited from invasive monitoring before, during or after the operation.

- Up to 16% of this sample had an indication for ICU or HDU care but did not receive it.

- The value of postmortem examinations for education and audit is poorly recognised.

- Anaesthetic departments did not review 70% of deaths. It would appear that many anaesthetic departments do not understand that a review of deaths can detect both organisational and clinical problems locally.

- That gynaecologists did not discuss 79% of their deaths is particularly poor.

The process for the collection of data is described in Appendix E. This section of the report reviews some of the anaesthetic and combined surgical specialties data for 10% of the deaths reported to NCEPOD from 1st April 1999 until 31st March 2000. Where appropriate the data will be compared to those from the 1990 NCEPOD Report[36] or the 'Then and Now' NCEPOD Report of 1998/99[13]. The full data from the anaesthetic and surgical questionnaires can be obtained, as a separate document, on direct application to NCEPOD or on the NCEPOD web-site (www.ncepod.org.uk).

COMPLETION OF QUESTIONNAIRES

All surgical questionnaires were completed either by the consultant surgeon or by a NCCG surgeon or surgical trainee. The consultant surgeon with responsibility for the care of the patient during their final operation subsequently reviewed most of the questionnaires. A consultant surgeon did not review 70 (4%) questionnaires. In 211 (13%) cases it is not known whether the consultant surgeon reviewed the questionnaire. Potentially, the consultant in charge of the case did not review 281 (17%) of the questionnaires.

An anaesthetist involved with the case completed the questionnaire in 64% of cases. A proxy anaesthetist, usually on behalf of a trainee anaesthetist, completed 35% questionnaires, but interestingly a trainee who was not involved in any way completed 14 questionnaires (Figure 6.1). NCEPOD is grateful to the proxy anaesthetists for the support that they give to this enquiry. It is surprising that a proxy completed 94 questionnaires for cases when the most senior anaesthetist at the start of the operation was a consultant and only three of these consultants were likely to have retired. The reason why consultants did not complete the questionnaire for a case in which they were involved is not known. Nevertheless, it does mean that an opportunity to reflect on their personal practice was lost on this occasion, as is additional information from personal recall of the circumstances surrounding the case.

HOSPITAL AND FACILITIES

Table 6.1	Type of hospital in which the final operation took place		
		1999/00	**1998/99**
District general	1169	73%	69%
University teaching	373	23%	26%
Limited surgical specialties	39	2%	2%
Independent	16	1%	1%
Others/not answered	9	<1%	2%
Total	**1606**		

Table 6.1 presents the types of hospitals in which the final operation took place and compares the percentage of the sample in each type of hospital with the data from the 1998/99 NCEPOD report. The distinction between district general and university teaching hospitals is not clear-cut. There are a large number of regional training programmes during which postgraduate trainees rotate through university teaching and district general hospitals, and consultants at both these types of hospitals are involved in their training. Moreover, the training status of a hospital does not indicate a level of facilities; for example, a response from a university teaching hospital reported that the hospital had no daytime emergency lists for general surgical patients, and no acute pain service. For acute hospitals, definitions based on the numbers of surgical beds might be more appropriate.

Critical care facilities

Table 6.2 compares the percentage of patients that had critical care facilities available in the hospital of their final operation with those in 1998/99.

Table 6.2	Special care areas in the hospital where the final operation took place* *(answers may be multiple n=1606)*	
	1999/00	**1998/99**
Recovery area or room	97%	97%
24-hour recovery area	81%	76%
High dependency unit	69%	61%
Intensive care unit	97%	96%
Coronary care unit	82%	N/A

Recovery area or room

Forty-two (3%) respondents to the surgical questionnaire did not indicate the presence of a recovery area in the appropriate tick box. Thirty-five of these were from district general or university

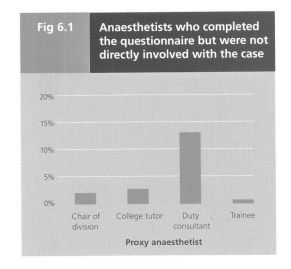

Fig 6.1 **Anaesthetists who completed the questionnaire but were not directly involved with the case**

Proxy anaesthetist (Chair of division, College tutor, Duty consultant, Trainee)

teaching hospitals so presumably this was an error of omission. Clearly a recovery area is now almost universally available. Twenty-one percent of anaesthetic questionnaires and 15% of surgical questionnaires indicated that there was in their hospital a recovery area that was not staffed 24 hours a day and seven days a week. The difference in reporting is probably one of perception of the local organisation of recovery services for out-of-hours patients. For those hospitals without a full-time recovery it would be timely to review their procedures for postoperative recovery of patients out-of-hours with reference to guidance published by the Royal College of Anaesthetists[38]. Immediately after their operation all patients not returning to a special care area (e.g. an ICU or HDU) need to be nursed until they are in a stable physiological state by nursing staff who are trained and practised in postoperative recovery care. If there are separate arrangements for staffing the operating theatres out-of-hours, these must include the provision of specialised recovery staff.

An 85-year-old, ASA 2 patient with a pelvic abscess and peritonitis underwent a laparotomy and Hartmann's procedure out-of-hours in a hospital with a part-time recovery area. The anaesthetist was a SHO 2. The operation finished at 22.30 and the patient was recovered by this anaesthetist for 15 minutes, and then returned to the ward at 22.45. The patient died on postoperative day seven.

These sorts of local arrangements are clearly not acceptable.

Intensive care and high dependency facilities

An ICU is now almost standard in hospitals in which acute surgery is undertaken. This is not so for an

Figure 6.2 shows the NCEPOD data on the percentage of patients that had an HDU in the hospital of their final operation, by year since 1990. Since 1994/95 there has been a commendable steady increase in HDU facilities. Of those patients whose operation was in a hospital without an HDU, 77% were in a district general hospital and 18% were in a university teaching hospital. The lack of an HDU facility for 31% of patients remains a cause for concern to NCEPOD[13, 25, 36, 39,] surgeons and anaesthetists[40]. All hospitals, where major acute surgery is undertaken, should have a critical care facility that is appropriate for level 2 patients. A level 2 patient is defined as one requiring more detailed observation or intervention including support for a single failing organ system or postoperative care, and those 'stepping down' from higher levels of care[37]. Patients should be made aware when this facility is not available.

The following deaths were in hospitals where HDU care was not available.

A 68-year-old, ASA 3 patient was scheduled for a Whipple's procedure. General anaesthesia was supplemented with thoracic epidural analgesia. During the operation there was persistent hypotension with a systolic arterial pressure of 80 mmHg or less, despite doses of ephedrine. After the operation the patient returned to the general ward. By postoperative day one a positive fluid balance of 12 litres was recorded and the patient was then admitted to the ICU where he died six days later.

A 77-year-old, ASA 3 patient was admitted for a laparotomy and drainage of a pelvic abscess. Coexisting medical disorders included hypertension, abdominal sepsis and anaemia with a haemoglobin of 9.1 gm/dl. After the operation the patient returned to the ward. The responding anaesthetist thought that the patient would have benefited from HDU care but this is not available in their hospital. Death was on the first postoperative day.

It is difficult to understand why some hospitals deny HDU facilities to selected patient groups.

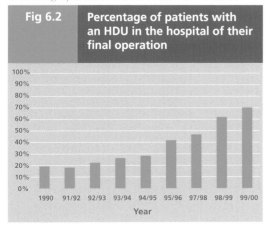

Fig 6.2	Percentage of patients with an HDU in the hospital of their final operation

Case Study 12

A 55-year-old had an operation for a second primary carcinoma of the colon some 16 years after two previous abdominal operations. During the operation technical difficulties were encountered. Thirty hours postoperatively, peritonitis was evident. The hospital has an HDU for medical patients only; it is the surgeon's opinion that an HDU facility could have resulted in the earlier recognition of this postoperative complication.

Case Study 13

A 92-year-old, ASA 3 patient had an operation for insertion of an Austin Moore prosthesis. Both the surgeon and anaesthetist commented that the hospital has an HDU, but orthopaedic patients are not allowed access to it.

Emergency operating theatres

Table 6.3	Availability of daytime emergency lists for urgent cases			
	General surgery		**Trauma /orthopaedic**	
	1999/00	**1998/99**	**1999/00**	**1998/99**
Available	1143 78%	75%	1280 87%	86%
Not available	317 21%	24%	173 12%	13%
Not answered	7 <1%	1%	14 1%	1%
Total	**1467**		**1467**	

NCEPOD has collected this data on daytime emergency lists for 1998/99 and 1999/00 only (Table 6.3). It is perhaps too soon to see a pattern of change but there is the suggestion that the number of cases in hospitals with general surgery emergency lists is increasing. This data is from the anaesthetic questionnaire, which also asked about anaesthetic staffing. Figure 6.3 shows the grade of anaesthetist providing cover for the emergency lists most of the time and Table 6.4 allows comparison of anaesthetic staffing for this sample with 1998/99 data.

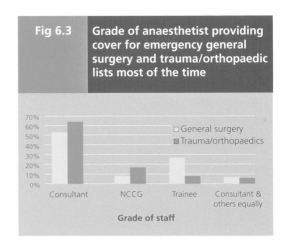

Fig 6.3 Grade of anaesthetist providing cover for emergency general surgery and trauma/orthopaedic lists most of the time

Table 6.4	Grade of anaesthetist providing cover for the emergency lists most of the time, comparison with 1998/99			
	General surgery		**Trauma /orthopaedics**	
	1999/00	**1998/99**	**1999/00**	**1998/99**
Consultant	605 53%	48%	819 64%	60%
Other grades	431 38%	48%	337 26%	37%
Consultant and other grades equally	93 8%	2%	112 9%	2%
Not answered	14 1%	2%	12 1%	1%
Total	**1143**		**1280**	

From Table 6.4 it would appear that consultant anaesthetic involvement with these lists, in which high-risk patients undergo operations, is increasing. This change is to be encouraged. Whilst comparable surgical data is not yet available, it is to be hoped that consultant surgical involvement is following a similar trend. NCEPOD is currently acquiring core data on the number and staffing of emergency operating lists.

It is of concern that trainee and NCCG anaesthetists provide cover most of the time for 38% of the emergency general surgical and 26% of emergency trauma/orthopaedic lists in the hospitals of these patients. It is recognised that training and experience in emergency anaesthesia are valuable, but senior anaesthetists are better able to deal with the organisational problems associated with running emergency operating lists, as well as providing greater clinical experience. It is the responsibility of each anaesthetic department to ensure that the anaesthetists running emergency lists are of sufficient experience, and to provide appropriate consultant supervision.

PATIENT PROFILE

Age and sex

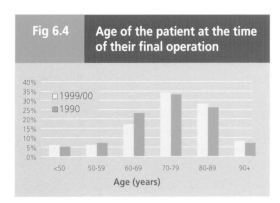

| Fig 6.4 | Age of the patient at the time of their final operation |

The age profile (Figure 6.4) repeats the trend seen in the 'Then and Now' NCEPOD Report[13] that patients who die after their operation are older compared to those in 1990[36]. Seventy percent of patients in this sample were aged 70 years or older compared with 65% in 1990. Fifty-two percent of patients were male.

Preoperative status

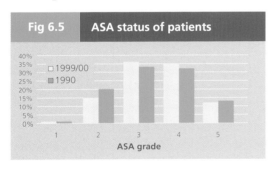

| Fig 6.5 | ASA status of patients |

Figure 6.5 repeats the trend seen last year, that patients who die after their operation are of poorer physical status compared to those in 1990. Eighty-three percent of the sample was ASA 3 or poorer compared to 78% in 1990.

From the anaesthetic questionnaires, 95% of patients had coexisting medical problems at the time of the operation.

The data in the first column of Table 6.5 is from the anaesthetic questionnaires. Compared with the 1998/99 data there is, apparently, an increase of cardiac, respiratory, neurological, alimentary and septic disorders. This may not be a true increase; rather the result of an increased recognition of the presence of these disorders. Under reporting of disorders has been suspected previously, for example the opinion of the 'Then and Now' NCEPOD Report[13] was that

Table 6.5	Coexisting medical problems at time of the final operation *(answers may be multiple)*		
	Anaesthetic questionnaire *(n=1467)*		Surgical questionnaire *(n=1606)*
	1999/00	1998/99	1999/00
Cardiac	72%	66%	46%
Respiratory	55%	37%	30%
Neurological	39%	33%	-
Alimentary	23%	16%	13%
Endocrine	19%	18%	14%
Sepsis	18%	13%	11%
Renal	16%	14%	16%
Haematological	10%	10%	9%
Musculoskeletal	10%	9%	8%
Hepatic	5%	5%	-
Other	15%	14%	-
None	-	6%	-
Not answered	-	2%	-

sepsis was under reported. An increased recognition of coexisting disorders is to be commended; it is likely to result in improved patient management.

The data in the last column is from the surgical questionnaires. Some of the responses by the anaesthetists and surgeons are markedly different, for example the cardiac and respiratory problems. This may be because the wording of the enquiry into coexisting disorders in the anaesthetic questionnaire differs from that in the surgical questionnaire. In the anaesthetic questionnaire *"coexisting medical symptoms, signs or diagnoses at the time of the final operation"* was requested. However, in the surgical questionnaire *"coexisting problems other than the main diagnosis at the time of operation"* was requested. It might be, for example, that controlled or previous cardiac or respiratory disorders were not viewed by the responding surgeon as a problem, and hence not reported. Not all the 'disorder' categories are directly comparable; for example the surgical questionnaire asks for neurological and psychiatric disorders separately. The wording of this and some other questions within the questionnaires makes comparisons between the surgical and anaesthetic data difficult. It is a weakness that NCEPOD recognises and will address.

The most common coexisting cardiac disorders and respiratory disorders as cited in the anaesthetic questionnaires are presented in tables 6.6 and 6.7 respectively.

Table 6.6	Coexisting cardiac disorders (n = 1467, answers may be multiple)
Previous MI/ischaemic heart disease	60%
Hypertension	29%
Chronic cardiac failure	19%
Angina	18%
Atrial fibrillation	17%
Peripheral vascular disease	15%

Table 6.7	Coexisting respiratory disorders (n = 1467, answers may be multiple)
COPD	19%
Chest infection	12%
Asthma	7%

NCEPOD has not previously been able to separately identify patients with either a previous myocardial infarction or ischaemic heart disease; in 1998/99 it could only estimate that 42% of patients had one or more cardiac conditions that indicated myocardial ischaemia[13]. This year NCEPOD has identified that 60% of the patients had known ischaemic heart disease at the time of their final operation; an incidence higher than has previously been identified. National Statistics [41] identified that for the year 2000, 20% of all deaths had ischaemic heart disease reported as the main cause of death. However, National Statistics under represent ischaemic heart disease, as importantly, they do not include co-morbidity, i.e. section II of the Medical Certificate of Death.

ADMISSION AND OPERATION

Admission category

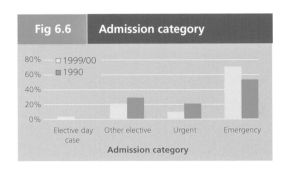

Fig 6.6 — Admission category

The type of operation and, admission data is from the surgical questionnaires. Figure 6.6 repeats the trend seen in the 'Then and Now' NCEPOD Report[13], that patients who die are more likely to be admitted as an emergency.

For the first time, this year's elective admissions were subdivided into those planned as day case admissions and other elective admissions. Twenty-three (1%) patients were elective day case admissions. The ASA of elective day case patients is presented in Table 6.8.

Table 6.8	ASA status of elective day case operations (n = 1606)
ASA 1	6
ASA 2	5
ASA 3	8
ASA 4	3
Not specified	1
Total	23

The 'Who Operates When' NCEPOD Report[42] identified that in 1995/96, 36% of all cases were elective day case operations; this figure now has probably increased. This figure of deaths (Table 6.8) after elective day case operations may slightly underestimate the true number of deaths; as patients who die at home do not always get reported to NCEPOD. Nevertheless, they suggest that very few of the patients that are admitted for elective day case operations die and that overall there is appropriate patient selection and assessment. The three ASA 4 patients were reviewed. One underwent dilatation and laser treatment of an oesophageal carcinoma, which was performed regularly at four-weekly intervals. Two underwent cataract surgery. One was an 80-year-old with cardiac and respiratory problems but no information was given as to whether these were longstanding problems, or of their severity. The other was a 74-year-old with non-Hodgkins lymphoma who had the operation at a specialist eye hospital. He had been unwell for six days before the operation and four days afterwards his medical team admitted him to hospital because of abdominal masses, splenomegaly, lymphadenopathy and jaundice; clearly these medical complications were missed at his preoperative assessment. This last case was the only one considered inappropriate.

Admission route

The main routes of admission were as follows: 31% of patients were referred from their general medical practitioner, 30% directly from A&E and 15% were admitted following an outpatient appointment. Thirteen percent were transferred from another hospital and this compares with 12% in 1990. In total 213 were transferred from another hospital to that of their final operation and details of these other hospitals are presented in Table 6.9. Of these, 25 were transferred from a hospital outside the region.

Table 6.9	Patients transferred from another hospital	
	1999/00	**1990**
District general hospital	132	189
University teaching hospital	31	33
Community hospital	13	36
Nursing home	12	
Independent hospital	11	6
Limited surgical specialty	7	19
Defence secondary care unit	1	3
Other		14
Not answered	6	13
Total	**213**	**313**

In 18/213 (8%) cases the patient's condition deteriorated during the transfer. Regional specialisation of services has concentrated surgical expertise in centres of excellence for specialist procedures. However, this does require some patients to be transferred between hospitals in order that they receive the best care for their condition. It is inevitable that some patients will be in an unstable condition and may deteriorate on transfer, for example patients with a leaking aortic aneurysm travelling to a vascular unit (six patients) or those with a severe head injury travelling to a neurosurgical centre (four patients). Nine of these 18 patients were already critically ill with an ASA 5. Some cases may be

affected by insufficient availability of ICU beds. The availability of ICU beds is something that requires local audit and remedy when indicated.

Case Study 14

A 62-year-old, ASA 5 patient with a leaking abdominal aortic aneurysm was admitted to a hospital without a vascular service. The patient waited "several hours" in the admitting hospital, whilst several hospitals tried to find an ICU bed. Although haemodynamically stable in the initial hospital, the patient arrived badly shocked at the hospital of referral and the situation was by then probably irretrievable. There was still no ICU bed available after the operation so the patient's lungs were ventilated in recovery until one became available. The surgeon commented that "lack of ICU beds nationally costs lives on a regular basis - this is one of them".

Operation

The surgical specialties for the operations are presented in Table 6.10 and the percentages of each specialty as a percentage of the whole sample are similar to those in 1998/99.

Table 6.10	Surgical specialty of the operation	
General surgery	703	44%
Orthopaedic	358	22%
Vascular	222	14%
Urology	81	5%
Cardiothoracic	75	5%
Neurosurgery	74	5%
Gynaecology	25	2%
Paediatric	23	1%
Otorhinolaryngology	21	1%
Plastic surgery	10	<1%
Ophthalmology	7	<1%
Oral/maxillofacial	7	<1%
Total	**1606**	

The classification of the urgency of the final operation is presented in Figure 6.7.

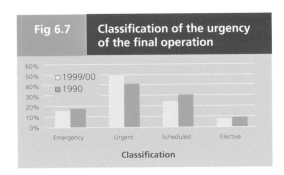

Fig 6.7 — Classification of the urgency of the final operation

Classification: Emergency, Urgent, Scheduled, Elective
Legend: □ 1999/00 ■ 1990

Sixty-seven percent of operations were classified as emergency or urgent compared with 60% in 1990 (Figure 6.7). This repeats the trend seen in the last NCEPOD report that patients who die after an operation are more likely to have undergone emergency or urgent surgery. Fifty-one percent had urgent surgery; this compares with 42% in 1990.

The anticipated operative risk is presented in Table 6.11 and follows the pattern of classification of the urgency of the final operation. This has not changed over the past 10 years.

Table 6.11 — The anticipated risk of death related to the proposed final operation		
	1999/00 (n=1606)	1990
Not expected	15%	14%
Small but significant risk	22%	24%
Definite risk	54%	50%
Expected	8%	3%

Delays to operation

From the anaesthetic questionnaire, 329/1467 (22%) patients had their operation delayed in order to improve their medical condition. The systems that required attention are presented in Table 6.12.

Table 6.12 — System(s) needing attention before operation (n = 329, answers may be multiple)	
Cardiac	51%
Metabolic	38%
Respiratory	27%
Haematological	25%
Other	8%

From the surgical questionnaire, 100/1606 (6%) patients had their operation delayed due to factors other than clinical. The numbers of cases delayed for each specialty, and these expressed as a percentage of the total number of cases in that specialty, are

presented in Table 6.13. From this it would seem that orthopaedic patients are more likely to suffer delays for non-medical reasons than patients in other specialties are. Information provided by surgeons and anaesthetists allowed NCEPOD to identify 69/1606 (4%) patients whose operation was delayed due to limited operating theatre availability and 13/1606 (1%) whose operation was delayed due to unavailability of an ICU or HDU bed. Delays to operation due to the availability of emergency operating time or critical care facilities requires close monitoring locally. An inadequacy of critical care facilities is detrimental to patient care.

Table 6.13 — Delays for non-clinical reasons and presented as a percentage of deaths for that specialty		
Orthopaedic	43	12%
Cardiothoracic	6	8%
Vascular	15	7%
General surgery	30	4%
Others	6	
Total	**100**	

Consent for the operation

The grade of the most senior surgeon taking consent from the patient is presented in Table 6.14.

Table 6.14 — The grade of the most senior surgeon taking consent from the patient		
Consultant	571	36%
Associate specialist	21	1%
Staff grade	48	3%
SpR	417	26%
SHO	350	22%
Pre-registration house officer	108	7%
No consent taken	43	3%
Other	6	<1%
Not known	11	<1%
Not answered	31	2%
Total	**1606**	

Obtaining informed consent appropriately is one of the fundamental aspects of good surgical practice [43, 44, 45]. In 28% of cases the person who obtained consent was not present during the operation. The General Medical Council has published guidance for those delegating the seeking of consent for operations and other invasive procedures[46] and the specific issue of consent was discussed in the 'Then and Now' NCEPOD Report [13]. The taking of a patient's consent for treatment should only be delegated in exceptional circumstances. If consent is delegated to one *not* undertaking the procedure it is the responsibility of the operating surgeon to ensure that:

- the person to whom this responsibility is delegated is suitably trained;

- they have sufficient knowledge of the proposed investigation or treatment;

- they understand the risks involved and possess the appropriate communication skills;

- they act in accordance with the GMC guidance.

Consent was not obtained in 3% of cases and these were when the patient was physically or mentally unable to provide it. On 108 (7%) occasions the person who obtained consent was a pre-registration house officer. The specialties where consent was by a pre-registration house officer were general surgery 65/703 (9%) (53 patients undergoing a laparotomy); vascular 29/222 (13%); urology 7/81 (9%) and orthopaedic 7/358 (2%). The physical status of the patients where consent was by a pre-registration house officer is presented in Figure 6.8.

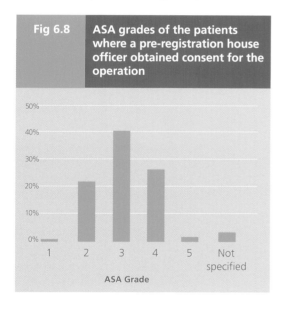

Fig 6.8 — ASA grades of the patients where a pre-registration house officer obtained consent for the operation

On 78/108 (72%) occasions when a pre-registration house officer obtained consent, the physical status of the patient was ASA 3 or poorer. It is hoped that all junior doctors that obtain consent have knowledge of, or have discussed with the senior surgeon, the specific complications of the procedure and communicate these to the patient. However, it must be questioned as to whether the most junior member of the team is the appropriate person to obtain consent in patients of poor physiological status and when there is an anticipated risk of death.

STAFFING

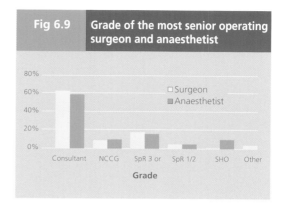

Fig 6.9 — Grade of the most senior operating surgeon and anaesthetist

Surgeons

A consultant was the most senior operating surgeon present in the operating room for 63% of cases and either a consultant or associate specialist was consulted before operation in 93% of cases. This is a commendably high senior surgical involvement in the decision to operate. The 'other' surgeons shown in Figure 6.9 were mostly locum appointments for service or training, or visiting SpRs of unknown grade.

In this sample there were 36 cases where the most senior surgeon was stated not to have a higher surgical diploma (36/1606, 2%). This is the same percentage as in the 1998/99 NCEPOD report (30/1518, 2%) in which we questioned its accuracy[13]. However, the consistency of the percentage suggests that the figure may be true. The grade and specialty of these surgeons are presented in Table 6.15. It seems unlikely that the surgeons in some of these grades would not have a higher surgical diploma. However, if the statements are true, then there appears to a problem, particularly in orthopaedic and general surgery. In these specialties individuals without a higher diploma are apparently holding senior surgical posts, including posts that usually have responsibilities for training.

Table 6.15	Grade and specialty of most senior operating surgeon for whom no higher surgical diploma was indicated		
Most senior operating surgeon	**Specialty of surgeon in charge**	**1999/00**	**1998/99**
Consultant	Orthopaedic	0	1
	General surgery	1	1
	Vascular	0	1
	Neurosurgery	0	1
	Cardiothoracic	2	0
Associate specialist	Orthopaedic	4	2
	General surgery	1	0
Staff grade	Orthopaedic	8	8
	General surgery	1	3
SpR 4+	Orthopaedic	1	0
	General surgery	1	1
	Neurosurgery	1	0
SpR 3	Orthopaedic	1	1
	General surgery	0	1
	Neurosurgery	1	0

Anaesthetists

A consultant was the most senior anaesthetist for 59% (860/1467) of cases. However, senior anaesthetic involvement was less apparent than was senior surgical involvement; a consultant or associate specialist anaesthetist was involved in some way in 77% of cases. Of the 569/1467 cases where the senior anaesthetist was not a consultant or associate specialist grade, advice was sought on only 212/569 (37%) occasions. When advice was sought, for 77% of these cases it was sought from a consultant, compared to 64% in 1998/99. This level of consultant input into the anaesthetic care of these patients, who were generally of poor physical status and at risk of death, is far too low. The supervision of anaesthetic trainees was fully discussed in the 'Then and Now' NCEPOD Report[13] and has been a recurring concern of all the NCEPOD and CEPOD reports.

The qualifications of the most senior anaesthetists were: 75% had the anaesthetic fellowship and 6% had no higher diploma in anaesthesia. In 1990 these figures were 66% and 6% respectively.

Operations by a SHO surgeon or anaesthetist

There were 48 patients who were operated on by an SHO and 141 patients who were anaesthetised by an SHO. The ASA grade of these patients is presented in Figure 6.10.

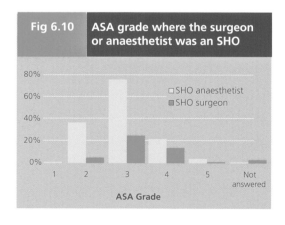

| Fig 6.10 | ASA grade where the surgeon or anaesthetist was an SHO |

SHO surgeons

The surgical specialties of the 48 patients operated on by an SHO were orthopaedics 17; general surgery 17; vascular 5; urology 2; maxillofacial 2; neurosurgery 3 and otorhinolaryngology 2. Of the 12 general surgical cases, 11 were ASA 3 or poorer.

The 1999 'Extremes of Age' NCEPOD Report[1] recommended that the experience of the anaesthetist and surgeon should be matched to the physical status of the elderly patient, as well as to the technical demands of the procedure. The technical abilities of these trainees to perform the operation are not being questioned. However, a senior surgeon is more likely to have a shorter operating time and is able to take responsibility for difficult decision-making if, or when, untoward events occur.

The following cases were discussed with a consultant surgeon before the operation. It must be questioned whether these consultants were aware of the poor physical status of the patients.

Case Study 15

A 59-year-old, ASA 3 patient with ischaemic heart disease, diabetes mellitus and thyroid disease was operated on at 21.40 for a perineal abscess. His preoperative haemoglobin was 10.1 gm/dl and serum creatinine 186 micromol/l. The surgeon was an SHO with seven months' experience and no higher diploma in surgery. The anaesthetist was a second year SHO. The patient received a general anaesthetic and the lungs were ventilated using a laryngeal mask airway. One hour into the procedure the patient suffered a cardiac arrest. He was initially resuscitated but died the following day.

Case Study 16

A 76-year-old, ASA 4 patient with CCF, shortness of breath, pleural effusion, dementia and a previous CVA underwent a simple closure of a dehisced colostomy stoma at 17.00. The surgeon was an SHO with more than two years' experience and had part 2 of the surgical Fellowship. The anaesthetist was a consultant. The patient suffered a fatal cardiac arrest 1 h 50 min into the operation, from what was presumed to be either acute left ventricular failure or a pulmonary embolus.

In the following case the consultant surgeon was clearly aware of the patient's poor physical status.

Case Study 17

An 80-year-old, ASA 5 patient developed peritonitis and hypoxaemia five days after a hemiarthroplasty for a fractured neck of femur. Preoperative haemoglobin was 9.1 gm/dl, serum urea 17.2 mmol/l and creatinine 169 micromol/l. Laparotomy revealed ischaemic colitis, and a partial left colectomy and transverse colostomy were performed. The surgeon had been an SHO for 36 months and had the surgical Fellowship. The anaesthetist was an associate specialist with the DA. No HDU existed in the hospital and the patient died in the recovery area one hour after the operation. The consultant who completed the surgical questionnaire commented that there was only a remote chance of survival.

In some cases, as illustrated in cases 18 and 19, SHO surgeons were both experienced and well qualified. It must be questioned as to whether it was appropriate for them to be occupying an SHO training post.

Case Study 18

A 74-year-old patient developed peritonitis 11 days after a right hemicolectomy for colonic carcinoma. The consultant was on leave but commented that the trainees were slow to react to the peritonitis. The case was discussed with a consultant who was providing cover. It was suspected that there was ileal ischaemia. The SHO who was deputed to operate had passed the FRCS three years previously. There was an associate specialist in the hospital to provide support. The patient suffered a cardiac arrest in the anaesthetic room, was resuscitated and the laparotomy went ahead. A further ileal resection and primary anastomosis was done. The patient did not survive 24 hours.

Case Study 19

A 79-year-old patient had a laparotomy to oversew a perforated duodenal ulcer. The surgeon was an SHO with the FRCS who had previously worked as an SpR. The consultant was at home. The patient died from cardiac complications three weeks after surgery.

SHO anaesthetists

The responsibilities of trainees in anaesthesia were discussed in detail in the 'Then and Now' NCEPOD Report[13] and so the following comments will be brief.

The surgical specialties of the 141 patients' anaesthetised by an SHO were: orthopaedics, 60; general surgery, 60; vascular, 14; urology, 4, plastic surgery, 2 and otorhinolaryngology, 1. Of the orthopaedic cases 57 had a fractured hip or femur and 41/57 (72%) were ASA 3 or 4. Of the general surgery cases 51 involved a laparotomy and 36/51 (71%) were ASA 3, 4 or 5. This picture of the physical status of patients who are being anaesthetised by SHOs is not reassuring. All anaesthetic departments need to review whether their most junior trainees are assuming responsibilities appropriately.

OPERATIVE MONITORING

Table 6.16 presents the patient monitoring that was used during the operation.

Table 6.16	Monitoring devices were used during the management of this anaesthetic (n = 1467, answers may be multiple)	
Pulse oximetry	1457	99%
Indirect arterial pressure	1176	80%
ECG	1442	98%
Capnography	1314	90%
Vapour analyser	1191	81%
Urine output	781	53%
Temperature	445	30%
CVP	642	44%
Direct arterial pressure	618	42%
Pulmonary artery pressure	66	4%

The first five monitors in this list are essential to the safe conduct of anaesthesia[47]. Only one patient had no operative monitoring.

Case Study 20

An 86-year-old, ASA 5 patient was undergoing femoral embolectomy under local anaesthesia that was provided by the operating surgeon. When the patient became agitated an SHO anaesthetist, who had not previously assessed the patient, was called upon to provide sedation. There was no monitoring during the procedure and no anaesthetic chart was completed.

In almost all cases pulse oximetry and ECG were monitored. If those patients having either direct or indirect arterial pressure monitoring are analysed, blood pressure was also monitored in almost all cases. The percentage of cases in which capnography was monitored was lower, but 81/1467 (8%) had local anaesthesia alone and some patients had intravenous sedation and face mask oxygen, making the monitoring of expired CO_2 difficult. Only 13/1467 (<1%) questionnaires complained of a lack of monitoring equipment. NCEPOD recognises the commendable efforts by anaesthetists and managers to achieve this. However, non-invasive blood pressure was not present in the anaesthetic room for one case, capnography was not present in the anaesthetic room for one case and in the operating room for two cases, and a vapour analyser was not present in the operating room for five cases. Of concern was case 21:

Case Study 21

A 55-year-old, ASA 5 patient with a chest infection, shortness of breath and CCF had a flexible bronchoscopy performed. An experienced SpR anaesthetist with the CCST provided the general anaesthesia in an environment that had no facility for ECG monitoring. The patient died three days later.

The environment for this general anaesthetic must be questioned.

The 'Recommendations for Standards of Monitoring During Anaesthesia and Recovery'[47] state explicitly that a pulse oximeter, non-invasive blood pressure monitor, electrocardiograph and capnograph in the anaesthetic room, and these four plus vapour analyser in the operating room, are essential for the safe conduct of anaesthesia. If it is necessary to continue anaesthesia without a particular device then the anaesthetist must clearly record the reasons for this in the anaesthetic record.

CVP monitoring was used in 44% of patients who died. Peer review suggested that a further 13% might have benefited from invasive monitoring, mostly CVP monitoring, before, during or after the operation. The following cases are examples.

Case Study 22

A 78-year-old, 51 kg, ASA 4 patient with faecal peritonitis, tachycardia and tachypnoea was admitted to a hospital without an HDU. Coexisting disorders included ischaemic heart disease with angina. There was ECG evidence of bundle branch block. The operation was a laparotomy, washout of the abdomen, drainage of an abscess and loop ileostomy. A staff grade anaesthetist with part 1 of the anaesthetic Fellowship and working with an SHO 2 provided general anaesthesia for the operation that lasted 1 h 45 min. No temperature or CVP monitoring was used and 3500 ml of fluid were infused. The anaesthetist declared that no critical incidents occurred during the anaesthesia. But immediately postoperatively the patient was transferred to the ICU where he was in a poor general condition and required ventilation to the lungs. He was hypotensive,

oliguric, had metabolic acidosis, needed inotropic support, developed pulmonary oedema and died on postoperative day two.

Case Study 23

A 75-year-old, ASA 2 patient weighing approximately 60 kg was admitted with a bowel obstruction. The patient had COPD and was 'frail' but otherwise had been fit. The patient received fluid resuscitation overnight that was not guided by CVP monitoring, and the next morning her operation was delayed for more than five further hours because the emergency theatre was busy with other cases. An SHO 2 anaesthetist with part 1 of the anaesthetic Fellowship provided general anaesthesia for the operation, a subtotal colectomy and ileosigmoid anastomosis, that lasted 3 h 45 min. Operative monitoring did not include urine output or CVP. The patient had a persistent tachycardia of greater than 100 per minute during the operation, despite receiving 3100 ml of intravenous fluid. Before the end of the operation this case was discussed with a consultant anaesthetist. After 30 minutes in a recovery area the patient was transferred to an HDU where she developed septicaemic shock accompanied by acute renal failure and metabolic acidosis. Death was in the ICU on postoperative day six.

It would appear that these patients were severely unwell with sepsis before their operation, and one also had severe coexisting cardiovascular disease. It was predictable that a CVP might be useful to guide fluid replacement during the operation. It was also likely to help guide fluid and drug treatment afterwards. Why then was it not inserted at the start of the anaesthetic? Does the absence of an HDU and/or the ability of the ward to manage or monitor a CVP line affect the decision to use, what would appear to be, appropriate invasive monitoring? If so, is it acceptable to have these sorts of restrictions placed on the way such patients are managed? Further discussion on this issue can be found in the section on perioperative care and the involvement of critical care teams.

POSTOPERATIVE CARE

ICU and HDU care

Admission

Four percent (63/1606) of this sample died in the operating theatre and 1% (24/1606) died in the recovery room. Immediately postoperatively 32% (521/1606) went to an ICU, 8% (130/1606) went to an HDU and one patient went to a coronary care unit. From the anaesthetic questionnaire, 6% (89/1467) of respondents were unable to transfer a patient to an ICU or HDU when they thought that this was indicated, mainly because these units were full. Peer review of cases suggests that for a further 10% of this sample there was an indication for ICU or HDU care.

From the surgical questionnaires NCEPOD knows of 21 (1%) patients who underwent an inter-hospital transfer preoperatively specifically for ICU care, either because there was no staffed and available ICU bed or no ICU facility in the referring hospital. NCEPOD does not know how many patients were transferred postoperatively because critical care facilities were not available.

Case Study 24

A 74-year-old, ASA 4 had an operation for perforated peptic ulcer. Postoperatively she required an ICU bed, but no bed was available and she was transferred to another hospital. She required a second operation for gastric outlet obstruction.

Case Study 25

A 68-year-old patient, ASA 4 had an operation for a perforated duodenal ulcer. No ICU bed was available after the operation so he was transferred to another hospital. He was transferred back to the original hospital's ICU and required re-operation for an abdominal washout three days before he died.

It is evidently unsatisfactory to transfer patients to another hospital for ICU care immediately postoperatively when they are likely to be in an unstable physiological status. The unenviable task of determining priorities, such as which patient is to be transferred because of insufficient ICU beds, falls to the intensive care physician and NCEPOD respects

their decision; it should not need to be made.

Forty-one patients were admitted to an ICU/HDU after they had initially been admitted to a ward.

Case Study 26

A 74-year-old, ASA 2 patient underwent a laparoscopy and subsequent open cholecystectomy for an inflamed gall bladder. Following surgical difficulties an HDU bed was requested. Another patient also needed the one remaining HDU bed and, after consultation with the HDU consultant and another anaesthetic consultant, this postoperative patient was deemed a lower priority and returned to the ward. Ward care in that hospital precluded epidural analgesia. Sputum retention, hypoxaemia and sepsis were established by the following morning when the patient was admitted to ICU. The patient died from multiple organ dysfunction on day eight.

Evidence from this sample is that clinicians can experience difficulty in securing admission for patients to ICU/HDU facilities. Failure to secure a critical care bed postoperatively often results in a delayed admission with a subsequent protracted ICU stay. The under-provision of critical care beds, and its impact on mortality, morbidity and length of hospital stay, seems to make very little sense in either clinical or economic terms.

Discharge

The reason for discharge of patients from ICU or HDU is presented in Table 6.17.

Table 6.17	Reason for discharge of patients from ICU and HDU	
Death	395	(57%)
Elective transfer to the ward	182	(26%)
Pressure on beds	13	(2%)
Not answered/not known	102	
Total	**692**	

NCEPOD knows of 13 patients that were discharged from ICU or HDU because of the pressure on beds. However, often the reason for discharge from a critical care facility is not documented in the clinical notes and the number is probably higher. Patients who die within 30 days of an operation represent a high-risk group that should be well provided for with critical care facilities and the data presented here reaffirms the persisting national shortfall in that provision.

The Audit Commission report, 'Critical to Success'[48] and the Department of Health's review, 'Comprehensive Critical Care'[37], reviewed critical care services nationally and made recommendations. At a local level hospitals undertaking acute surgery should collect the type of data that is presented in this section in order to identify and quantify inadequacies in their critical care facilities. The solutions to this inadequacy are not simply increased beds, manpower and funding. There is interdependency between the use of critical care and ward based care. Once areas of inadequacy in the critical care service have been identified discussions between intensive care consultants, surgeons, physicians, senior nursing staff and senior hospital management can agree organisational changes across the hospital that may improve its use (see section 6 on perioperative care).

POSTOPERATIVE COMPLICATIONS

The complications after operation reported in the anaesthetic questionnaires are presented in Table 6.18.

From the surgical questionnaire 502/1606 (31%) cases had shared care with another medical specialty; of these for 93/1606 (6%) patients it was with another surgical specialty and for 371/1606 (23%) patients it was with a medical specialty. The postoperative ward care of patients is discussed more fully in section 6 on the organisation of perioperative care.

Table 6.18	Complications after operation (n = 1476, answers may be multiple)	
Cardiac		44%
Ventilatory		42%
Renal failure		28%
Septicaemia		23%
Progress of surgical condition		17%
Haematological including blood loss		14%
Central nervous system failure		14%
Hepatic failure		4%
None		5%
Not answered		11%

POSTMORTEM

Sixty-two percent (993/1606) of deaths were reported to the coroner and a coroner's postmortem was performed on 425/993 (43%) of the deaths reported to them. Of the remaining cases, a hospital postmortem was undertaken on 79/1181 (79%). (Table 6.19)

Table 6.19	Postmortem examinations (n = 1606)	
Coroner's postmortem	425	(26%)
Hospital postmortem	79	(5%)
No postmortem	930	(58%)
Not answered or not known	173	(11%)

Thus, in total for 31% of cases there was a postmortem examination and this compared with 41% in 1990.

The surgical team was apprised of the date of the postmortem for 141/503 (27%) cases when a postmortem was being performed. On 62/141 (44%) occasions no one from the surgical team attended, and a consultant attended only 23/141 (16%), despite being informed that the examination was taking place. The hospital postmortem rate and the interest of clinicians in their findings appear low. The value of postmortem examinations for education and audit is poorly recognised. One surgeon commented that no postmortem was requested because there was *"no surgical problem"*. Is there then little interest in postoperative medical complications? The postmortem did not confirm the clinical impression in 43 cases, and in a further 61 there were additional unexpected findings; thus there was something to be learned from 104/503 (21%) of postmortem examinations. Five hundred and sixty-four patients died in an ICU or HDU and only 217/564 (38%) of them had a postmortem. One hundred and ninety-three of these 217 (89%) had a coroner's postmortem and 25/217 (11%) had a hospital postmortem. It is hoped that intensive care physicians are being involved in the decision to request postmortems of patients treated in their units, and are taking an interest in the findings (see Section 9).

AUDIT

Seventy-seven (5%) deaths were in hospitals in which the anaesthetic department still has no morbidity/ mortality review meetings. That there are anaesthetic departments without morbidity/mortality review meetings is unacceptable in the current climate of clinical governance and risk management. Whether such departmental meetings exist was not asked in the surgical questionnaire. The percentage of cases discussed at anaesthetic and surgical departmental audit meetings is presented in Figure 6.11.

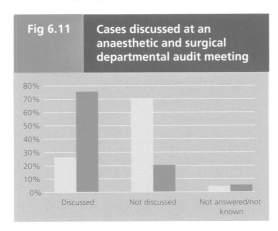

Fig 6.11 — Cases discussed at an anaesthetic and surgical departmental audit meeting

That anaesthetic departments did not review 70% of patients who died is deplorable. The advice in 'Good Practice: a Guide for Departments of Anaesthesia'[49] is explicit; there should be a monthly review of deaths, complications, unexpected outcomes and critical incidents. This NCEPOD report contains a plethora of examples in which organisational problems affected outcome. It would appear that many anaesthetic departments do not understand that a review of deaths can detect both organisational and clinical problems locally.

There are clear recommendations that surgeons must take part in surgical audit[43]. Despite this, surgical departments did not discuss 20% of deaths. The comments concerning the value of audit in anaesthesia must also apply to surgery. The breakdown of the numbers for each surgical specialty is presented in Table 6.20

The percentage of patients discussed at audit in the last two reports has remained unchanged at 75% compared with 64% in 1990. However, the use of audit varies between the specialties (Figure 6.12).

There has been maintenance of standards in many specialties and a marked improvement in some. The audit of deaths in the specialty of gynaecology is particularly poor and this anomaly needs to be addressed in the light of clinical governance.

Table 6.20 — Cases that were not discussed at a surgical audit meeting by specialty and the percentage of deaths for that specialty not discussed

	Not discussed	% of deaths
Orthopaedic	107	30%
General surgery	102	14%
Vascular	28	13%
Urology	22	27%
Neurosurgery	18	24%
Gynaecology	15	60%
Cardiothoracic	8	11%
Otorhinolaryngology	7	33%
Ophthalmology	5	24%
Others	9	
Total	**321**	

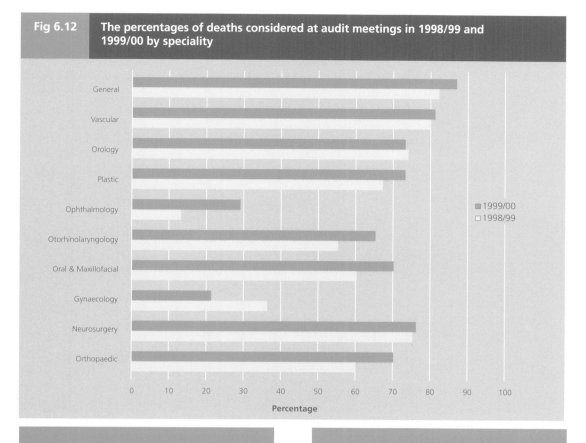

Fig 6.12 The percentages of deaths considered at audit meetings in 1998/99 and 1999/00 by speciality

Recommendations

- Immediately after their operation all patients not returning to a special care area (e.g. an ICU or HDU) need to be nursed by those who are trained and practised in postoperative recovery care. If there are separate arrangements for staffing the operating theatres out-of-hours, these must include the provision of specialised recovery staff.

- All hospitals where major acute surgery is undertaken should have a critical care facility that is appropriate for level 2[37] patients. Patients should be made aware when this facility is not available.

- It is the responsibility of each anaesthetic department to ensure that the anaesthetists running emergency lists are of sufficient experience, and to provide appropriate consultant supervision.

- Delays to operation due to the availability of emergency operating time or critical care facilities require close monitoring locally.

- Where there is a definite risk of death and patients are in a poor physiological condition, junior doctors in training (SHO or pre-registration house officers) should not obtain consent for surgery.

- Medical Directors should review the responsibilities of those consultant and NCCG surgeons who do not hold a higher surgical diploma.

- There needs to be a much higher level of involvement of anaesthetic consultants in the care of those patients who are in a poor physical state and at risk of death.

- Hospitals should identify and quantify inadequacies in their critical care facilities. If inadequacy exists discussions between intensive care consultants, surgeons, physicians, senior nursing staff and senior hospital management can agree organisational changes across the hospital that may improve its use.

- Medical Directors should ensure that morbidity/mortality meetings are held in all specialities.

GENERAL ANAESTHESIA WITH REGIONAL ANALGESIA

Key points

- A regional anaesthetic technique can provide good analgesia, both during the operation when combined with general anaesthesia, and postoperatively. NCEPOD supports both techniques.

- Regional analgesia combined with general anaesthesia may precipitate hypotension, especially in those who are septic or dehydrated.

For some years NCEPOD has been concerned about operative hypotension and the measures and/or timeliness of its treatment. This section reviews the relationship between regional analgesia with general anaesthesia and hypotension in specific patient groups.

Type of anaesthesia

Table 6.21 presents the type of anaesthesia used for the patients in this report and compares this with that used in 1990.

Table 6.21	Types of anaesthesia		
		1999/00	1990
General alone		914 62%	83%
Local infiltration		7 <1%	<1%
Regional alone		74 5%	3%
General and regional		301 21%	7%
General and local infiltration		75 5%	2%
Sedation alone		4 <1%	<1%
Sedation and local infiltration		5 <1%	<1%
Sedation and regional		81 6%	4%
Not known/Not answered		6 <1%	-
Total		1467	

Compared with 1990, there has been a move away from general anaesthesia alone, towards general and regional techniques. The use of these techniques, both during the operation and for pain relief after the operation was applauded in the 1990 NCEPOD Report[36] and is so now. Of the 301 patients who had general anaesthesia combined with regional analgesia, 195 patients had general anaesthesia combined with epidural analgesia and 21 patients had general anaesthesia combined with spinal analgesia. Epidural analgesia is particularly valuable postoperatively for patients who have undergone major vascular, abdominal or thoracic operations and, in conjunction with the achievements of local acute pain services, provides safe and effective analgesia on the general ward. Good postoperative pain control may improve patient outcome [50, 51]. However, the incautious use of regional techniques in association with general anaesthesia during an operation can lead to excessive vasodilatation and hypotension. Each year NCEPOD reviews cases where the use of general anaesthesia with regional analgesia was associated with persistent hypotension during the operation. Some of these cases are presented here.

General and regional anaesthesia in association with dehydration or sepsis

Case Study 27

An 82-year-old, 76 kg, ASA 4 patient with no coexisting medical disorders underwent a laparotomy for peritonitis. On arrival in the anaesthetic room the patient was dehydrated, hypotensive with a blood pressure of 76/50 mmHg and hypoxic with a SpO$_2$ of 86%. The SHO anaesthetist with more than two years' experience did not discuss the case with someone of greater experience before the operation. Invasive monitoring, CVP and arterial lines, and an epidural at the L1/L2 level were established with the patient awake. A test dose of 3 ml of 0.5% bupivacaine was followed by 20 ml of 0.125% bupivacaine into the epidural space. The subsequent hypotension (systolic arterial pressure of between 70-100 mmHg) persisted for 1 h 20 min before and during the operation despite bolus doses of ephedrine. However, almost total small bowel infarction was found and, after consultation with a consultant anaesthetist and surgeon, the operation was abandoned and a diamorphine infusion was started.

Case Study 28

A 70-year-old, male, ASA 3 patient weighing 45 kg required oversewing of his perforated duodenal ulcer. He had alcohol-related cachexia, was 'dry', had a possible right hilar lung mass and a preoperative haemoglobin 9.1 gm/dl. A consultant provided the anaesthesia for the operation that lasted for 1 hr 45 min. Following induction of anaesthesia a CVP and a thoracic epidural were sited. The first recorded blood pressure was 110/60 mmHg. After 5 ml of 0.125% bupivacaine with morphine was given into the epidural space the blood pressure decreased to 80/45 mmHg. A further 10 ml of epidural 0.125% bupivacaine with morphine and 1000 ml of fluid were given over the next 30 minutes. The blood pressure had by then decreased to 45/30 mmHg. Fifteen minutes later, when the blood pressure was 50/30 mmHg, a final 5 ml of epidural 0.125% bupivacaine with morphine was given. The blood pressure remained at 60/25 mmHg for the following 40 minutes during which time a further 1500 ml of intravenous fluid and, when the haemoglobin was 4.8 gm/dl, two units of blood were given as well as 6 mg ephedrine. The CVP, which was 6 mmHg at the start of the operation, had increased to 20 mmHg by the end of the operation. Towards the end of the operation the patient had increasing arterial desaturation and a postoperative chest X-ray showed a "collapsed left lung" After the operation the patient was nursed on a general ward. He developed a supra-ventricular tachycardia and ST segment changes on his ECG monitor and died on postoperative day five. No postmortem was requested but the surgeon recorded that he died of a myocardial infarction.

Case Study 29

A 62-year-old patient with a carcinoma of the lung and ischaemic heart disease required a laparotomy for closure of a perforated duodenal ulcer. A junior SpR anaesthetist with the Fellowship, and working with an SHO, provided the anaesthesia. The case was discussed with a consultant who was available by telephone. The patient was resuscitated in the anaesthetic room between 21.00 and 22.45. His baseline blood pressure was 120/60 mmHg. Two thousand ml of intravenous fluid was given and then a thoracic epidural was established at the level of

T10. Following a test dose of 3 ml of 0.5% bupivacaine into the epidural space, the blood pressure decreased to 80/40 mmHg. After 15 minutes a further 5 ml of 0.25% bupivacaine was given into the epidural space. During the next hour the blood pressure remained between 80/40 mmHg and 90/50 mmHg despite another 500 ml of intravenous fluid, 18 mg ephedrine and 6 mg methoxamine. Following this, the first CVP reading of minus 2 mmHg was recorded. Anaesthesia was induced at 22.45 and the hypotension persisted throughout the 45 minute operation, during which time a further 1000 ml of intravenous fluid was given. After the operation the part-time recovery ward was closed and so the patient was returned directly to the general ward at 23.45. The epidural was not used for postoperative analgesia; instead the patient received intermittent subcutaneous morphine. The patient remained haemodynamically unstable overnight and died 14 h 30 min after the operation.

Case Study 30

A 72-year-old, ASA 3 patient with bowel obstruction and weighing 37 kg required a laparotomy for a sigmoid colectomy, left oophorectomy and salpingectomy. She had COPD. The anaesthetist, a first year SHO with no anaesthetic qualification did not discuss the case with someone of greater experience before the operation. The patient's preoperative blood pressure was 107/49 mmHg. The operation started at 19.00. Following induction of anaesthesia an attempted epidural at the L2/3 level resulted in a dural tap. An epidural was subsequently established at the L3/4 level. Ten ml of 0.5% bupivacaine was given into the epidural space and an epidural infusion of 0.125% bupivacaine was run at 20 ml/hr throughout the operation. During the operation that lasted for 2 h 45 min, the blood pressure remained at 80/40 mmHg and the heart rate was between 105-110 per minute. Three thousand ml of intravenous fluid was infused but no vasoconstrictors were used. Following tracheal extubation the patient went into pulmonary oedema and respiratory failure, the trachea was re-intubated and the patient was then nursed in the ICU where she died three days later.

Hypotension resulting from the vasodilator effects of local anaesthetic in the epidural space could have been expected in these patients who were dehydrated and, in some instances, possibly septic. It cannot be proved that the operative hypotension these patients suffered was a direct cause of their deaths. Nevertheless, most anaesthetists would consider this degree of hypotension unacceptable. The above cases highlight that the use of epidural analgesia during general anaesthesia for urgent operations requires caution in the dose of local anaesthetic that is used. Trainee anaesthetists managed some of these patients and this highlights the need to ensure that they are trained in the prompt and appropriate management of operative hypotension.

General and regional anaesthesia in association with other medical disorders

Case Study 31

A 69-year-old male, ASA 2 patient weighing 61.5 kg required an abdominoperineal resection. He had angina that had been recently stabilised. A consultant anaesthetist, working with an associate specialist, provided the anaesthesia. A CVP and thoracic epidural at the level of T10/11 were established with the patient awake. The preoperative blood pressure was 140/70 mmHg. After induction of anaesthesia and an epidural test dose of 3 ml of 1% lignocaine, the arterial pressure decreased to about 70/35 mmHg for one hour, during which time 24 mg of intravenous ephedrine was given. After one hour the blood pressure increased to 100/70 mmHg. At this time a further 12 ml of bupivacaine 0.5% was given into the epidural space, followed shortly afterwards by ST segment changes and hypotension unresponsive to epinephrine. The patient suffered a fatal cardiac arrest during the procedure one hour later.

Case Study 32

A 76-year-old, ASA 3 male patient required a sliding hip screw for a fractured left hip. His medical history included ischaemic heart disease, angina, three previous CVAs, confusion, dementia and several TIAs. A second year SHO with part 1 of the Fellowship provided the anaesthesia. The patient's blood pressure preoperatively was 180/100 mmHg at which time 1.6 ml of heavy 0.5% bupivacaine and 20 micrograms of fentanyl were injected into the

subarachnoid space at the level of L3/4. During the anaesthetic the patient breathed spontaneously through a laryngeal mask airway. At the start of the anaesthetic the blood pressure decreased to 50/20 mmHg. After 20 minutes it spontaneously increased and it remained between 90/40 mmHg and 110/50 mmHg for the next 1 h 15 min. During the operation 2000 ml of crystalloid was infused. The patient suffered a CVA six hours after the operation.

Case Study 33

An 86-year-old, ASA 3 female patient underwent an operation for insertion of a Thompson's prosthesis following a fractured neck of femur. Her weight was not recorded. She had severe angina, confusion and a previous CVA. An associate specialist with the DA provided anaesthesia. The preoperative blood pressure was 148/91 mmHg. After induction of anaesthesia a femoral and lateral cutaneous nerve block was established using 40 ml of 0.5% bupivacaine (200 mg). During the operation the patient breathed spontaneously through a laryngeal mask airway. During the one-hour operation the blood pressure remained between 50/20 mmHg and 70/30 mmHg, no vasoconstrictors were given and 1000 ml of crystalloid fluid was infused. Postoperatively on the ward the blood pressure stayed between 90/60 mmHg and 100/65 mmHg, and the patient received 4300 ml of intravenous fluid, but did not pass urine before she died 16 hours after the operation. Although the weight of the patient is not known, this dose of bupivacaine seems large.

In these cases, the choice of anaesthetic, a combination of regional analgesia with general anaesthesia, was not criticised by NCEPOD. However, the management of the resulting hypotension in these patients, all three of whom had known coronary arteriopathy and two had cerebrovascular disease, could be questioned. It is a matter of opinion, but it is difficult to avoid the conclusion that the management of the regional technique was 'heavy handed'. When using combined general anaesthesia with regional analgesia the incidence of complications is probably the sum of each technique, and hypotension is more likely when the general anaesthetic has a tendency to vasodilatation. Could better or more prompt treatment of the subsequent hypotension then, have avoided these adverse events?

Recommendations

- Anaesthetists should be cautious about the dose of local anaesthetic used for a regional technique in those patients who are predisposed to hypotension.

- Operative hypotension demands an appropriate and timely response, especially for those patients who have a coexisting disease such that hypotension is potentially harmful.

AORTIC STENOSIS

Key points

- An asymptomatic cardiac murmur may indicate significant cardiac disease.

- Patients with a large aortic valve gradient or small aortic valve area, particularly in association with a reduced ejection fraction, have an indication for invasive monitoring, ICU/HDU care and excellent postoperative pain control.

As people are living longer so disorders associated with age become more common. Aortic stenosis is mostly secondary to degenerative valve disease and is becoming increasingly prevalent. Approximately thirty percent of those aged 80 years or older who have a postmortem examination have evidence of degenerative changes in their aortic valve, inevitably some of these will be clinically important aortic stenosis. This section of the report discusses their operative management

Aortic stenosis and operative risk

In 1977 Goldman and co-workers[52] identified critical aortic stenosis as an operative risk factor. Recent studies by Lee and co-workers of postoperative cardiac complications in patients undergoing major non-emergency surgery have failed to confirm this correlation, and so aortic stenosis has been removed from the Revised Cardiac Risk Index[35]. However, in their study, aortic stenosis was present in only 5/2893 (0.2%) patients and with such small numbers, finding a correlation with adverse outcome was unlikely. This does not mean that aortic stenosis is no longer a worrying prognostic factor, indeed it is likely to be important for the sorts of patients within this Enquiry who often are undergoing emergency surgery and/or have other coexisting medical problems. The risk factors that were identified within the Revised Cardiac Risk Index were high risk surgery (intraperitoneal, intrathoracic or supra-inguinal vascular operations), a history of ischaemic heart disease, a history of congestive heart failure, cerebrovascular disease, preoperative treatment with insulin and a serum creatinine >177 micromol/l.

The 1994/95 NCEPOD Report[39] expressed concerns about the assessment and management of patients with aortic stenosis. Aortic stenosis in the Western World is now less often secondary to rheumatic fever and more commonly bicuspid, calcific, or what is termed 'senile degenerative' disease in the valve. Although rheumatic aortic stenosis may progress slowly, the progression of calcific aortic stenosis can be rapid. Symptoms of aortic stenosis can present late in the disease process, and patients often remain asymptomatic despite having moderate to severe aortic stenosis. Aortic stenosis occurs most often in elderly patients, who are also more likely to have coexistent cardiac and/or other systemic diseases. It is therefore evident that patients with aortic stenosis should be carefully assessed preoperatively. Those with coexisting risk factors should be considered for invasive monitoring during and after their operation. In this sample NCEPOD identified 22 patients who had aortic stenosis and died after non-cardiac surgery. This is a sample of 10% of deaths. Extrapolating from this there will be approximately 220 patients with aortic stenosis that die postoperatively each year; this equates to one patient within each Trust per year. Of the 22 patients, two were not diagnosed until a post mortem examination.

Case Study 34

A 74-year-old, ASA 2 patient underwent a right shoulder replacement. An asymptomatic murmur was detected preoperatively that was thought to arise from the mitral valve. No echocardiography was performed. The patient had a cardiac death six days after operation. Postmortem examination revealed severe aortic stenosis.

Case study 35

A 73-year-old, ASA 2 patient with COPD and shortness of breath underwent a sigmoid colectomy. General anaesthesia was supplemented with lumbar epidural analgesia. No invasive monitoring was used. One hour after the start of the operation, when the blood loss was 200 ml and 2500 ml of fluid had been infused, the patient suffered a fatal cardiac arrest. Postmortem examination revealed left ventricular hypertrophy and senile calcific aortic stenosis.

An asymptomatic cardiac murmur may indicate significant cardiac disease and should be investigated preoperatively by echocardiography.

Preoperative assessment

The 1994/95 NCEPOD[39] Report recommended that *"A patient with an ejection systolic murmur in association with evidence of left ventricular hypertrophy or myocardial ischaemia requires referral to a cardiologist preoperatively for assessment of the aortic valve."* The questionnaires for this sample do not allow us to identify clearly how many of the 20 patients with known aortic stenosis had a preoperative medical review. We can identify three that did and they are presented below.

Case Study 36

An 83-year-old, ASA 5 patient with known ischaemic heart disease and aortic stenosis, but no other medical problems, was anaesthetised by a consultant for a left cemented Thompson prosthesis. The operation was delayed for a preoperative medical review of the aortic stenosis that included echocardiography. The severity of the aortic stenosis was not reported to NCEPOD. The patient received a general anaesthetic, but no invasive monitoring was used during the operation that lasted for two hours. The patient entered the recovery area and was then returned to the ward almost straight away. Cardiogenic shock ensued and the patient died on postoperative day two.

Case Study 37

An 86-year-old, ASA 4 patient with ischaemic heart disease, angina, known moderate to severe aortic stenosis, confusion and deafness required a hemiarthroplasty. The operation was delayed for a medical opinion, but no echocardiography was performed. Anaesthesia was provided by an SHO of more than two years' experience with the DA who had asked advice from a consultant. The patient received a spinal anaesthetic, but no invasive monitoring was used. The patient returned to the ward and died three days after the operation. The cause of death was recorded as cardio-respiratory failure secondary to cardiac failure, pulmonary oedema, aortic stenosis and mitral regurgitation.

The support and advice this trainee received would appear to be inappropriate.

Case Study 38

An 88-year-old, ASA 3 patient with known aortic stenosis and bundle branch block on the ECG, dementia and confusion, required internal fixation of a displaced fracture of the proximal femur. The operation was delayed for a medical opinion but no echocardiography was performed. An associate specialist with the DA provided the general anaesthetic. No invasive monitoring was used during the operation that lasted for 2 h 5 min. The patient died on postoperative day 27.

It would appear that these patients who received a medical referral were recognised as having serious medical problems. For two out of three of these patients, although their medical treatment was reviewed, the severity of their aortic stenosis was not assessed by echocardiography. From a medical point of view perhaps it was judged that this was not indicated, although its findings might have influenced the anaesthetic management. There is no reason why a physician should understand the risks of aortic stenosis in relation to anaesthesia, or that an accurate assessment of its severity can influence the operative and postoperative anaesthetic management. Patients with a large aortic valve gradient (>50 mmHg) or small aortic valve area (<1.0 cm^2) particularly in association with a reduced ejection fraction have an indication for invasive monitoring, ICU/HDU care and excellent postoperative pain control. These cases illustrate the paramount importance of clear communication between the anaesthetist, surgeon and physician on the aims and benefits of all medical referrals. In many hospitals it is a technician who performs the echocardiography and anaesthetists have direct access to that service. Whenever possible, the anaesthetist of a patient with aortic stenosis should obtain a preoperative echocardiographic assessment of the aortic valve.

Six out of the 20 (30%) patients with known aortic stenosis before their operation had a preoperative echocardiogram. Nine percent of all the patients in this report (excluding those patients that underwent a heart operation) had a preoperative echocardiogram. This is a very low percentage in this sample where 72% of patients who died after their operation had a cardiac disorder. NCEPOD recognises that many echocardiography services are under pressure from a spiralling increase in workload. However, the clear relationship between preoperative cardiac disorders and postoperative death demands that the echocardiography service is accorded an appropriate priority in the funding and development of plans by Trusts/hospitals. Anaesthetists should help to promote this.

Operative and postoperative care

Patients with aortic stenosis require close control of their heart rate, arterial and venous filling pressures, both during and after their operation. Invasive monitoring is so readily available to the technically competent, modern anaesthetist that its appropriateness should be considered for each individual with this disorder. Some of the cases in this section of the report can be criticised on the lack of invasive monitoring, despite the presence of known aortic stenosis in association with serious cardiac or systemic disorders. Eleven out of the 20 patients with known aortic stenosis did not have any invasive monitoring during their operation.

Case Study 39

An 81-year-old, ASA 4 patient with aortic stenosis, uncontrolled AF, CCF and renal impairment (serum creatinine 179 micromol/l) was scheduled for a sigmoid colectomy. Preoperative echocardiography confirmed aortic stenosis and revealed an ejection fraction of 49%. The AF was controlled preoperatively with a loading dose of amiodarone and maintenance continued with oral amiodarone 200 mg daily. A consultant provided the general anaesthesia but did not use invasive monitoring. During the operation, which lasted for 1 h 25 min, the heart rate was 110 per min and systolic arterial pressure was 90 mmHg. After the operation the patient spent 20 minutes in recovery before returning to the general ward. Overnight the heart rate remained elevated at 120 per minute and the patient was in a 2000 ml positive fluid balance 18 hours after the operation when he suffered a fatal cardio-respiratory arrest.

Case Study 40

An 80-year-old, ASA 3 patient with a history of four previous myocardial infarctions, aortic

stenosis and a serum creatinine of 181 micromol/l was anaesthetised by a consultant for a scheduled right hemicolectomy. There was no preoperative echocardiographic assessment. The patient received a general anaesthetic without invasive monitoring. Postoperatively he was nursed in the ICU and died of a perioperative myocardial infarction ten days later.

It is recognised that for patients with known aortic stenosis who are admitted for emergency operations, preoperative echocardiography may be impractical. For these patients, their anaesthetic management, including their monitoring and perioperative care, should be based on the assumption that the lesion is moderate or severe.

Case Study 41

An 84-year-old, ASA 3 patient with known aortic stenosis, a cardiac pacemaker and serum creatinine of 225 micromol/l required repair of a strangulated inguinal hernia. No preoperative anaesthetic assessment was made but a preoperative haemoglobin of 16.6 gm/dl suggested probable dehydration. A SpR with the CCST provided general anaesthesia at 21.15. No invasive monitoring was used during the operation that lasted for 1 h 25 min. The patient was returned to the general ward, without going to a recovery area, at 23.40 where he remained anuric and hypoxaemic. He developed acute LVF and died 18 hours after the operation. Despite the obvious organisational problems, this case was not discussed at an anaesthetic audit meeting.

For patients with aortic stenosis, the appropriate level of postoperative care needs to be considered preoperatively. The patients cited above with known aortic stenosis were all aged 80 years or older. Irrespective of their age, for many of the cases cited above, intensive monitoring and HDU or ICU care would have been appropriate. Nine out of the 20 patients with known aortic stenosis were admitted to an HDU or ICU after their operation.

Case Study 42

An 82-year-old, ASA 4 patient with IHD and aortic stenosis was admitted for a scheduled anterior resection of rectum and end colostomy. Preoperative assessment included echocardiography. A consultant provided general anaesthesia for the four-hour operation. Anaesthetic management included CVP, direct arterial and pulmonary artery pressure monitoring. Postoperatively the patient was nursed in the ICU. Unfortunately the patient suffered a perioperative myocardial infarction and died on postoperative day three.

Case Study 43

An 85-year-old, ASA 3 patient with aortic stenosis and AF required a subtotal colectomy and ileostomy. No preoperative echocardiographic assessment was made. A staff grade with the Fellowship, who had discussed this case with a consultant preoperatively, provided the general anaesthesia for the operation that lasted 3h 15min. The anaesthetic management included CVP and direct arterial pressure monitoring. After the operation the patient went to an HDU. The patient suffered a perioperative myocardial infarction and died on postoperative day three.

The two cases above are examples of indisputably excellent care. That they died despite this standard of care reflects serious anaesthetic risk for patients with aortic stenosis and coexisting ischaemic heart disease. This standard of operative care must minimise that risk.

Recommendation

● Whenever possible the anaesthetist of a patient with aortic stenosis should obtain a preoperative echocardiogram of the aortic valve.

● The availability of the echocardiography service for patients preoperatively should be accorded an appropriate priority in the funding and development plans of hospitals.

THE ORGANISATION OF PERIOPERATIVE CARE AND THE INVOLVEMENT OF CRITICAL CARE TEAMS

Key points

- Preoperative resuscitation of some patients was inadequate and/or poorly coordinated.

- Timing of operations was often inappropriate to the patient's physical state.

- Resuscitation plans were not always adhered to.

- Doctors in training can be slow to seek advice.

- CVP lines were poorly managed on the wards thus providing misleading information.

Patients step-up to or step-down from units with different nursing care levels, e.g. ICU to HDU, HDU to the general ward. However, irrespective of where they are nursed, patients require a continuum of levels of medical and nursing expertise. This section considers the interface between care on the general ward and care in a critical care facility. It explores ways of providing that continuum of medical and nursing expertise that is tailored to the patient's requirements. Included in this section are discussions on the use of critical care teams and ward based management by doctors in training.

Preoperative care

The perioperative status of patients is a continuous spectrum from the very well to the critically ill. It is obvious then that medical requirements of patients are also a continuum, both for levels of facilities and levels of medical expertise.

Within hospitals the facilities, specialised and general care units, are physically separate so a continuum of care levels is not easy to provide. A patient will step-up to or step-down from a care level. In addition, the presence of an ICU or HDU facility in a hospital does not mean that there is a bed within such a facility available for all patients when it is required. NCEPOD[13] and clinicians recognise that there is a chronic shortage of critical care beds, critical care clinicians and nursing staff. There is a need to make the best use of the existing facilities. This report includes the period of the ICU bed crisis in the winter of 1999/2000 and it is recognised that the cases reviewed may reflect the crisis as well as the ongoing national ICU/HDU bed shortage.

The issue of providing a continuum of medical and nursing expertise can be addressed. 'Critical to Success', a report by the Audit Commission[48] was published in 1999 and Comprehensive 'Critical Care'[37], was published by the Department of Health in May 2000. Both reports contain many recommendations on how the care of seriously ill patients might be improved, and the Department of Health has provided additional funding for critical care services. Many hospitals are using that funding to implement organisational changes, including critical care outreach teams. These changes should enable critical care expertise to be deployed outside the confines of the ICU or HDU facility.

This section of the report aims to promote change by illustrating and commenting on some aspects of perioperative care where NCEPOD sees deficits.

Preoperative assessment

The anaesthetic questionnaire enquired where the anaesthetist assessed the patient before the operation (Table 6.22). This gives some indication of where patients were managed and resuscitated preoperatively.

Table 6.22	Location of anaesthetic assessment*		
Ward		1132	80%
ICU/HDU		204	14%
A&E		62	4%
Outpatients		6	
Not known/not answered		5	
Total		**1409**	

Fifty-eight patients (4%) were not assessed preoperatively.

Eighty percent of patients were assessed on the general ward. Fourteen percent of patients were assessed on the ICU/HDU, few had been admitted specifically for preoperative resuscitation or optimisation and most of these patients had undergone a previous operation and/or were receiving ongoing treatment within the unit. Six percent of patients were assessed in the A &E department and then progressed rapidly to the operating theatre. Most of these were true emergencies for example, leaking abdominal aneurysms or acute intracranial pathology. But for some, the rapid progression to the operating theatre was inexplicable.

Case Study 44

An 87-year-old, ASA 5 patient with peritonitis was assessed in the A&E Department by an SpR 1/2 anaesthetist. Coexisting medical problems included a previous MI, angina, atrial fibrillation, a previous CVA and hypothyroidism. The patient was breathless due to LVF, and confused. Preoperative investigations revealed ECG evidence of bundle branch block and serum potassium of 2.6 mmol/l. The operation, a laparotomy for repair of a perforated transverse colon and tube caecostomy, was started at 02.30 by the same anaesthetist who did not seek more senior advice and a visiting SpR surgeon who discussed the case with their consultant. No invasive monitoring was used during the operation and after 40 minutes in recovery the patient was returned to the general ward at 04.45.

In this case there are questions to be asked about the timing of the operation and the grades of the operating surgeon and anaesthetist. The case was discussed at a surgical audit but not at an anaesthetic one.

Preoperative ward based resuscitation

The surgical team mainly undertakes the initial assessment of patients. They determine the investigation, resuscitation and referral needs of a patient before their operation. For urgent or emergency operations, referral to an anaesthetist should precede a joint decision on when the condition of the patient is optimal, within the constraints of the operative urgency. Following a consensus opinion, subsequent undue delay should not occur.

Case Study 45

An 87-year-old, ASA 3 patient was admitted for amputation of two infected and gangrenous toes. Coexisting medical problems included poorly controlled diabetes mellitus and atrial fibrillation. For four days the diabetes mellitus was managed using an intravenous potassium, insulin and dextrose/saline infusion. Preoperative investigations on the day of operation revealed serum sodium 129 mmol/l, serum potassium 3.7 mmol/l and blood glucose 2.0 mmol/l.

Case Study 46

A 90-year-old, ASA 3 patient with COPD, IHD, AF and confusion was admitted at 21.00 with a fractured hip. Preoperative investigations revealed a haemoglobin of 17.1 gm/dl. Over the next 12 hours the patient received 1000 ml of 0.9% saline. A consultant anaesthetist assessed that the patient was still dehydrated at 09.00 and recommended that the intravenous fluids be increased. By 16.00, the time of starting the operation, the patient had received only a further 200ml of dextrose/saline.

Case Study 2

An 86-year-old, ASA 5 patient with no coexisting medical disorders was admitted for a laparotomy and exploration of left femoral hernia. On the day of admission an ICU SpR reviewed the patient on the ward, advised on appropriate intravenous fluids and recommended that hourly urine output and CVP be measured. The patient was anuric for five hours overnight but none of the medical staff was informed. The next day the patient was admitted to ICU for preoperative resuscitation including intravenous fluids and inotropic therapy.

Clearly the resuscitation of these patients and others within this enquiry was inadequate and/or poorly coordinated between specialties, and the timing of the operations was inappropriate to the patient's physical state. For some reason the resuscitation plans were not adhered to. Preoperative resuscitation involves the skills of surgical, anaesthetic and nursing staff and its successful coordination, or otherwise, should be a subject of multidisciplinary case review.

The preoperative involvement of critical care teams

Resuscitation

Critical care teams by their outreach activities are increasingly being involved in the preoperative resuscitation of patients. The responsibility for referral of patients to critical care staff rests with ward based doctors. It is they who must identify which patients might benefit from the critical care team's early involvement. The process for appropriate referral of patients to critical care clinicians can be, and in some centres is, facilitated by guidelines or early warning systems[48]. The skills of ward based nursing and medical staff vary between hospitals, and even between wards within hospitals. It is therefore, important that guidelines to determine which patients should be referred to the critical care team should be developed locally and subsequently validated.

Specialised critical care teams are best equipped to identify which of the referred patients will benefit from ward based resuscitation, which require a period of intensive resuscitation on the ICU or HDU and when the patient has attained the best 'window of opportunity' for an operation to take place.

Case Study 47

An 87-year-old, ASA 2 patient was admitted with a strangulated femoral hernia accompanied by faeculent vomiting and confusion, but without any other coexisting medical problems. Preoperative investigations revealed a haemoglobin of 16.2 gm/dl and serum urea 26.3 mmol/l with a normal serum creatinine. The patient went to the operating theatre at 00.55, a few hours after admission. The SpR anaesthetist commented that the patient had not received

fluid resuscitation, but nevertheless continued with the anaesthetic. The patient received 500 ml of crystalloid fluid during the operation, returned to the general ward after the operation and died from congestive heart failure on postoperative day six.

Case Study 48

A 54-year-old without any coexisting medical disorders was admitted with a perforated peptic ulcer. The operation was delayed for three days for fluid resuscitation but this appeared inadequate and was not guided by invasive monitoring. By the time of the operation the patient's physical status was graded as ASA 5. After 2 h 20 min in recovery the patient was returned to the general ward and died of peritonitis on postoperative day 12.

These are the sort of cases that might benefit from the advice of a critical care clinician. This does not mean that the critical care team should take over ward based management. If the decision is to manage the patient on the ward then, for reasons of locality, the primary responsibility for the ongoing supervision of the resuscitation or postoperative care will most likely still remain with the ward based clinicians and nursing staff, albeit supported by the critical care team.

The anaesthetic and surgical questionnaires were not specific as to where patients were resuscitated, but NCEPOD could identify only 11 patients who were admitted to the ICU or HDU specifically for resuscitation before their operation.

Case Study 49

A 42-year-old, ASA 4 paraplegic patient was admitted for treatment of a gluteal ulcer and necrotising fasciitis. Preoperative resuscitation included invasive monitoring and inotropic treatment on the ICU before the operation for debridement of the ulcer that started at 23.00. The anaesthetist was a SpR 1/2 working with a second year SHO. There was no involvement by an intensive care or anaesthetic consultant preoperatively. The patient suffered a respiratory arrest before the operation and died in the ICU on postoperative day one.

Case Study 50

An 85-year-old, ASA 3 patient with IHD, COPD, NIDDM was admitted with a bowel obstruction. A medical SHO and a staff grade anaesthetist resuscitated the patient on the HDU overnight before a laparotomy and division of adhesions. A consultant anaesthetist was involved in the decision-making before the operation at 11.00 the following morning, but a SpR 1/2 anaesthetist who had not seen the patient preoperatively, provided the anaesthesia.

The management of these patients by the doctors in training is not criticised. However, adequate medical standards cannot be ensured when there is such a large reliance placed on junior medical staff in the management of critically ill patients. These situations are a result of the shortfall of suitably experienced critical care clinicians and that needs remedy[48].

Combined specialty decision-making

It must be recognised that some patients are so seriously ill that an operation, even with postoperative intensive care, is likely to be futile.

Case Study 51

A 60-year-old who was bed bound with TB suffered a severe gastrointestinal haemorrhage. Preoperatively his physical status was ASA 5. The surgeon thought that the patient had little chance of surviving the surgery, but his family insisted that he should receive an operation.

Case Study 52

An 87-year-old patient with severe cardiac disease had suffered six gastrointestinal bleeds that had been managed by medical treatment during the previous six months. Preoperatively his physical status was ASA 5 and, in the opinion of his physician, he was not fit for surgery. The surgeon agreed with this, but stated in the questionnaire that he had been persuaded to operate.

These cases illustrate difficult decisions that needed to be made before the operation and at the highest level. Consultation between the consultant surgeon and a consultant anaesthetist can best decide when a patient has little chance of surviving and therefore, is unlikely to benefit from an operation or ICU treatment. In such cases where both consultants agree, an explanation to the patient and their relatives may result in a decision made jointly by all parties.

The time to plan the ongoing intensive or high dependency care in critically ill patients is before the operation and with the full involvement and support of the critical care team.

Case Study 53

A 75-year-old, ASA 5 patient underwent a laparotomy for treatment of a perforated diverticular abscess. He had severe ischaemic heart disease, pulmonary oedema and hypoxaemia (PaO_2 6 kPa on a FiO_2 0.5). He went to theatre in the afternoon on the day following his admission, but without any obvious preoperative resuscitation. Postoperatively his trachea was extubated, his SpO_2 was 65% and he died in recovery.

A predictably difficult case with, apparently, no planning of how the patient's ongoing care would be organised.

The development of critical care outreach teams needs to be supported by developments in the skills of ward based staff. This was recognised in the Department of Health's review, 'Comprehensive Critical Care'[37] which recommended that 50% of ward based nursing staff should have received competence based high dependency training by March 2002 and 100% by March 2004. Similar arrangements for the training of ward based junior medical staff in high dependency medicine are also appropriate. If this is achieved then improvements in ward based care will result, and this should help to ease the pressures on critical care resources.

Postoperative ward based care

The responsibilities of ward based doctors in training

NCEPOD was critical when doctors in training were either inappropriately slow to seek advice or did not. This was not confined to any specialty; it applied to surgical, anaesthetic and medical clinicians.

Case Study 54

A 79-year-old, ASA 2 patient underwent sub-total colectomy. Seven days postoperatively he became acutely unwell coinciding with the onset of atrial fibrillation. A surgical HO and a medical SHO assessed the patient and diagnosed that he had suffered from a pulmonary embolus, even though the clinical picture suggested pneumonia. Without seeking more senior advice, they decided not to instigate any further treatment. The patient died later that day. Postmortem examination showed bilateral lower lobe consolidation with no evidence of pulmonary embolism.

Case Study 55

An 83-year-old, ASA 3 patient underwent a femoro-distal arterial bypass. He was known to be a high risk patient who had suffered a previous myocardial infarct accompanied by a cardiac arrest. The patient was treated on the HDU for the first day postoperatively. The next day he was transferred to the ward where two surgical SHOs supervised the management, with advice from a medical registrar. Over the first 24 hours on the ward the patient received five litres of fluid, despite a blood loss of only 300 ml, and developed oliguria that progressed to established renal failure. The consultant surgeon was not informed of the situation and was critical of the trainees. The patient died on the third postoperative day.

For doctors in training to see and assess a sick patient in the first instance, and to form an opinion is entirely appropriate; it is a good way to learn. However, recognising the limits of one's knowledge and experience and assuming a readiness to seek advice is a prime responsibility of all doctors. Serious questions arise when doctors in training inappropriately do not seek advice. Do they have unrealistic belief in their education and experience and so fail to recognise their limitations? If so, how much is this due to their own, perhaps over confident personality and how much a failure of their training? Do they have, or perceive that they have a lack of senior support, and so are reluctant to seek advice? How much is this a failure of supervision of the doctors in training by the consultant responsible for the care of the patient? Ultimately, it is the consultant's responsibility to ensure that the lines of communication are open between them and the doctors that are under their supervision, and that those doctors are acting appropriately.

Ward based central venous pressure monitoring

The maintenance of appropriate fluid balance in the perioperative patient, the prevention of severe dehydration or fluid overload, is of paramount importance. This was discussed in detail in the NCEPOD Report, 'Extremes of Age'[1]. A useful aid to guide fluid therapy is central venous pressure (CVP) monitoring. In the sample for this report, 642/1467 (44%) patients had CVP monitoring during and after their operation. However, peer review advised that there was a monitoring deficiency, mainly of CVP monitoring, in a further 13% of cases.

Case Study 56

An 81-year-old, ASA 4 patient was scheduled for abdominoperineal resection. Past medical history included four previous myocardial infarctions, and coexisting disorders included angina and hypertension. The operation was in a hospital with no HDU and the ICU was full. Knowing this, the consultant anaesthetist proceeded without invasive monitoring. After 56 minutes in recovery the patient returned to the ward where she suffered a further myocardial infarction and died on postoperative day two.

Case Study 40

An 80-year-old ASA 3 patient with a history of four myocardial infarctions, hypertension, aortic stenosis and serum creatinine 181 micromol/l was anaesthetised by a consultant for a right hemicolectomy. This consultant anaesthetist wrote on his assessment form "I have warned him of the consequences to have (sic) this operation prior to CABG". The patient received a general anaesthetic, but no invasive monitoring was used. The patient was nursed on the ICU for two days before discharge to the general ward where he died of a perioperative myocardial infarction ten days later.

NCEPOD considers it likely that, with increased involvement of critical care teams on the wards and an increase in patient optimisation, the use of CVP monitoring will increase. The reasons for an under use of CVP monitoring may include a lack of training in CVP line management amongst the ward based staff. The surgical advisors in particular emphasised that CVP lines were poorly managed by the nursing staff on their wards, and the information from them was often misinterpreted by their trainees. They were of the opinion that all patients who would benefit from CVP monitoring should be admitted to a critical care unit. However, there is a national shortage of HDU beds. An alternative approach is to develop training programmes to increase the skills of the nurses and doctors on the wards in CVP management and interpretation. This concept of monitored beds on the general ward is not entirely new, and some hospitals are already successfully practising ward based CVP monitoring. On these wards, CVP monitoring is viewed as merely an extension of already established ward monitoring practices.

A programme for the development and maintenance of ward based CVP monitoring skills within a hospital should include:

- the development of formal training schemes to ensure that sufficient ward based nurses receive training, and training update in the correct management of CVP lines;

- sufficient ward monitoring equipment with transducer pressure monitoring facility for accurate and continuous CVP monitoring;

- training for ward based surgical trainees in the insertion of CVP lines;

- special attention to all aspects of CVP interpretation within the basic surgical training programme. The understanding of fluid balance and the correction of problems in the perioperative patient already form part of the core basic surgical training requirements[53];

- the involvement of anaesthetists and critical care teams (both clinicians and nurses) in the training and support of ward based medical and nursing staff who are supervising the CVP monitoring.

More widespread use of ward based CVP monitoring should result in fewer patients competing for scarce critical care beds.

Recommendations

- Preoperative resuscitation of patients and the success of its coordination should form part of multidisciplinary case review involving surgical, anaesthetic and nursing staff.

- Guidelines to determine which patients should be referred to a critical care team should be developed locally and subsequently validated.

- It is the consultant's responsibility to ensure that there are open lines of communication between them and the doctors that are under their supervision, and to ensure that those doctors are acting appropriately.

- There should be more training programmes to increase the skills of nurses and doctors on the wards in CVP management and interpretation.

SURGERY IN GENERAL (EXCLUDING MALIGNANCY)

INTRODUCTION

Key points

- Formal shared care is increasing for elderly patients managed in orthopaedic and urological surgery.

- The majority of deaths occurred after emergency surgery.

- Radiologists increasingly have the ability to intervene in patient management using guided drainage of fluid collections. In the sickest patients, this may either provide definitive treatment or gain sufficient time so that their clinical status can be stabilised before surgery.

- The complications of diverticular disease are common and continue to be difficult to manage, particularly in the very elderly.

- There is a reluctance to catheterise patients with urinary incontinence.

- Trauma patients were more likely to suffer delays for non-medical reasons than patients in other specialities.

This section describes and discusses a variety of issues that arose during discussion of deaths occurring in many differing surgical specialties. Many issues apply generally and are covered in other sections of this report, for example audit performance. The deaths in some specialties followed wholly appropriate delivery of care, provided no new lessons and thus are not discussed further, for example burns patients and head and neck surgery. The care of patients suffering from malignancy is considered in a separate section.

In general surgery a total of 703 cases were reviewed. Forty-seven percent (332/703) had some form of malignancy and are considered separately in the section on oncology. The remaining 371 patients, those without malignant disease, are considered here.

In orthopaedic surgery there were 358 deaths reviewed in comparison with 420 in 1990 and 341 last year. There was a noticeable change in the age distribution compared to previous reports. Ninety-three percent of patients were aged between 70 and 99 in this sample compared with 88% in the 1990 group and 92% in 1998/99. This represents an increase in a vulnerable group of patients. The male to female ratio was 1:2, very similar to 1990 and 1998/99. The emergency admission rate in orthopaedics remained high at 83% and the range of procedures performed was similar to previous years, with the majority being performed for hip fracture.

There were 81 deaths following urological surgery. The majority of patients were aged between 60 and 99 years (73/81, 90%). This is similar to the age distribution seen in other years (89% in 1998/99 and 93% in 1990). The sex ratio was male: female 3:1. Approximately half the admissions in urology were urgent or emergencies.

The sample of gynaecological surgery this year showed a similar age range to previous years with 88% (22/25) being over 60 years old. Emergency or urgent admissions accounted for half the sample and most procedures were undertaken for patients with gynaecological malignancy, or where malignancy was suspected.

There were 74 neurosurgical deaths in the sample. The majority of the neurosurgical patients were extremely sick, and in many, death was an inevitable consequence of the underlying condition. Thirty-six of the 59 (61%) non-oncology neurosurgery patients were classified as ASA 4 or 5. The indication for surgical intervention in this group of patients was often unclear.

Supporting sections of interest to surgeons in general are 'General information about anaesthesia and surgery' and the 'Organisation of perioperative care' (both in section 6).

QUALITY OF QUESTIONNAIRES

The quality of completion of the questionnaires varied. Some questionnaires provided comprehensive and valuable information, others were poorly completed and from these it was difficult to detect whether there were deficits in facilities or standards of care. The questionnaires are a confidential disclosure. NCEPOD relies on their accuracy in order to make its recommendations, not to criticise individuals. Clinicians are reminded that it is an important clinical governance issue that questionnaires are filled in carefully and conscientiously.

PROCEDURES PERFORMED

In general surgery, procedures were categorised into general abdominal, hepatobilary and pancreatic, colorectal, hernias and a miscellaneous group of procedures. A number of patients had more than one procedure performed during their operation and in total there were 409 procedures performed in 371 patients. The most common procedures were Hartmann's procedure, laparotomy for small bowel ischaemia and repair of perforated duodenal ulcer.

For 12/35 general surgery patients, who had a 'laparotomy' only, no operation note was sent and the questionnaires were so poorly completed that it was impossible to determine the reason for the laparotomy. The operation note and a summary are important inclusions that help NCEPOD understand events. They should be submitted with the questionnaire. Amongst these laparotomies there were cases of peritonitis (cause uncertain), bowel ischaemia and pancreatitis. There were several misdiagnoses; in one laparotomy the abdomen was entirely normal, one patient had a pseudo-obstruction, another had a distended liver due to severe right heart failure and one had bilateral hydronephrosis presenting as an acute abdomen.

In orthopaedic surgery the range of procedures performed was similar to previous years, with the majority being performed for hip fracture.

DELAYS

Orthopaedic patients continue to have their operations delayed for non-clinical reasons and the figure in this sample is no different from last year's

(43/358, 12% compared to 40/341, 12% last year). These delays will often militate against a good outcome.

TRANSFER

Patients with severe trauma do not travel well, and neurosurgical units should have an adequate number of ICU beds to prevent the need for inappropriate transfer. In one instance, a 17-year-old ASA 4 patient with severe head injury had to be transferred because the receiving neurosurgical unit did not have an ICU bed. The severity of this patient's injuries made survival unlikely, but his chances were not improved by having to travel.

CLINICAL CONSIDERATIONS

Perioperative care and fluid management

Most cases admitted under general surgeons were emergencies and required an emergency or urgent operation. Many patients had suffered some intra-abdominal catastrophe with accompanying dehydration. Many were likely to develop multiple organ dysfunction, be dependent on careful fluid management and require high level or critical care. The interface between critical care units and ward based care, and the problems of fluid management are discussed in detail in the section on the 'Organisation of perioperative care', (see section 6). All surgeons with responsibility for the care of acute surgical patients should read that section.

A urinary catheter was placed in only 83/358 (23%) of orthopaedic patients despite the fact that fluid balance charts revealed many wet beds and hence inaccurate fluid 'balance'. Presumably many of these incontinent patients may have gone on to develop pressure sores. Failure to maintain adequate fluid requirements was a major problem within the orthopaedic sample.

Radiological support for an acute surgical unit

There were some cases where it was thought that radiological diagnostic or therapeutic intervention might have obviated an operation or might have been more appropriate than the operation. This Enquiry does not know the supporting radiological services available to all acute surgical units. Nor does it know the denominator data and details of those patients who had non-surgical intervention, either successfully or unsuccessfully, for a similar disorder. Nevertheless, it can raise questions and suggest standards of support that should be provided by radiology departments.

Water soluble contrast investigations of the GI tract

Three patients underwent a diagnostic laparotomy for obstruction during which pseudo-obstruction was diagnosed. The resulting operations were caecostomy, colostomy and abdominal closure without any further procedure. In each case a water soluble contrast enema might have been diagnostic and identified whether these patients would have been better managed with non-operative treatment.

CT scanning

Case Study 57

A 90-year-old, ASA 4 patient with ischaemic heart disease and dehydration was admitted with a working diagnosis of peritonitis due to a perforated peptic ulcer. However a raised serum amylase was noted. Nevertheless, the patient underwent a laparotomy at 21.55 on the day of admission. Operation revealed acute pancreatitis. After the operation the patient returned to the general ward and died within 24 hours.

Case Study 58

A 63-year-old, ASA 4 patient with severe mitral incompetence, cardiomyopathy and right heart failure was admitted with a history of colicky abdominal pain and tenderness in the right upper quadrant. A laparotomy was performed at 23.00, at which the only abnormality was a very distended liver. The patient died of cardiac and renal failure on the third postoperative day.

In these two cases, a CT scan might have confirmed the diagnosis and obviated the need for a laparotomy. In both cases the operation was performed out-of-hours. Was emergency CT scanning available?

Ultrasound investigation

Case Study 59

An 87-year-old, ASA 3 patient with diabetes mellitus was admitted with an acute abdomen. Preoperative investigations revealed a haemoglobin 9.1gm/dl, white cell count $15.7 \times 10^9/l$ and serum creatinine of 600 micro mol/l. Two days later a laparotomy revealed bilateral infected hydronephroses that were drained. The patient returned to the general ward and died there on the seventh postoperative day.

An ultrasound scan could have made the diagnosis and been used for percutaneous drainage.

Case Study 60

A 75-year-old, ASA 4 patient with diabetes mellitus and a mucocoele of the gall bladder, which was failing to resolve, was admitted for an urgent cholecystectomy. After a 50 minute operation the patient was admitted to ICU and died on the third postoperative day.

Would an ultrasound-guided aspiration of the gall bladder have enabled surgery to be avoided?

These are just some examples where radiological procedures, as alternatives to surgery, could have been considered.

Planning the radiology service

The NHS in its plan for investment and reform[54] is committed to delivering a consistently high standard of care to all patients, and investing in staff and facilities. It specifically mentions updating existing and purchasing new CT scanners. Many aspects of elective and urgent admissions can be measured and compared, as can changes in their standards. It is less easy to quantify the care of emergency patients. Nevertheless, sensible plans can be drawn up; the benefits of which will be recognised by the pragmatist. The above cases highlight possible problems in the radiological facilities and skills available for the acute surgical patient both in and out-of-hours, and poor recognition of the potential for intervention radiology. Hospitals may wish to consider the following:

- Within all hospitals there should be a multidisciplinary review of the organisation of acute surgery and radiology services. This review should define what is currently available, and what is desired and should be planned for.

- All hospitals admitting patients with intra-abdominal emergencies should be able to provide radiological investigations including ultrasound, CT and water-soluble contrast investigations of the gastrointestinal tract 24 hours a day.

- Radiologists increasingly have the ability to intervene in patient management using guided drainage of fluid collections. In the sickest patients this may either provide definitive treatment or gain sufficient time so that their clinical status can be stabilised before surgery. There should be sufficient skilled radiologists to provide interventional radiology for emergency cases both in and out-of-hours.

Perforated peptic ulceration

Thirty-one patients presented to general surgeons with perforated peptic ulceration.

Case Study 61

A 78-year-old, ASA 4 patient with a past history of a previous perforated peptic ulcer was admitted with another perforated duodenal ulcer. There was a four day delay between admission and the operation that finally started at 21.00. A partial gastrectomy was performed. After a 2 h 20 min operation the patient was admitted to the ICU and died there two days later.

Was this definitive operation appropriate, given the patient's poor physical status?

Case Study 62

An 89-year-old ASA 4 patient with ischaemic heart disease and a history of transient ischaemic attacks was admitted with an acute abdomen. The patient had been unwell for several days

and preoperative investigations revealed a serum creatinine of 225 micromol/l. A diagnosis of perforated peptic ulcer was made and at 22.00 on the day of admission the patient had a laparotomy and the perforated duodenal ulcer was oversewn. The patient returned to the ward and died two days later.

Case Study 63

A 78-year-old, ASA 3 patient with COPD, hypoxia, ischaemic heart disease and a previous CVA was admitted with a diagnosis of an acute perforated ulcer. Preoperative investigations revealed a haemoglobin of 16.1 gm/dl, white cell count of 2.0 x 10⁹/l and creatinine 145 micromol/l. The patient had a laparotomy and oversew of a perforated duodenal ulcer at 17.30, which was within 30 minutes of arriving in the hospital. Trainee surgeons and anaesthetists managed the patient during the operation without any consultant involvement. Postoperatively the patient returned to the general ward, was admitted to ICU when problems supervened and died there on the eighth postoperative day.

All these patients were operated on and anaesthetised by trainee surgeons and anaesthetists late in the day. The experience of these trainees in the management of perforated peptic ulcer can be questioned. There is ongoing controversy amongst experienced surgeons about the most appropriate operative approach for acute perforated peptic ulcers. The incidence of perforated peptic ulcer has declined in association with the increased treatment of chronic peptic ulceration using anti-secretory drug therapy; histamine₂ receptor blockers and proton pump inhibitors, and with the control of helicobacter pylori infections. The availability of these treatments postoperatively can influence the extent of the operative procedure for perforated peptic ulceration, particularly for patients of poor physical status[55]. Moreover, it is recognised that some perforated peptic ulcers heal spontaneously[56] and that when diagnosis is delayed, unless there is persistent leakage, operative treatment is not always indicated and careful non-operative management can result in comparable outcomes[57].

As part of their governance responsibility, general surgeons could review the clinical evidence and formulate local guidelines for the management of acute perforated peptic ulceration for both stable and unstable patients. This should clarify the appropriate management of these patients who are admitted as emergencies. NCEPOD recommends the referenced papers as a useful starting point.

Inappropriate operations in surgery

There were a number of patients where it was thought that the operative management was inappropriate. This applied to all specialties. This has been commented on in previous reports. The problems can be summarised as:

- inexperience on the part of the surgeon;

- patients with little chance of survival;

- misdiagnosis;

- too major or an inappropriate procedure.

Pancreatitis

Deaths occurred following operations for acute pancreatitis. Patients with pancreatitis are often severely ill and treatment is primarily medical, unless complications supervene that require surgical intervention. Three operations in patients with acute pancreatitis were considered inappropriate as no CT imaging was done. CT scanning in equivocal cases of pancreatitis can be diagnostic and these three laparotomies might have been prevented by CT scan examination.

There are UK guidelines for the management of acute pancreatitis. These state that severity stratification should be made in all patients within 48 hours[58]. A simple mnemonic 'PANCREAS' has been suggested for remembering the criteria used in assessing severity[59]:-

The reader is referred to the original publication for details on the interpretation of these results. Those who are assessed as having severe pancreatitis should not only be treated on an HDU or ICU, but consideration should also be given to referral to a pancreatic specialist.

Diverticular disease

Forty-six patients died following an emergency operation for diverticular disease. Of these 21 had a Hartmann's procedure. Hartmann's procedure is not always simple and straightforward; in particular complications with a colostomy performed as an emergency do seem to be more common than when a stoma is created electively. Three patients had problems of either retraction or necrosis of the colostomy and required a further laparotomy and re-fashioning of the colostomy.

Perforated diverticulitis is accompanied by an overall high mortality of between 20-25%[60]. Intra-abdominal abscess formation has a mortality of 12%, purulent peritonitis 27% and faecal peritonitis 48%[61].

In an attempt to predict severity and outcome, two risk assessment systems for scoring patients with peritonitis have been devised.

The Mannheim Peritonitis Index (MPI) devised by Billing and colleagues gives a weighted score for age >50 years, female gender, organ failure, malignancy, duration >24 hours, generalised peritonitis and a purulent or faecal exudate[62]. A score of 21-29 is associated with a mortality of 22%; this rises to 59% when the MPI score is greater than 29[63].

The Peritonitis Severity Score (PSS)[64] devised by Biondo and colleagues gives a weighted score for age >70 years, ASA of 3 or 4, organ failure, immuno-compromise, ischaemic colitis and peritonitis.

Mnemonic Letter	Criteria	Positive when
P	PaO$_2$	<60 mmHg
A	Age	>55 years
N	Neutrophils (white blood cell count)	>15 x 10^8/l
C	Calcium	<2 mmol/l
R	Raised urea	>16 mmol/l
E	Enzyme (lactic dehydrogenase)	>600 units/l
A	Albumin	<32 g/l
S	Sugar (glucose)	>10 mmol/l

Mortality based on the PSS score ranges from 0% with the minimum score of 6 to 100% with a score of 13 (maximum score 14). The overall mortality in this series was 22.4%. There was a significant difference between those aged <70 years (15.3%) and >70 years (37.2%) (p=0.01) and between those graded ASA 1-2 (9.4%), ASA 3 (38.1%) and ASA 4 (64.7%) (p<0.0001 for ASA 4 compared with ASA 1-2).

The Physiological and Operative Severity Score for the Enumeration of Morbidity and Mortality (POSSUM) has also been applied to diverticulitis[65] but its main use is as a retrospective audit tool. However, like the other scoring systems age >71 years and faecal peritonitis are scored highly (4 and 8 respectively). Although not specifically designed for it, the APACHE II (Adult Physiology and Chronic Health Evaluation) score has also been used to assess the outcome of patients with peritonitis. Mortality increased from 4.8% with a score below 15 to 46.7% with a score above 15. Mortality was significantly greater in those patients over 65 years or with four-quadrant peritonitis, diabetes mellitus or organ failure[66].

Age does have an impact on mortality from peritonitis. In a 5 year audit of the acute complications of diverticulitis[67] the overall mortality was 17.7% whilst in those patients over 80 years' of age, it rose to 72% (p=0.01). ASA 4 was associated with a mortality of 89% and patients who were shocked on admission had a mortality of 71%.

There is no doubt that an increasing number of patients aged 80 years or older will present to surgical units with peritonitis[68]. What advice then can be offered about their management and probable outcome? The MPI and PSS have demonstrated that a patient over 70 years' with generalised or faecal peritonitis of more than 24 hours duration, an ASA score of 3-4 and evidence of single organ failure is most unlikely to survive surgery. The decision not to operate on a sick patient who will die without surgery is difficult and should be made by a consultant after discussion with relatives, nurses and, where possible, the patient. If a decision is made to operate, there must be an agreement to care for the patient on ICU afterwards. If the chance of survival is negligible due to age, multi-organ failure, co-morbidity and faecal peritonitis of more than 24 hours duration, then there may be a place for accepting the inevitable, carrying out no further procedure and withdrawing support other than effective analgesia.

Upper GI haemorrhage

There were some examples of problems with the management of upper GI haemorrhage. There were examples of high risk elderly patients where an injection of the bleeding point via gastroscopy should have been considered but was not.

One was a patient with very profuse bleeding from a gastric ulcer who vomited during gastroscopy and died shortly after, presumably as a result of inhalation of vomit. Perhaps, in patients with severe gastrointestinal haemorrhage like this, it would be safer to perform a gastroscopy after induction of anaesthesia and endotracheal intubation by an experienced anaesthetist in order to make the airway secure.

There were also examples of patients with bleeding from oesophageal varices who might have benefited from treatment in a specialist unit with a full range of therapeutic options.

The reader is reminded of the guidelines for good practice in the management of upper gastrointestinal haemorrhage[69]. This is being updated and is due to be published on the British Society of Gastroenterology's Web site by the end of the year (2001)[70].

There is concern, that with the increasing management of upper GI cancer in specialist centres, surgeons in district general hospitals may have a problem maintaining the necessary skills required to manage patients with upper gastrointestinal haemorrhage, as they are increasingly unlikely to be familiar with gastric and oesophageal problems.

Use of staples in the presence of intestinal obstruction

There were a number of patients who had a right hemicolectomy or small bowel resection done as an emergency, in the presence of intestinal obstruction, where the operation note indicated that staples were used at the anastomosis. There were six patients who had a right hemicolectomy (all were in the oncology group) in whom it was noted that staples were used and two out of these six had an anastomotic leak. There were also a further two small bowel anastomoses in the presence of obstruction where staples were used and which subsequently leaked.

The question was raised as to whether a sutured anastomosis might be safer than staples in the presence of obstructed and oedematous bowel, although we were unable to find any references alluding to this. Is there a place for a thoughtful and well-constructed trial to be invoked?

Shared care in orthopaedic and urological surgery

There has been a steady increase in formal shared care. In 1990 21% of cases were managed under formal shared care. By 1998/99 this had increased to 30% and the present sample showed that 39% (139/358) of patients were managed jointly by orthopaedic surgeons and another specialty, usually general or elderly medicine. Given the increasingly elderly nature of these orthopaedic patients and the incidence of comorbidity (50% had cardiac disorders, 35% respiratory disease and 19% psychiatric disturbances), such joint management should become the norm.

In urology 40% of the patients (32/81) were managed on a formal shared care basis. This is a considerable improvement on the figure reported last year (20/73, 27%).

Recommendations

- Early consideration of diagnostic or therapeutic radiological procedures might avoid surgery in some high risk patients.

- Acute hospitals should continually review their radiological provision to ensure the availability of appropriate and modern methods for the investigation and treatment of emergency cases.

- Fluid balance and urinary incontinence should be proactively managed especially in orthopaedic patients.

VASCULAR SURGERY

Key points

- Correction of coagulopathy, including the use of platelets, is important in the management of bleeding associated with surgery for ruptured abdominal aortic aneurysms.

- MRSA infection is a hazard for surgical patients.

There were 222 questionnaires relating to deaths after vascular surgery. The majority were over the age of 70 (72%). Twenty-three percent were in their sixties and only 5% of those who died after vascular operations were under the age of 60. There were twice as many men as women.

There was a high instance of coexisting medical problems with 62% of patients (137/222) having cardiac problems, 27% (61/222) respiratory problems, 21% (47/222) renal problems and 18% (40/222) with diabetes mellitus.

QUALITY OF QUESTIONNAIRES

A high proportion of the vascular surgical questionnaires were poorly completed making it very difficult for the NCEPOD Vascular Advisors (who are nominated by the Vascular Surgical Society of Great Britain and Ireland) to analyse the data received. Vascular surgeons are reminded that the object of the exercise is to improve the quality and delivery of care to patients. The NCEPOD questionnaires should be filled in carefully and conscientiously.

PROCEDURES

The procedures performed are shown in Table 7.1. This table shows that the most frequent operations amongst the reported perioperative deaths were repair of leaking abdominal aortic aneurysm and above knee amputation.

Table 7.1 Procedures in Vascular Surgery (n=222, procedures may be multiple)

Procedure	Number
Abdominal aortic aneurysm surgery	
(including iliac and thoracic aneurysms presenting to vascular or general surgeons)	
Leaking (ruptured) aortic aneurysm	63
Elective abdominal aortic aneurysm	8
Urgent /elective surgery for non-leaking abdominal aortic aneurysm	7
Suspected AAA - other pathology found	4
Leaking iliac aneurysm	3
Endovascular repair of AAA	2
Removal of infected aortic graft	2
Leaking thoracic aneurysm	2
Miscellaneous aortic procedures (including one each of: elective repair of thoracic aneurysm, repair of aorto-enteric fistula, exploration of thrombosed aortic graft)	3
Aortoiliac surgery for occlusive disease	
Aorto-femoral bypass	6
Axillo-femoral bypass	5
Femoro-femoral bypass	3
Ilio-femoral bypass	1
Iliac endovascular stent	1
Peripheral vascular surgery	
Femorotibial bypass	9
Femoropopliteal bypass	7
Brachial embolectomy	4
Femoral thromboembolectomy	4
Popliteal tibial bypass	3
Ligation of popliteal aneurysm	1
Removal of infected arterial prosthesis	1
Amputation surgery	
Above knee amputation	38
Below knee amputation	15
Debridement of toes or leg ulcer	11
Gritti-Stokes amputation	3
Miscellaneous	
Carotid endarterectomy	4
Operation to revascularise ischaemic bowel	4
Fasciotomy	4
Suture of bleeding point following angioplasty	2
Repair of vascular catheter damage	1
A-V fistula for dialysis	1
Angiogram only	1
Angioplasty	1

TRANSFER OF PATIENTS, DELAYS AND CANCELLATIONS

There were six patients who were transferred from another hospital and whose condition was considered to have deteriorated during the transfer. All six were patients with a ruptured abdominal aortic aneurysm. In three, no reason was given for the need to transfer; in one, transfer was because the admitting hospital had no vascular surgical service and in the remaining two cases, although the hospital had a vascular surgical service, there were no available ICU beds. It is inappropriate to repair an aneurysm unless the full backup of intensive care, including ventilation, is going to be applied. One of these patients was haemodynamically unstable and would undoubtedly have been more likely to survive if the operation had been performed at the initial hospital, had an ICU bed been available. Perhaps an operation at the initial hospital with transfer later when the patient was stable might have been better in this particular case, although, this cannot be seen as best practice.

Of the fifteen cases that were delayed, three were elective operations cancelled because there was no HDU/ICU bed available (two were abdominal aortic aneurysms and one was an aortofemoral bypass). In order to provide a proper vascular service it is essential that there are an adequate number of ICU/HDU beds to support a satisfactory emergency service and avoid cancelling elective operations.

In a further patient, who was subsequently found to have an aorto-enteric fistula, the diagnosis was delayed because the endoscopy list was full.

INAPPROPRIATE OPERATIONS

Ruptured aneurysms

There were seven patients who underwent ruptured aortic aneurysm repair in which the decision to operate was questioned. There were four patients who were over 80 years old and moribund. Two others had considerable comorbidity.

Case Study 64

An 82-year-old, ASA 5 patient with ischaemic heart disease (angina and orthopnoea) and a known abdominal aortic aneurysm was admitted following rupture of the aneurysm. Preoperatively the patient was shocked with an arterial pressure of 60/30 mmHg. An experienced consultant general surgeon who had an on-call commitment for vascular emergencies and had done three similar cases in the past 12 months performed the operation, which lasted for four hours. However, the bleeding was never controlled and the patient had persistent hypotension, despite an epinephrine infusion. The patient died in theatre.

Would a specialised vascular surgeon have started this case, or carried on so long with an evidently failing cardiovascular system?

There is a need to identify those patients who have little or no chance of survival. A scoring system has been suggested using a multiple organ dysfunction score (MOD)[71]. In this study of 56 patients from the University of Berne in Switzerland, seven patients, who scored badly, died. These patients consumed a quarter of all the ICU bed-days and three-quarters of the ICU bed-days of patients who died.

Elective aortic surgery

There were three patients who underwent elective aortic surgery where the decision to operate was questioned. Two had poor cardiac function; one of these patients also had chronic renal failure.

Case Study 65

An 82-year-old, male, ASA 4 patient was admitted to a teaching hospital for a scheduled endo-luminal repair of an 8.5 cm infra-renal aortic aneurysm. A cardiologist, who had been investigating his poor heart function, referred the patient. Coexisting disorders included severe ischaemic heart disease (occluded right coronary artery and poor left ventricular function), aortic stenosis with a gradient across the valve of 60 mmHg, CCF, hypertension and chronic renal impairment (bilateral reduced kidney perfusion with a creatinine 157 micromol/l). A consultant surgeon working with a consultant radiologist performed the operation that lasted for 3 h 40 min. Immediately postoperatively the patient developed acute renal failure for which he required dialysis. Subsequently he developed a chest infection and severe heart failure such that he no longer tolerated dialysis. He died on the thirteenth postoperative day.

This questionnaire and the enclosures for this case were very detailed for which NCEPOD is grateful. It is evident that the operation was carefully planned and the postoperative care of this patient was of the highest standard. Interventional radiology is pushing back the frontiers of technical feasibility. Nevertheless, patients must be assessed individually for operability. This patient obviously had a very high operative risk and, excluding the risk of the aneurysm rupturing, his co-morbidity alone gave him a life expectancy of about one year. Was it appropriate then to advise that he had this operation? The influence of aortic stenosis on operative risk is discussed more fully in section 6.

The third case is presented below

Case Study 66

An 83-year-old ASA 2 patient was investigated for intermittent claudication of his buttocks. His aortogram revealed a 4.3 cm infra-renal aortic aneurysm with a right iliac artery occlusion and multiple stenosis in the right femoral artery. Coexisting medical problems were hypertension, an asymptomatic 50% right internal carotid artery stenosis and renal impairment with a serum creatinine of 185 micromol/l. The operation, an aorto-bifemoral graft with a jump graft to the right profunda artery, lasted for nine hours and was complicated by massive blood

loss and consequent worsening haemodynamic status. Postoperatively the patient required re-exploration for a thrombosed right limb of the graft and a right femoro-popliteal arterial graft was performed. Unfortunately the patient developed multiple organ failure and died four days later.

The UK Small Aneurysm trial has shown that there is no benefit to be gained from an operation on an aneurysm less than 5.5 cm in diameter[72]. An extra-anatomic bypass may have been a better option if surgery was required at all for his claudication.

Patients not fit for operation?

There were six patients in whom it was questioned whether they were fit enough to withstand the operation. Five of these had critical leg ischaemia.

Case Study 67

A 77-year-old, male, ASA 5 patient was admitted with a critically ischaemic leg and peripheral gangrene. Three weeks previously he had suffered a myocardial infarction that was accompanied by left ventricular failure. The surgeon recognised the operative risks and recorded that death was "expected". A femoro-tibial arterial bypass was performed. It was difficult to establish good flow down the graft and the operation lasted for 4 h 20 min. Postoperatively the patient developed increasingly intractable left ventricular failure and died on day eight.

Considering his clinical status, was a lesser operation considered; for example amputation or good palliative care?

Patients with critical limb ischaemia are difficult to manage. They are often very unwell, and it is a fine clinical balance between doing too much or too little. The levels of intervention are well known. It should be remembered that primary amputation, although initially difficult for the patient to contemplate, is sometimes the best form of pain relief for a patient with critical limb ischaemia. Also, compared with a dubious arterial reconstruction, the prospects for ambulation may be better after a successful amputation[73].

However, there are undoubtedly some patients who would be best treated by analgesia and palliation, thus allowing their inevitable death to take place peacefully[73].

The sixth patient, whose fitness for operation was questioned, was said to be pre-terminal. Nevertheless debridement of leg ulcers was performed. If the patient was pre-terminal then why was the operation done? Alternatives are available such as larval therapy.

LACK OF SUPERVISION

Consultant input in theatre was generally good and a consultant was involved in the decision to operate in almost all patients, and was present in operating theatre for a high proportion of procedures. Nevertheless, there were some cases where it was thought that the supervision should have been better. Three patients had an emergency repair of a ruptured abdominal aortic aneurysm performed by SpRs with no consultant supervision. In one of these cases the patient lost 22 units of blood. In another, a straight tube graft was performed which was later revised to a bifurcated graft to both iliac arteries. In neither case was any request made for the consultant to come and help. Is it ever appropriate for an SpR to repair a ruptured aneurysm on his own? Certainly, if an SpR is going to repair a ruptured aortic aneurysm, the consultant should be immediately available to help and, until the SpR has demonstrated his proficiency, the consultant should be scrubbed up and assisting with the operation. If an SpR has never reached this level of proficiency then the first time that he has to do this procedure will be when he is a newly appointed consultant. In this situation, the newly appointed consultant should ask for help. The concept of consultant invincibility is outmoded; surgical units should be organised to provide support for newly appointed surgeons, who as a result of shortened time in training and reduced junior doctor hours are likely to be less experienced in the future.

PREOPERATIVE INVESTIGATION

Ninety-eight percent of patients (218/222) were appropriately investigated and prepared for vascular surgery. There were four cases out of the 222 where preoperative investigations were considered deficient, two patients had cardiac problems and two had renal failure.

INFECTION AND MRSA

There were two patients who had PTFE grafts inserted in the presence of infection. Both subsequently developed prosthetic graft infections. Synthetic grafts should be avoided whenever possible for femoro-popliteal or femoro-tibial arterial bypass in the presence of infection. In such cases, if a long saphenous vein is unavailable, alternative sources of autologous vein such as arm veins or deep leg veins may be considered as conduits.

There were four cases of documented MRSA infections. Hospital acquired infections are an increasing hazard and are causing great concern [74, 75]. It has been shown that the incidence of MRSA transmission in hospital can be reduced by conscientious hand hygiene using spirit based antiseptic hand rubs[76]. Has the time come for spirit based hand rubs to be available at each surgical bed space?

RETROPERITONEAL HAEMATOMA FROM SUPERFICIAL FEMORAL ANGIOPLASTY

There was one death following a retroperitoneal haematoma complicating an angioplasty. The diagnosis was made, the haematoma was evacuated and the cavity packed. The patient subsequently died of cardiac failure.

The NCEPOD report on Interventional Vascular Radiology[77] stated that it is dangerous to cannulate the femoral artery above the inguinal ligament, because of the risk of retroperitoneal haematoma. This is particularly likely to occur in the antegrade puncture that is used for subintimal angioplasty of the superficial femoral artery. The danger is greater when the block comes up to the origin of the superficial femoral artery, and where its origin is high and therefore close to the inguinal ligament. The incidence of cannulating the vessel above the inguinal ligament during antegrade puncture for subintimal angioplasty of the superficial femoral artery is not known, nor is the incidence of retroperitoneal haematoma when this occurs. Likewise we do not know the mortality rate of this complication. Problems can be avoided if the artery is not cannulated above the inguinal ligament.

RUPTURED ABDOMINAL AORTIC ANEURYSM

This continues to be the operation associated with most vascular surgical deaths. There are a number of aspects to be considered under this heading.

Specialty of surgeon

There continue to be general surgeons, who do not have vascular surgery as a subspecialty, who repair leaking abdominal aortic aneurysms. This is despite the fact that they perform little if any elective aortic graft replacements. This would appear to be due to on-call service requirements irrespective of the surgeon's specialist interest. This situation presumably arises because, in some hospitals, there are insufficient surgeons with a sub-specialist vascular surgical practice to provide a vascular on-call rota.

Case Study 68

A 67-year-old, ASA 4 patient was admitted at 04.00 with a diagnosis of a ruptured aortic aneurysm. Coexisting medical disorders were asthma and a three month history of hypertension. Preoperative arterial pressure was 128/81 mmHg and heart rate 115/min. The surgeon was a consultant with an interest in upper gastrointestinal surgery and had performed one similar operation in the past 12 months. The operation, a tube graft replacement of the aorta, took 4 h 30 min, during which time the patient received 30 units of blood and the haemodynamic status deteriorated. Bleeding continued postoperatively and the patient died later that day.

This situation should not continue. Those hospitals admitting vascular emergencies should now take steps to ensure that there are sufficient surgeons of appropriate ability to provide an acceptable emergency vascular surgical rota.

General surgeons seeking for help from vascular surgeons

If a general surgeon is not familiar with the vascular problem that he is facing, then it would be good practice to seek help and support from a more experienced colleague. There was at least one example of a general surgeon who was having difficulty and, quite correctly, called for help. Unfortunately there were also several other examples where, even though the surgeon was getting into difficulty, there was apparently no attempt to contact a specialist vascular surgeon.

Ischaemic leg

There were several examples of patients undergoing emergency surgery for ruptured abdominal aortic aneurysms, or having elective surgery to repair an aneurysm, where one limb was ischaemic at the end of the operation but this problem was not recognised at the time. It is important to recognise and correct such ischaemia before the patient leaves the operating theatre. If the problem is not detected until the following day there is a high probability that irreversible damage will occur, resulting in amputation or death. If the operating surgeon has insufficient experience to assess the lower limb circulation then it is essential to seek the help of a specialist vascular surgeon.

Case Study 69

A 72- year-old patient had an elective repair of an infrarenal abdominal aortic aneurysm. Overnight he developed ischaemic legs but the problem appears to have been overlooked. Once diagnosed the patient was returned to theatre where a thrombosed aortic graft was found and a thrombectomy and distal embolectomy done. Unfortunately, one leg was unsalvageable and the patient rapidly deteriorated. Death occurred 48 hours after the initial surgery.

Case Study 70

A 71-year-old patient had a repair of a leaking abdominal aortic aneurysm. The day after surgery, one leg was noted to be ischaemic and a femoral embolectomy and femoro-femoral crossover graft was done. The patient died three days later from acute renal failure. All the surgery was done by a gastrointestinal surgeon who did not request the help of a vascular surgeon, even when complications developed.

Coagulopathy, platelets and packing

There were several cases of patients developing coagulopathy during repair of ruptured abdominal aortic aneurysm. In two of these, fresh frozen plasma was given but the anaesthetists were unable to obtain platelets even though the platelet count was low. Ideally platelets should be given prior to the release of the vascular clamps rather than waiting for uncontrollable haemorrhage to confirm a low platelet count. NCEPOD recommends that blood banks ensure that platelets are readily available for such cases. The use of an abdominal pack may also help in these cases. The abdomen is closed with the pack in place so compressing the bleeding site and the pack removed two to three days later.

Because abdominal aortic aneurysm repair is associated with high mortality and morbidity, NCEPOD recommends that the specialist societies should conduct a more detailed audit of abdominal aortic aneurysm surgery, both elective and ruptured.

- At the end of an aortic operation it is essential to assess the adequacy of the circulation in both legs and, if deficient, to correct it before the patient leaves the operating theatre.

- Blood banks should have platelets readily available for the correction of coagulopathy for ruptured AAA cases.

Recommendations

- There needs to be sufficient ICU/HDU beds so that major elective arterial operations are not cancelled and emergency admissions can be cared for without the need to transfer the patient to another hospital or discharge another patient from the unit too early.

- Those hospitals admitting vascular emergencies should now take steps to ensure that there are sufficient surgeons of appropriate ability to provide an acceptable emergency vascular surgical rota.

- The concept of consultant invincibility is outmoded; surgical units should be organised to provide support for newly appointed surgeons, who are likely to be less experienced in the future.

- There is a need for a scoring system to assess the likelihood of survival of a patient with a ruptured abdominal aortic aneurysm.

MANAGEMENT OF MALIGNANCY

INTRODUCTION

> ### Key points
>
> - The system is failing patients with a cancer, particularly those who present as an emergency. Currently the picture is one of varying expertise, poor compliance with recommendations and failure to collect data and run adequate multidisciplinary teams.
>
> - Many of the recommendations of the Calman-Hine report have not been implemented.
>
> - Patients are being managed in units and centres with very different case-loads and experience levels. Some case-loads are very low and it is doubtful whether clinicians are able to maintain clinical skills.
>
> - Some patients are being subjected to lengthy and complex surgical procedures for palliation, where the benefits of surgery are unclear.
>
> - Data collection appears to be deficient, and many clinicians are unable to demonstrate knowledge of simple demographic data about the cancer being treated, including survival data.

> - In some specialties, rates of cancer staging are very low.
>
> - Some patients are receiving inappropriate diagnostic operative procedures, because of a failure to use appropriate preoperative imaging modalities, or because of a lack of resources for diagnostic facilities.

A total of 512 cases reported had a diagnosis including a cancer at the time of admission. These cases have been studied in some detail in order to assess the quality of care for patients admitted and undergoing a surgical procedure, whilst they had a diagnosis of cancer. In the majority of cases (77%) the final procedure was undertaken in relation to the cancer. However, in some cases, patients underwent a procedure which was not directly related to the cancer.

The report 'A Policy Framework for Commissioning Cancer Services' (Calman-Hine report) was published in 1995[78]. This report identified apparent variations in recorded outcomes of treatment for cancer. It noted that improved outcomes were associated with specialised care, particularly for uncommon cancers.

It is perhaps worth reiterating some of the general principles outlined in the Calman-Hine report:

- *"All patients should have access to a uniformly high quality of care... to ensure the maximum possible cure rates and best quality of life. Care should be provided as close to the patient's home as is compatible with high quality, safe and effective treatment."*

- *"Patients, families and carers should be given clear information about...treatment options and outcomes available to them."*

- *"Effective communication between sectors, professionals and patients is imperative."*

- *"Psychosocial aspects of cancer care should be considered at all stages."*

- *"Cancer registration and careful monitoring of treatment outcomes are essential."*

The report made a number of recommendations

about the configuration of cancer services in order to

achieve these goals:

- *"The new structure should be based upon a network of expertise in cancer care reaching from primary care through cancer units in district hospitals to cancer centres."*

- *"Integration with relevant non-cancer services is essential."*

- *"Designated cancer units should be of a size to support clinical teams with sufficient expertise and facilities to manage the commoner cancers."*

- *"Designated cancer centres should provide expertise in the management of all cancers."*

- *"Cancer units or cancer centres, which use different methods of treatment, should be expected to justify them on scientific or logistical grounds."*

- *"Surgical sub-specialisation in the cancer sites is essential and a hospital should only seek to function as a cancer unit if the volume of work, related to each cancer site, is sufficient to maintain such sub-specialisation."*

- *"All specialties with responsibility for cancer care should form a network for audit with other cancer units and centres."*

- *"There will need to be flexibility to allow for emergency presentations of cancers in hospitals without cancer units."*

- *"Multidisciplinary consultation and management are essential and each cancer unit should have in place arrangements for non-surgical oncological input into services."*

- *"Nursing services must be structured to ensure access to specialist nurses and care at ward and outpatient level must be planned and led by nurses who have benefited from post-registration education in oncology."*

- *"The services of the cancer unit/centre should include palliative medicine."*

- *"Cancer units are expected to engage in appropriate clinical research."*

This study examines to what extent the principles and recommendations set out in the Calman-Hine report of 1995 have been implemented for patients with cancer who died within 30 days of a procedure in the data collection year 1999/00.

OVERVIEW OF CANCER SERVICES

Questionnaire completion

Overall, the standard of the data provided in the oncology questionnaire was rather poor due to failure to correctly complete all questions, and in particular, the failure to use the free text options in order to give advisors an accurate 'pen picture'.

Those questions requesting details about demographic data concerning the cancer concerned were particularly poorly answered. Should clinicians be expected to have a reasonable grasp of basic facts about specific cancers? NCEPOD believes that they should.

Admission category

The majority of patients with a cancer diagnosis were admitted either urgently or as an emergency (Figure 8.1). This is of importance, because the emphasis on organisation of cancer services is to accommodate patients attending following elective referral for cancer from the primary sector. It is not well designed to serve those patients who are admitted as emergencies.

Consequently many patients, who are admitted with the complications of malignant disease, fail to benefit from multidisciplinary teams (MDTs), or sub-specialised surgical teams throughout their acute admission. Paradoxically, it is this group of patients, requiring complex management decisions, who have most to benefit from experienced MDTs.

The Calman-Hine report sets out in considerable detail, recommendations for the configuration of services necessary to maximise the equality and quality of care available for cancer patients. However, in relation to those patients presenting as emergencies, the report simply acknowledges the need for "flexibility" in managing these patients presenting at hospitals without cancer units. There is evidence from this study that even when patients are admitted as emergencies to hospitals designated as a cancer unit or cancer centre, they are not receiving a uniformly high quality of cancer care. NCEPOD believes that more guidance is required, to ensure that this significant group of cancer patients also receive access to uniformly high quality, specialist cancer care.

The major burden numerically for this group of patients falls upon the general surgeon as shown in Table 8.1

Table 8.1	Distribution by speciality and classification of urgency of procedure *Included in this group of general surgeons are those with specialised interests other than vascular surgery.*			
Specialty	Total Oncology Cases	Urgent and Emergency Procedures	Scheduled and Elective Procedure	Not answered
General*	332	170	159	3
Orthopaedic	53	37	16	-
Urology	50	14	36	-
Gynaecology	20	2	17	1
Neurosurgery	15	9	6	-
Otorhinolaryngology	10	2	8	-
Vascular	9	8	1	-
Paediatrics	4	2	2	-
Plastic	1	0	1	-
Cardiothoracic	15	7	8	-
Oral & Maxillofacial	2	0	2	-
Ophthalmology	1	0	1	-
Total	512	251	257	4

Some problems could be alleviated by surgeons recognising the benefit of cross-referral to colleagues with a sub-specialised oncology interest at an early stage in the process. However, there remains a problem over the provision of specialised care 24 hours a day, seven days a week.

Most district hospitals (including designated cancer units) have insufficient numbers of sub-specialised staff to cover around the clock even for the common cancers. Junior doctors' hours and European Working Time Directives will often mean that no

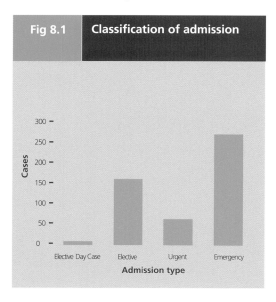

Fig 8.1 — Classification of admission

Cases (y-axis: 0, 50, 100, 150, 200, 250, 300)
Admission type (x-axis: Elective Day Case, Elective, Urgent, Emergency)

member of the specialist team is available out of working hours. In a number of cases, consultants commented that they were now on-call all the time for their sub-specialty, because other surgeons felt that they had become de-skilled.

More emphasis needs to be placed upon developing the concept of clinical networks as outlined in the Calman-Hine report. The cosmetic designation of hospitals as cancer units or centres does nothing to enhance the quality of patient care.

Clinical networks should be designed to try and ensure that every patient has access to the appropriate level of expertise. At one extreme this may involve Trusts reaching mutual agreement to concentrate on their strengths and withdraw from certain services where expertise cannot be maintained. Depending upon circumstances, 24-hour advice may be available from specialist teams or admission or transfer policies agreed, so that patients are treated in the most appropriate hospital. Geographic considerations will need to be taken into account when configuring local clinical networks.

Basic cancer data

Overall 112/512 (22%) questionnaires were unanswered in relation to staging and in a further 118/512 (23%), no stage was recorded in the notes. Two hundred and seven questionnaires (40%) did not indicate how many new cases were seen by the team each year; only 193/512 (38%) supplied peri-operative mortality rates; and only 109/512 (21%) could supply the incidence of the particular cancer in their area.

Perhaps of most concern, only 108/512 (21%) supplied five-year survival rates.

The Calman-Hine report set out the following principle:

"Patients, families and carers should be given clear information about...treatment options and outcomes available to them."

It is difficult to know how clinicians could fulfil these obligations without having a basic grasp of the demographics of a particular cancer, and without employing a recognised staging system in the management of the patient.

Multidisciplinary teams (MDTs)

Overall 313/512 (61%) of patients were not considered by a MDT. A further 58 questionnaires failed to answer this question, and only 141/512 (27%) of patients were identified as having been seen by such a team.

Of the 141 patients discussed by a MDT, the non-surgical make up of the teams was as shown in Figure 8.2.

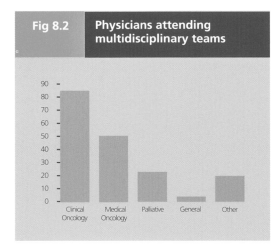

Fig 8.2 Physicians attending multidisciplinary teams

In 30/141 (21%) cases neither a clinical oncologist nor a medical oncologist were members of the MDT. Despite the small number of palliative care physicians attending MDTs, in those cases where the aim of treatment was palliation (either wholly or in part), only 14/196 (7%) indicated that there was inadequate support from the palliative care team.

Transfer to a hospice was considered appropriate in 69/512 (13%) of cases but bed availability was only confirmed in 38/69 (55%). In 14/69 (20%) no bed was available. Fifteen questionnaires were unanswered and two did not know. Home care with palliative support was considered in 89 cases and of these support was thought to be inadequate in only 8/89 (9%).

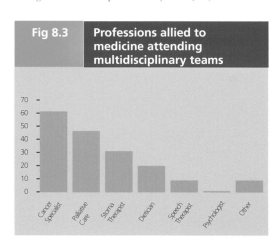

Fig 8.3 Professions allied to medicine attending multidisciplinary teams

Although radiologists and pathologists were infrequently cited as members of the MDT, in 51% of cases joint clinico-radiology meetings were held and in 55% joint clinico-pathology conferences were held. Sub-specialised pathology was only available in 49% of cases. Specialised radiology and pathology is an important component of any multidisciplinary team.

Cancer status of hospital

Despite the relatively low number of patients being seen by MDTs and the low number of patients who were considered at clinico-pathological or radiology meetings, 73% of hospitals were designated as either cancer centres or cancer units. In only 35 cases was chemotherapy administered on the surgical ward, and in all but one case medical and nursing staff had had specific training for this.

Guidelines for GPs

There were 201 questionnaires where the question asking if referral guidelines were available for general practitioners (GPs) was unanswered. Four questionnaires (all seen by consultants) stated that they did not know. Of those remaining who responded, 160 did provide referral guidelines for GPs, but 147 stated that they did not.

Continuing professional development

Just under half (45%) of the surgeons undertaking treatment of cancer patients indicated membership of an appropriate specialist oncology association. One hundred and nineteen (23%) indicated that they were not members of a relevant specialist association, and in 182 cases the question was either unanswered, or the clinician completing the form did not know. Membership of a relevant specialist association does not guarantee effective CME. However, surgeons who are not members of a specialist association may be at danger of not keeping abreast of developments.

Nursing

Overall only 95/512 (18%) answered the question about the percentage of ward staff who held an appropriate higher qualification in oncology care. Of those, 31/95 (32%) indicated that none of the nursing staff were in possession of an appropriate qualification. Only 17/95 (18%) indicated that more than 30% held a relevant qualification.

There is a great deal to be done to meet the

aspiration that all cancer patients should be cared for in units with access to nurses with appropriate post-basic qualifications in oncology care.

Questionnaire deficiency

The questionnaire was identified as deficient, in that it failed to ask sufficiently specific questions about preoperative investigations and their findings. It was often suspected, but only confirmed in a few cases, by free text that preoperative investigation of acute cases was inadequate, particularly in terms of appropriate use of imaging. In a number of cases where diagnostic laparotomy was performed, more thorough preoperative assessment might have prevented the need for surgical intervention.

Aims of treatment

Question 21 asked what the aim of treatment was. Table 8.2 details the responses. It is disappointing that in 110 questionnaires, this question was not answered. Is this a reflection of a lack of clarity about the reason for surgery?

Table 8.2	Aim of treatment
Aim	**Cases**
Palliation	176
Curative Intent	156
Diagnosis	38
Palliation and Diagnosis	10
Palliation and Cure	8
Cure and Diagnosis	5
Palliation, Cure and Diagnosis	2
Not answered	110
Not sure	7
Total	**512**

PATIENTS UNDERGOING SURGERY WITH PALLIATIVE INTENT

Palliation of symptoms alone was the object of surgery in 176/512 (34%) of cases overall, and in 151/395 (38%) where the procedure was directly related to the index cancer.

Whilst it is understood that a procedure, initially intended as diagnostic, could ultimately become palliative once the diagnosis became clear, it is less easy to understand the ten cases where the intent was both curative and palliative, given that: to palliate is by definition 'to lessen the severity of symptoms without curing'.

Only 35/176 (20%) of patients undergoing surgery with palliative intent were admitted electively.

Table 8.3	Symptoms being controlled in palliative only cases *(answers may be multiple)*
Symptom	Cases
Bowel obstruction (sic)	50
Pain/discomfort	50
Nausea and or vomiting	19
Bleeding	13
Immobility	10
Dysphagia	8
Jaundice	8
Anaemia	6
Diarrhoea / faecal incontinence	5
Dyspnoea	5
Weight Loss/anorexia	4
Urinary retention	4
Other	10
Not Stated	18

Bowel obstruction

There were 50 cases operated upon by general surgeons to palliate bowel obstruction. In the majority 38/50 (75%) death was either a definite risk or expected. Small bowel obstruction accounted for 24/50 and large bowel obstruction for 26/50.

Use of the term 'bowel obstruction' as a symptom means different things to different clinicians. Furthermore, the lack of standardised outcome measures for palliation of the variable symptoms of bowel obstruction makes comparison of surgical and medical techniques difficult. However, it is estimated that between 42-80% of patients with bowel obstruction have satisfactory surgical palliation, and between 10-50% of patients will re-obstruct following surgery [79].

Medical measures to control colicky pain, reduce constipation and control nausea and vomiting are often effective, and have the advantage of avoiding painful laparotomy scars and often avoid tying patients to intravenous lines and NG tubes.

Non-surgical methods of palliative control should be considered in patients who are terminally ill and particularly where death is regarded as a definite risk or is expected [80].

Procedures

There was a wide range of procedures undertaken to relieve bowel obstruction. At one extreme, a simple defunctioning colostomy was performed whereas at the other extreme, a major resection and anastomosis was undertaken to palliate bowel obstruction. In some cases, an extensive resection together with a colostomy or ileostomy was undertaken. The rationale for choice of procedure was not always clear.

Table 8.4	Procedures undertaken for palliation of bowel obstruction	
Procedures	No. of cases	
Resection and primary anastomosis	17	
Resection and stoma	8	
Bypass procedure	9	
Stoma alone	10	
Other	6	
Total	50	

Just over half 26/50 (52%) of procedures were classified as emergency or urgent (within 24 hours). Only six of these cases were discussed by a multidisciplinary team (MDT), and whilst disappointing, this is perhaps not surprising. However, of the remaining 24/50 (48%) of procedures classified as scheduled, only nine (37%) were considered by a MDT. Is it possible that some of these procedures could have been avoided, or at least been less radical, if the patient had had access to a multidisciplinary team? Is it possible to organise services for cancer patients so that those presenting acutely have access to the same level of expertise as those referred on an elective basis?

It is unfortunate that the Calman-Hine report fails to give specific guidance on the provision of service for this group of patients.

Case Study 71

An 83-year-old, ASA 4 patient was admitted to a district hospital (cancer centre) under the care of a surgical team with a sub-specialised interest in breast surgery. Two days following admission for small bowel obstruction the patient underwent a sub-total colectomy and ileorectal anastomosis, performed by a SpR 2. The procedure took 3h 30 min and was carried out with palliative intent for an extensive sigmoid carcinoma with hepatic metastases. The patient died of pneumonia five days after surgery. This team sees four colon cancer cases per year and the consultant operates on two cases per year. The patient was not considered by a MDT, and this surgical team is not involved in audit or research for colon cancer.

Should this patient have been referred to the colorectal cancer MDT? Was this procedure appropriate for palliation? Was the seniority and experience of the surgeon appropriate?

Pain or discomfort

Pain or discomfort was usually associated with other symptoms. In 11 cases, pain or discomfort was the only symptom that the procedure intended to palliate. Procedures performed to palliate pain are shown below. Of these procedures five were performed urgently or as emergencies, and six as scheduled or elective procedures. Six were considered by a MDT.

Nausea and vomiting

Of the 19 patients undergoing procedures for nausea and vomiting, only four (21%) were seen in a MDT. Seven patients underwent procedures classified as urgent and the remaining 12 were classified as scheduled.

Of the patients undergoing urgent procedures, only two were seen by a MDT and only 2/12 (16%) of the scheduled patients were seen by a MDT. It seems strange that in some hospitals patients have access to a MDT even when undergoing an urgent procedure, whereas in the majority of patients undergoing scheduled surgery, where more time is available, and where the procedure was recognised as having palliative intention, these patients were not seen by MDTs. This is particularly noteworthy given that non-surgical methods of palliation for nausea and vomiting are often very effective.

Six patients underwent pancreatico-biliary procedures to palliate nausea and vomiting. Only two of these patients were considered by a MDT. Table 8.6 shows the wide range of procedures undertaken to palliate nausea and vomiting.

Table 8.5	Procedures undertaken to palliate pain or discomfort
Site of Primary	**Operation**
Breast	Closed reduction and intra-medullary nail humerus
Finger	Debridement arm wound and bilateral humeral nails
Leukaemia	Drainage perianal abscess
Prostate	Humeral intramedullary nail
Rectum	Laparotomy for peritonitis
Rectum	Laparoscopic assisted loop sigmoid colostomy
Sezary syndrome-leukaemic	Incision and drainage of abscess, marrow harvest
Stomach	Laparotomy
Stomach	Exploratory laparotomy
Uterine cervix	Paracentesis
Unknown	Drainage of ascitic fluid under local anaesthesia

Bleeding

Four of these patients underwent procedures classified as emergency or urgent (Table 8.7). Eight patients had scheduled procedures and one patient had an elective cystoscopy and TURBT. Only 3/9 of the scheduled or elective group were seen by an MDT.

Dysphagia

Only one out of eight patients, admitted for dysphagia, underwent an urgent procedure. The remainder underwent scheduled procedures. The site of tumour and operation performed are shown in Table 8.8.

Six of these eight patients with dysphagia were

considered by a MDT. It is interesting to note the wide range of techniques and procedures available for managing this symptom. Is it right to consider major surgery to palliate dysphagia?

Immobility

All the patients who were palliated for immobility were managed by orthopaedic surgeons. The distribution of primary site and procedure undertaken is shown in Table 8.9. The three patients with breast cancer and one with lung cancer had been seen by a multidisciplinary team, but the remaining six patients had not.

It is interesting that immobility is a relatively

Table 8.6	Wide range of procedures undertaken to palliate nausea and vomiting
Site of Primary Tumour	**Operation**
Caecum	Right hemicolectomy
Common bile duct	ERCP - dual approach with radiology & insertion of endoprosthesis
Gastric antrum	Laparotomy + high gastrojejunostomy
Head of pancreas	Cholecystectomy + gastrojejunostomy
Hepatic flexure of colon	Palliative loop ileostomy + omental biopsy
Pancreas	Palliative gastroenterostomy (mini-laparotomy)
Pancreas-head	Biliary and gastric bypass
Pancreas-head	Laparotomy for haemorrhage from gastroenterostomy
Pancreatic/biliary	Laparotomy
Rectum	Laparotomy
Sigmoid colon	Sigmoid colectomy, end colostomy, caecostomy, biopsy of lesion of colon
Sigmoid colon	Laparotomy/Hartmann's procedure/small bowel resection
Stomach	Laparotomy, no palliative procedure possible
Stomach	Gastrojejunostomy
Stomach	Total gastrectomy and splenectomy
Stomach (antrum)	Gastrojejunal bypass
Stomach (pylorus)	Laparotomy, gastroenterostomy
Transverse colon?	Endoscopic insertion of nasojejunal feeding tube
Unknown	Bilateral salphingo-oophrectomy + omental biopsy

Table 8.7	Procedures undertaken to palliate bleeding
Site of Primary Tumour	**Operation**
Bladder	Cystoscopy + TURBT (3 Cases)
Colon	Cystoscopy + clot evacuation, biopsy and diathermy
Corpus of uterus	Truncal vagotomy, gastroenterostomy, feeding jejunostomy
Hepatic flexure	Right hemicolectomy
Left kidney	Left radical nephrectomy
Prostate	Flexible sigmoidoscopy
Rectum	Minilaparotomy - left iliac colostomy
Splenic flexure	Percutaneous cricothyroidotomy
Stomach	Laparotomy, palliative distal gastrectomy
Stomach invading the transverse colon	Laparotomy + oesophagojejunal anastomosis
Suspected pancreas	OGD

common reason cited for a palliative procedure. Yet many of the surgical procedures used to palliate other symptoms do in themselves produce immobility, by virtue of tying the patient to lines and giving them uncomfortable (mainly abdominal) scars, which also have effects on respiration as well as immobility. It is likely that most of these immobile patients would also have pain and discomfort, and orthopaedic procedures would palliate this as well. Orthopaedic surgery is not always indicated however, and other non-operative methods of palliating pain and discomfort caused by bony metastases should be considered.

Orthopaedic surgeons are involved in the management of patients with cancer arising from many primary sites. Despite this they were not cited as being involved in any of the MDTs. There needs

to be a mechanism whereby orthopaedic surgeons are involved in the decision making process of the MDT particularly for those cancer sites with a predilection for bony metastases.

Jaundice

Jaundice was cited as the reason for palliative surgery in eight cases (Table 8.10). Only half of these patients were seen by a MDT. Half of these patients were classified as having scheduled surgery and half as urgent or emergency. Classification of procedure made no difference as to whether the patient was seen by a MDT. Five cases were treated in cancer centres and three in cancer units. The average number of new cases of these cancers seen by the teams per year was 16 (range 10-25).

Table 8.8	Procedures undertaken to palliate dysphagia
Site of Primary Tumour	**Operation**
Hypopharynx	OGD and dilatation PEG feeding tube
Oesophagus	OGD and dilatation
Oesophagus	OGD + laser
Middle third of oesophagus	OGD + laser + radiological stent insertion
Bronchus invading oesophagus	OGD and dilation + covered stent insertion
Lower third oesophagus	OGD + stent
Lower third oesophagus	OGD and dilatation + micro-selectron therapy
Oesophago-gastric junction	Oesophago-gastrectomy

Table 8.9	Procedures undertaken to palliate immobility
Site of Primary Tumour	**Operation**
Breast	Total hip replacement
Breast	Hemiarthroplasty
Breast	Rush nail humerus
Lung	Intramedullary nail humerus
Ovary	Hemiarthroplasty
Penis	Dynamic condylar screw and plate femur with cement augmentation
Prostate	Intramedullary nail femur
Prostate + rectum	Dynamic hip screw
Ureter	Acetabular reconstruction & THR with Bich Scheider reinforcement ring
Unknown	AO screws to hip

Table 8.10	Procedures undertaken to palliate jaundice
Site of Primary Tumour	**Operation**
Bile duct	Endoscopic retrograde cholangio pancreatogram + change of stent
Common bile duct	ERCP - dual approach with radiology & insertion of endoprosthesis
Gallbladder/pancreas	Open cholecystectomy
Head of pancreas	ERCP
Head of pancreas	ERCP abandoned
Pancreas	Laparotomy stent bile duct, gastrojejunostomy, biopsy metastases
Pancreas head	Biliary and gastric bypass
Pancreatic/biliary	'Open and close' laparotomy

Anaemia

None of the patients who had surgery to palliate the symptoms of anaemia were seen by a MDT. One procedure was performed as an emergency and one urgently, the remainder being classified as scheduled (Table 8.11). There was a definite risk of death in four out of six of these patients. All had major abdominal surgery for palliation of anaemia.

Diarrhoea

All of these procedures were classified as scheduled. Only one patient was seen in a MDT. Diarrhoea can usually be well controlled with medication[81]. Involvement of palliative care physicians as part of an MDT may prevent unnecessary palliative operations.

Weight loss or anorexia

This group of patients (Table 8.13) all had scheduled procedures and none were seen by a MDT.

Case Study 72

A 65-year-old, ASA 2 patient was admitted for weight loss and anorexia, resulting from an adenocarcinoma of the stomach. A radical gastrectomy was planned, but surgery was delayed for one week because of the unavailability of ICU beds. The intention of surgery was to "effectively palliate weight loss". Despite being in hospital for almost a month, the patient did not have the benefit of a MDT. At operation, the tumour was found to be more extensive than predicted by preoperative imaging, and an extended right hemicolectomy

and splenectomy were performed in addition to the gastrectomy. The patient died of septicaemia and bilateral pleural effusions, 22 days after surgery.

Would this patient have benefited from a MDT opinion and involvement of a dietician, or nutrition team? Was this extensive surgery justified to palliate weight loss?

Dyspnoea

Only one of these procedures (Table 8.14) was classified as urgent, the remainder being scheduled or elective. Only one patient was seen by a MDT.

Simple aspiration may be appropriate for palliation, however medical therapy is also available for this distressing symptom and should be considered by the MDT.

Urinary retention

All but one procedure was scheduled, and half of the patients were seen by a MDT (Table 8.15). Death was expected in two patients.

Table 8.11	Procedures undertaken to palliate anaemia
Site of Primary Tumour	**Operation**
Body of stomach	Radical total gastrectomy, splenectomy and extended right hemicolectomy
Caecum	Right hemicolectomy
Hepatic flexure	Right hemicolectomy and gastrojejunostomy
Splenic flexure	Re-laparotomy for bleeding and hypotension
Kidney	Radical nephrectomy
Rectum	Anterior resection and ovarian cystectomy

Table 8.12	Procedures undertaken to palliate diarrhoea
Site of Primary Tumour	**Operation**
Hepatic flexure	Right hemicolectomy
Prostate	Defunctioning loop colostomy
Rectum	Abdominoperineal excision of rectum
Rectum	Loop ileostomy
Recto-sigmoid	Anterior resection, left iliac fossa end colostomy

Orthopaedic surgery

Orthopaedic surgeons were involved in the management of 53 patients with a diagnosis of cancer. In 23 of those cases, the orthopaedic procedure was stated to be directly related to the index cancer. All but one procedure was undertaken with the intent of palliating symptoms, mainly pain and immobility, following pathological fracture. Orthopaedic surgeons were therefore involved in the management of patients with cancers from a wide range of primary sites. Despite this, only 12/23 cases had been considered by a MDT.

The reader is referred to the British Association of Surgical Oncologists 'Guidelines for the Management of Metastatic Bone Disease in the United Kingdom' [82].

Table 8.13	Procedures undertaken to palliate weight loss or anorexia
Site of Primary Tumour	**Operation**
Hepatic flexure of colon	Palliative loop ileostomy, omental biopsy
Stomach (body)	Radical total gastrectomy, splenectomy, extended right hemicolectomy
Stomach (pylorus)	Laparotomy, Gastroenterostomy
Transverse colon (uncertain)	Endoscopic insertion of nasojejunal feeding tube

Table 8.14	Procedures undertaken to palliate dyspnoea
Site of Primary Tumour	**Operation**
Gut	Ascitic tap
Left kidney	Radical nephrectomy
Oesophagus (mid third)	OGD drainage of pleural effusion + talc pleurodesis
Ovary	Paracentesis

Table 8.15	Procedures undertaken to correct urinary retention
Site of Primary Tumour	**Operation**
Bladder	Cystoscopy, bladder washout, prostatic/pelvic mass biopsies
Chronic lymphatic leukaemia	Laparotomy, with view to splenectomy
Prostate	Cystoscopy, laparotomy, ureteric catheters and attempted bladder & prostatic urethral diversion
Rectum	Minilaparotomy - left iliac colostomy

PATIENTS UNDERGOING SURGERY WITH CURATIVE INTENT

Distribution of cancers

The majority of patients receiving treatment with curative intent were managed by general surgeons (Table 8.16).

In contradistinction with those patients undergoing procedures with palliative intent, the majority of patients (103/156, 66%) undergoing procedures with curative intent were admitted electively.

Table 8.16	Distribution by specialty and classification of urgency of procedure		
Specialty	**Cases**	**Elective Admission**	**Urgent or Emergency**
General	114	74	40
Urology	14	12	2
Gynaecology	9	5	4
Cardiothoracic	6	5	1
Otorhinolaryngology	5	4	1
Neurosurgery	2	0	2
Oral and maxillofacial	2	2	0
Paediatric	2	1	1
Vascular	1	0	1
Orthopaedic	1	0	1
Total	**156**	**103**	**53**

Rectal and rectosigmoid carcinoma

The largest group of cancers treated with curative intent by general surgeons was colorectal 77/114 (68%). Thirty-five of these were rectal or rectosigmoid and the remaining 42 were other colon sites.

Multidisciplinary teams

A MDT considered 11/35 (31%) of the rectal or recto-sigmoid cases treated with curative intent. Seventeen of the 35 were operated upon either as emergencies or urgently, the remaining 18 being classified as scheduled or elective.

Staging

Despite the relatively low number of MDTs, the use

of staging for this cancer site was high (Table 8.17).

Table 8.17	Staging of rectal and recto-sigmoid carcinoma
Staging	**No. of cases**
Dukes only	23
TNM + Dukes	10
No Stage	2
Total	**35**

Cancer status of hospital

Twelve patients were treated in cancer centres or associate centres, 21 in cancer units and two in other hospitals. Fifteen cases were treated in units or centres with access to sub-specialised pathology services.

Basic cancer data

Five questionnaires supplied no demographic data. However, of the remaining 30, the mean population served by the units or centres was 299,000 with a range of 100,000 to 550,000. The mean number of new cases of rectal or rectosigmoid cancer seen per unit was estimated at 70, with a range between 12 to 300. Only 12 respondents answered the question about the incidence of this cancer in the population. The answers given ranged from 16.3/100,000 to 84/100,000. The published rates of new rectal cancer registrations for 1997 were 23.4/100,000 for males and 17.1/100,000 for females[83].

Outcomes

Five-year survival figures for units were only returned in five questionnaires, and ranged from 30% to 60%. Perioperative mortality rates were disclosed by 21 units, and ranged from 1% to 10% with a mean of 4.6%. The recommended standards for perioperative mortality for curative colorectal cancer are less than 20% for emergency surgery and less than 5% for elective surgery[84]. Can those units unable to supply this simple data satisfy the Calman-Hine recommendation to give patients *"clear information about...treatment options and outcomes available to them?"* Why are units unable to supply this simple data? Is it because of lack of knowledge by clinicians who are not sub-specialised? Is it because there is a lack of support for data collection and management in cancer units and centres?

Guidelines for GPs

In 24/35 cases, the centres or units claimed to provide written guidelines to GPs.

Audit/research

All but one unit was involved in audit. Eleven were confined to local unit audits, 20 both regionally and locally and only two units were involved in national audits. Calman-Hine recommended all specialties with responsibility for cancer care should form a network for audit with other cancer units and centres.

Nursing

Only three units responded to the question about percentage of nursing staff with appropriate specialist qualifications. Answers ranged from 1% to 50% of ward staff having appropriate higher qualifications in oncology care. The draft manual of cancer services standards[85] suggests that colorectal nurse specialists should be available to all patients with a stoma, and should have obtained the ENB 216.

Chemotherapy was only administered on one of the surgical wards, and medical and nursing staff were appropriately trained on this ward.

Continuing professional development

In 13 cases, the consultant in charge was not a member of any specialist oncology association. Of the remainder, 12 were members of the Association of Coloproctology of Great Britain and Ireland, five were members of The British Association of Surgical Oncology, one a member of the specialist section of the Royal Society Medicine and four did not state which association they belonged to.

Procedures

Table 8.18	Procedures undertaken with curative intent for rectosigmoid cancers	
Procedure	**Number of cases**	
Abdominoperineal resection	3	
Anterior resection alone	4	
Anterior resection + stoma	6	
Hartman's procedure	3	
Other resection + stoma	5	
Stoma only	4	
Other procedure	10	
Total	**35**	

As can be seen from Table 8.18, a wide range of procedures and modifications of procedures were undertaken. It is notable that only a small number of patients in this sample of 30-day deaths received an abdominoperineal (AP) resection,

for the curative management of patients with rectosigmoid carcinomas. Is the small number of AP resections in this sample simply a reflection of the decreased indications for AP resection, or could it indicate that the indication for anterior resection has been over extended to a level where the mortality rate has risen?

Quality of life is an important consideration. However it was noted that a significant number of patients in this group either had, or advisors strongly suspected they had, anastomotic leaks following low anterior resections. Are surgeons becoming too reluctant to produce a stoma? Are some patients being treated by inexperienced surgeons due to lack of sub-specialisation?

Case Study 73

A 65-year old, ASA 4 patient was admitted electively one week following neoadjuvant radio-therapy for a Dukes C rectal carcinoma. An anterior resection was performed, and the patient sent to HDU. Postoperatively the patient became hypotensive on HDU and a gastrograffin enema demonstrated a leak.

Should this patient have had a covering stoma in view of the preoperative radiotherapy?

Colon

Multidisciplinary teams

Excluding rectum and recto-sigmoid, a further 42 cases of colon cancer were treated with curative intent. Only 6/42 (14%) of cases were seen by a MDT. 23/42 cases were classified as emergency or urgent procedures and 18 as schedules or elective, with one case not being classified.

Staging

All but one patient in this group had been staged appropriately (Table 8.19).

Table 8.19	Staging of colon carcinoma
Staging	**No. of cases**
TNM + Dukes	22
Dukes only	17
TNM only	2
No stage	1
Total	**42**

Cancer status of hospital

Twelve patients were treated in cancer centres or associate centres, 15 patients were treated in cancer units, and five in other hospitals. Half (21) of the patients were treated in units or centres with access to sub-specialised pathology services.

Basic cancer data

Three units supplied no demographic data for this cancer site. However of the remaining 39, the mean population served was 262,000, with a range of 105,000 to 600,000. The mean number of new cases seen per unit was 86/year with a range of 5-290. It is possible that this question was interpreted differently by different clinicians. Even so, there is a very wide variation in the number of new cases of colon cancer seen in units. Only 10 questionnaires gave an indication of the incidence of colon cancer, and the answers given ranged from 5/100,000 to 100/100,000. The published registration rates for colon cancer were in fact 34.6/100,000 for males and 35.5/100,000 for females for 1997. Only two questionnaires gave figures within ±10/100,000 of the actual reported figures.

Outcomes

Overall five-year survival figures were only produced in 7/42 questionnaires and ranged from 10% to 80%. The overall five-year survival rate published in the UK is in the region of 38% for all colo-rectal cancers[84]. Only three of the questionnaires gave responses within 10% of published survival data.

Audit/research

Five questionnaires stated that no audit was undertaken for cancer patients, and in four questionnaires the question was unanswered. In the remaining 33 questionnaires, 13 were engaged in local audit only, four in regional audit only, 13 were involved both locally and regionally and three were involved in local and national audits.

Twelve units were either not involved in clinical trials or failed to answer the question. Of the remaining 30 units, 27 were involved in national clinical trials and four in international trials.

Nursing

Only five units responded with regard to the qualifications of nursing staff. One stated that no nurses had appropriate higher qualifications in oncology care and the others ranged from 10% to 75%.

Continuing professional development

In 16 cases the consultant was not a member of a relevant specialist association or the question was not completed. Of the remaining 26, 19 were members of the Association of Coloproctology of Great Britain and Ireland and 11 were members of the British Association of Surgical Oncology.

In all but three cases where the question was not completed, the questionnaire was either completed by the consultant or was agreed by him/her.

Procedures

Table 8.20	Procedures undertaken with curative intent for other colonic cancers
Procedures	**Number of cases**
Resection + primary anastomosis alone	22
Resection + stoma	3
Bypass	4
Stoma alone	5
Other	8
Total	**42**

Case Study 74

An 82-year-old, ASA 4 patient was admitted electively for a right hemi-colectomy performed with curative intent. The patient was on warfarin for a previous deep vein thrombosis. No preoperative preparation was undertaken. Postoperatively the patient became hypotensive, anuric, and developed a coagulopathy. There was no active intervention, and the patient succumbed to intra-abdominal exsanguination.

Having taken a decision to treat with curative intent, could the preoperative preparation of this patient have been improved upon, and subsequently should an attempt have been made to arrest the haemorrhage?

Case Study 18

A 74-year-old patient had been admitted electively and undergone a right hemi-colectomy for a T4N3M1 carcinoma of the ascending colon, performed by an associate specialist on a colorectal firm. The procedure was carried out with curative intent. However, the patient had not been seen by a MDT. Eleven days later the patient developed peritonitis and after an unsuc-

cessful attempted resuscitation for 16 hours, underwent a laparotomy and further resection and primary anastomosis. This procedure was performed by an SHO. The consultant was on annual leave and a 'non-colorectal' general surgeon was available for advice. The hospital provided a service for a relatively small population of 105,000.

Would this patient have benefited from a clinical network, so that specialist colorectal expertise was available even when the Trust's own specialist was on leave? Surely this difficult case should not have been left to an SHO?

Upper gastrointestinal cancer

Multidisciplinary teams

There were 24 upper GI cases managed with curative intent, 23 of which were treated by general surgeons, and one by a thoracic surgeon. Only seven of these cases were seen by a MDT. Eight cases were treated as urgent or emergency procedures and the remaining 16 were either scheduled or elective.

Staging

In 19 cases the TNM staging system was used, in four cases the stage was not recorded in the medical records, and in one questionnaire the question was left uncompleted.

Cancer status of hospital

Fifteen patients were treated in cancer centres or associate centres, eight were treated in cancer units and one was treated in another hospital. In 13 cases there was a sub-specialised pathology service.

Basic cancer data

Two questionnaires contained no demographic data, but of the remaining 22 units, the median population served was 320,000, with a range of 140,000 to 4,000,000 (with the exception of the one centre claiming a catchment population of 4 million the range was 140,000 - 800,000). The mean number of new cases seen per year was 39, and ranged from 10 to 120.

Twelve of the questionnaires gave figures for incidence. Two questionnaires gave outlying figures of 77/100,000 and 150/100,000 for oesophageal cancer, but the median incidence was 14.5/100,000, and the remaining 10 units gave incidences ranging from 10 - 20/100,000 which is within

±10/100,000 for both stomach and oesophageal cancer registrations in England and Wales.

Survival figures were provided in only five questionnaires, and ranged from 10 - 30% five-year survival.

Nursing

Only five questionnaires responded to this question. Two units indicated that none of the nurses had a relevant postgraduate qualification and the maximum number in one unit was 20%.

Audit/research

Three questionnaires gave no detail about audit, and only one unit undertook no audit for cancer patients. Ten units conducted local audit only, and a further 10 units were involved in both local and regional audit for these patients. Half of the units were involved in nationally based clinical trials, and one unit was involved in multinational trials.

Continuing professional development

Fifteen consultants were members of relevant specialist associations, 13 were members of the Association of Upper Gastro-Intestinal Surgeons and seven were members of the British Association of Surgical Oncology.

Procedures

Table 8.21	Procedures undertaken with curative intent for upper GI cancers	
Site of Primary Tumour	Operation	Number of Cases
Gastric	Gastrectomy	5
Gastric	Other	5
Gastro-oesophageal	Oesophagogastrectomy	4
Oesophagus	Oesophagogastrectomy	6
Oesophagus	Other	4
Total		24

Case Study 75

A 49-year-old, ASA 4 patient was admitted electively, and underwent a transhiatal oesophagectomy with curative intent. The surgeon performed five oesophagectomies per year, working in a district hospital with no MDT and a catchment of 220,000. On day five postoperatively, the patient developed chest pain. He was admitted and discharged from ICU on three occasions. On day ten he underwent a laparotomy for a possible appendicitis. He died of septicaemia. No postmortem was undertaken, and no cause of death given.

Should this patient have been seen by a MDT and managed in a centre or unit where there was sufficient throughput of similar cases to maintain the expertise of the team? Could there have been an anastomotic leak heralded by the chest pain at day five? Unfortunately we will never know, because the form was incomplete, and no post mortem was conducted.

Gynaecology

Multidisciplinary teams

There were a total of nine patients with cancer who underwent a procedure where the intention was to achieve cure. Five of the nine patients were considered by a MDT, there was only one emergency procedure and the remainder were all classified as scheduled. Only one centre and one unit did not have access to sub-specialised pathology services.

Staging

All cases except one were staged using the FIGO staging system. Five of the nine cases were treated in cancer centres and the remaining four in cancer units.

Basic cancer data

All but two units were able to supply some demographic data. Four centres served populations ranging from 500,000 to 3.5 million (median 1.75 million). The three cancer units who completed this section served a median population of 150,000 ranging from 138,000 to 230,000. For ovarian cancer, the median number of new cases seen per year was

35 ranging from 32 to 70 for the cancer centres, and from 6 to 35 for the cancer units. Only one unit and one centre completed the question on incidence, and both stated that the incidence of ovarian cancer was 20/100,000. This is close to the registration rate of 23/100,000 in England and Wales for 1997.

Survival figures were produced by only two units who reported 20% and 30% five-year survival for ovarian cancer, and two cancer centres who reported five-year survival figures of 60% and 62%. When asked about perioperative mortality, two cancer centres quoted 1% and one reported 7%. Three units reported figures ranging from 1% to 5%.

Guidelines for GPs

Three cancer centres and one cancer unit had written referral guidelines for GPs.

Audit/research

All units and centres were involved in either regional or local audit. Four of the five centres, and two of the units were involved in national clinical trials.

Nursing

Four of the five centres reported between 1% and 10% of ward nurses had appropriate specialist qualifications. The question was not answered by any of the units.

Continuing professional development

Four of the surgeons in centres belonged to the British Gynaecological Cancer Society, together with one surgeon from a unit. Three centre surgeons also belonged to the International Gynaecological Cancer Society.

Table 8.22	Gynaecological procedures undertaken with curative intent
Site of Primary Tumour	**Operation**
Ovary	Total abdominal hysterectomy, bilateral salpingo-oophrectomy, omentectomy. stenting right ureter
Ovary	Laparotomy and omental biopsy only
Ovary	Laparotomy, partial omentectomy and bilateral salpingo-ovariectomy
Ovary	Laparotomy
Ovary	Laparoscopy, laparotomy, bilateral salpingo-oophrectomy, omentectomy
Ovary	Laparotomy, evacuation of clot, packing of upper abdomen
Ovary	Total abdominal hysterectomy, bilateral salpingo-oophorectomy, appendicectomy and omentectomy
Endometrial	Laparotomy & removal of omental tumour & bilateral oophrectomy
Unknown	Laparotomy, drainage of ascitic fluid, biopsy of ?ovarian tumour

Procedures

Table 8.22 shows gynaecological procedures undertaken with curative intent.

Case Study 76

A 74-year-old patient (ASA not stated) was admitted to a district hospital serving a catchment population of 150,000. Ultrasound and CT scan had failed to demonstrate the extent of ovarian carcinoma which was detected at laparotomy, conducted with curative intent. The patient was not seen by a MDT prior to surgery. The patient died two days after surgery from respiratory failure attributed to disseminated ovarian malignancy.

Could a more accurate diagnosis have been reached by an MDT? Could neoadjuvant chemotherapy have been employed?

Case Study 77

An 83-year-old, ASA 2 patient underwent total abdominal hysterectomy, bilateral salpingo-oophorectomy, omentectomy and ureteric stenting to debulk an ovarian tumour. The patient returned to a general gynaecological ward because HDU was not available. By the second postoperative day, the patient was in positive fluid balance of over six litres. When recognised mannitol was administered. The patient died of a myocardial infarction.

Should this patient have undergone extensive surgery without access to an HDU bed? Why do patients continue to suffer from poor postoperative fluid management?

Urology

Multidisciplinary teams

Ten of the 14 urology patients undergoing procedures with curative intent had bladder tumours, three had renal tumours, and one prostatic tumour. Only two cases were classified as urgent, the remainder being scheduled or in two cases elective. Only four cases (all bladder) were seen by a MDT.

Staging

All patients had been staged using the TNM system.

Cancer status of hospital

Three patients were treated in cancer centres or associate centres, the remaining 11 being treated in cancer units.

Basic cancer data

The two cancer centres served populations of 325,000 and 420,000. The associate cancer centre served a population of 260,000, and the cancer units served populations ranging from 100,000 to 500,000 (median 300,000). Five units had access to sub-specialised pathology services, but perhaps surprisingly, none of the centres had sub-specialised pathology.

For bladder cancer, the number of new cases seen per year ranged from 30 to 200 (median 100). Only two questionnaires gave details of incidence for bladder cancers namely 5/100,000 and 16/100,000. Data from the ONS indicates that the incidence of bladder cancer in England and Wales in 1997 was 33/100,000 for males and 13/100,000 for females. For renal carcinoma, only one unit indicated an incidence and this was 30/100,000. The published ONS data indicates an incidence of 12/100,000 for males and 7/100,000 for females.

Five-year survival figures were only produced for two patients with bladder cancer and were 70% and 50%. Only one questionnaire reported on five-year survival for renal carcinoma and this was 80%.

Guidelines for GPs

Six of ten hospitals treating bladder cancer had written referral guidelines for GPs. In contrast there were no guidelines for any of the hospitals dealing with renal cancer.

Audit/research

All units and centres undertook audit for cancer patients, but only six hospitals undertook audit on a regional or national basis. Eight units were involved in clinical trials, four involving national trials.

Nursing

Only four questionnaires gave details of relevant nursing qualifications. Two hospitals indicated that none of the nursing staff had additional qualifications, and two indicated 10% and 20%.

Continuing professional development

Eleven out of fourteen consultants were members of the oncological section of the British Association of Urological Surgeons.

Procedures

Table 8.23 shows Urological procedures performed with curative intent.

Case Study 78

An 86-year-old, ASA 2 patient with dementia underwent a thoraco-abdominal approach for a small T1 renal carcinoma. There was a staghorn calculus in the lower pole of the kidney. Consent for the procedure was obtained from the patient by an SHO 2. The patient was not seen by a MDT despite a three month delay for an operating list. The patient died seven hours later following a myocardial infarction.

Should this patient have been seen by the MDT? Was surgery appropriate and was the choice of approach appropriate? Was consent valid?

Head and neck

There were nine cases where a procedure was undertaken in relation to a head and neck index cancer. Two procedures were undertaken for palliation and the remaining seven cases were undertaken with curative intent.

Multidisciplinary teams

All but one of these cases was seen by a MDT, and all but one case was treated in a unit with access to sub-specialised pathology services.

Staging

In six out of nine cases, staging was undertaken using the TNM system, however in three cases there was no stage recorded in the notes.

Cancer status of hospital

Half of the cases were treated in cancer centres and half in cancer units (one questionnaire was incomplete).

Basic cancer data

One ENT unit claimed a catchment population of 50 million, but otherwise the catchments ranged from 380,000 to 1 million (median 775,000). There were a wide range of cancer sites covered in this section. Despite this, demographic data was mainly completed and in most cases accurately reflected the published data on incidence and survival.

Audit/research

All but two units were involved in audit of cancer patients, but only two hospitals were involved in clinical trials.

Nursing

Only six out of nine responded to this question. The number of nurses with appropriate additional qualifications in these units ranged from 0 to 75%.

Continuing professional development

Five of the nine consultants were members of the British Association of Head and Neck Oncologists (BAHNO) and one surgeon was a member of the British Association of Surgical Oncology. Three surgeons were not members of any relevant specialist association.

Table 8.23	Urological procedures undertaken with curative intent	
Site of Primary Tumour	**Operation**	**Number**
Bladder	Flexible cystoscopy	2
Bladder	Laparotomy, closure of faecal fistula, ligation of both ureters	1
Bladder	Cysto-urethrectomy, hystero-salpingo-oopherectomy, appendicectomy, ileal conduit	1
Bladder	Cystodiathermy	1
Bladder	Radical cystectomy	1
Bladder	TURBT	3
Bladder	Anterior pelvic exteriorisation and ileal conduit urinary diversion	1
Bladder	Total cystoprostatectomy, Ileal conduit urinary revision, appendicectomy	1
Left kidney	Radical nephrectomy	3
Total		**14**

Procedures

Table 8.24 shows head and neck procedures undertaken with curative intent

Although classified as 'curative' by the surgeon completing the questionnaire, some of these procedures would appear to be diagnostic rather than curative.

Case Study 79

> A 60-year-old, ASA 4 patient was initially admitted electively for excision of a presumed cutaneous squamous cell carcinoma on the nose. The patient was seen in a joint clinic comprising ENT surgeon, clinical oncologist, Macmillan nurse and social worker. There was no input from physicians. Postoperatively she developed a chest infection and underwent an elective tracheostomy under general anaesthesia. At the time of the tracheostomy her sodium was 120 mmol/l, haemaglobin 9 gm/dl, urea 58 mmol/l and creatinine 561 micromol/l. The pathology specimen reported a basal cell carcinoma.

Would this patient have benefited from a preoperative biopsy? Should this procedure have been undertaken without the benefit of managing her underlying medical problems prior to surgery?

This case does not appear in table 8.24, as in the opinion of the surgeon, the final procedure was not undertaken in relation to the management of the index cancer.

Cardiothoracic surgery

Six cases were treated with curative intent by cardiothoracic surgeons. One oesophageal cancer has already been considered under the upper gastrointestinal section.

Of the remaining five cases, four had primary lung tumours and one had a cardiac tumour. Only one of these patients was seen by a MDT. This is particularly surprising given that lung cancer is common, and yet the indications for surgery are relatively few. As one of the common cancers, one might expect MDTs to be more available for patients with a lung cancer. All except the cardiac tumour were treated as scheduled or elective procedures.

Neurosurgery

Only two neurosurgical procedures were undertaken with curative intent, out of a total of 11 neurosurgical procedures undertaken in direct relation to index tumours. The remainder were either diagnostic, palliative, or the aim was not stated. Neither of the two patients treated with curative intent was seen by a MDT. However, one patient was admitted as an emergency and the other urgently.

Paediatric surgery

There were only two children who underwent procedures for cancers with curative intent. One child with leukaemia had removal of a Hickman line, and one infant had insertion of a ventricular drain to control hydrocephalus during chemotherapy for a primary neuro ectodermal tumour. Both children had been considered by a MDT.

Orthopaedic and plastic surgery

There were no primary orthopaedic tumours in this sample, nor were any patients treated with curative intent under the care of plastic surgeons.

Table 8.24	Head and neck procedures undertaken with curative intent	
Specialty	**Site of Primary**	**Operation**
Oral/Maxillofacial	Maxillary sinus	Tracheostomy under LA, debridement of surgical defect + insertion of pack
Oral/Maxillofacial	Floor of mouth	Resection, neck dissection and free flap reconstruction
Otorhinolaryngology	Larynx	Panendoscopy
Otorhinolaryngology	Pyriform fossa	Laryngectomy, partial pharyngectomy and flap repair
Otorhinolaryngology	Pyriform fossa	Pharyngoscopy + biopsy
Otorhinolaryngology	Thyroid	Tracheostomy
Otorhinolaryngology	Nose	Total rhinectomy
Otorhinolaryngology	Nose	Orbital exenteration and free flap, tracheostomy
Otorhinolaryngology	Unknown	Superficial parotidectomy

PATIENTS UNDERGOING SURGERY FOR DIAGNOSIS

Thirty-eight procedures were performed for diagnostic purposes on patients with cancer.

Table 8.25	Distribution by specialty
Specialty	**Number of Cases**
General	19
Urology	8
Gynaecology	5
Cardiothoracic	2
Neurosurgery	2
Paediatric	2
Total	**38**

This group of procedures was performed predominantly on patients admitted urgently or as emergencies (84%). However, only 12/38 procedures were considered to be urgent or emergency. Of these, eight out of 12 were regarded as at definite risk of dying, or death was expected.

Multidisciplinary teams

The majority of patients, even when admitted with a degree of urgency, only underwent a diagnostic procedure on a scheduled basis. It is therefore a little surprising that only 8/38 (21%) were seen by a MDT, despite the fact that in 28/38 (74%) of cases the preoperative working diagnosis involved malignancy.

Cancer status of hospital

Twelve patients were managed in hospitals designated as cancer centres or associate cancer centres and 17 patients were managed in cancer units. The remaining nine patients were managed in hospitals not designated as cancer centres or units.

Basic cancer data

Only 12/38 (31%) completed the demographic data.

Audit/research

Audit for cancer patients was carried out in 24/38 (63%) of cases, but only 14/38 were involved in clinical trials.

Nursing

Only 11/38 (29%) answered the questions regarding levels of nursing qualification and two of these indicated that there were no nurses with appropriate post-basic qualification.

Continuing professional development

In this group 19/38 (50%) indicated membership of a specialist association.

There were a number of cases where diagnostic procedures appeared to be used inappropriately, either because the patient had not been seen by a MDT, or because diagnostic facilities or expertise were deficient. Because we did not specifically ask about preoperative diagnostic facilities, we are unable to give any statistical analysis. However, we give below examples, where the problem was highlighted in the free text section of the questionnaire.

Case Study 80

A 56-year old, ASA 1 Jehovah's Witness was admitted to a district hospital with a palpable pelvic mass. Ultrasound failed to distinguish between a fibroid and ovarian malignancy. There was no MDT, and it was felt inappropriate to wait two weeks for a CT scan. A diagnostic laparotomy was therefore undertaken. Extensive friable tumour was encountered, including liver metastases. Bleeding could not be controlled despite the assistance of a vascular surgeon who ligated both iliac arteries. The patient died of exsanguination.

Should this patient have been managed in a gynaecological cancer centre, with timely access to appropriate diagnostic facilities and expertise? Was a diagnostic laparotomy appropriate?

Case Study 81

A moribund 50-year-old patient graded ASA 5 underwent a brain biopsy with the stated intention of confirming to the family that no further treatment was possible. The working diagnosis was of high grade glioma, and the patient was not seen by a MDT.

Was this diagnostic procedure necessary? Might the family have been equally reassured by a MDT?

PATIENTS UNDERGOING SURGERY WHERE THE AIM STATED WAS "NOT SURE"

There were seven patients in whom the aims of the procedure were stated in the questionnaire as not clear. All of these questionnaires had been either completed or seen by the consultant. In addition there were a further 25 cases where multiple responses were given about the aims of treatment. For example, in eight patients, the aim was described as both palliative and curative. By definition these two aims are mutually exclusive. It is likely that some of these represent procedures where the initial intent was curative, but once the extent of the disease was fully appreciated the aim was changed to palliation. Unfortunately, the data completion for this group is poor and does not permit more detailed analysis.

The majority of this group 22/32 (69%) were admitted either urgently or as emergencies. As in other groups general surgeons are primarily involved.

Table 8.26	Indication for procedure given as "not sure" or multiple answers given.
Specialty	**Number of Cases**
General	22
Urology	5
Neurosurgery	2
Gynaecology	1
Otorhinolaryngology	1
Vascular	1
Total	**32**

Multidisciplinary teams

There were very few patients in this group who were seen by a MDT, only 5/32 (16%). This may well reflect why there was uncertainty about the aims of the procedure.

Staging

In only 50% of this group of patients was staging undertaken or recorded in the notes.

Cancer status of hospital

These patients were treated in cancer centres or associate centres in 11 cases, cancer units in 15 cases, and in non-cancer designated hospitals for the remaining eight cases.

Basic cancer data

Basic demographic data including five-year survival rates was completed in only 7/32 (22%) of questionnaires.

Guidelines for GPs

Only six units responded indicating that referral guidelines were available for general practitioners.

Audit/research

Whilst 23/32 (72%) units were involved in the audit of cancer patients, by contrast few were involved in clinical trials 13/32 (41%).

Nursing

Only six units responded to the question regarding qualifications of ward nursing staff. Only one unit claimed that any nursing staff held an appropriate post-basic qualification, and even here this was only by an estimated 10% of the ward nurses.

Continuing professional development

Twenty-three of the surgeons claimed membership of an appropriate oncological specialist association (72%).

Procedures

As would be expected, there was a wide range of procedures undertaken in this group. By way of example the following case indicates the concern that some patients had inappropriate procedures, which had the patient been seen by an appropriate MDT, might have been avoided.

Case Study 82

An 80-year old, ASA 5 patient was taken to theatre for a laparotomy at 21.00 hrs without any relevant preoperative investigation having been undertaken. At surgery, extensive tumour was identified, with "litres of liquid tumour". The surgeon comments "with the benefit of hindsight an alternative may have been to provide palliative care only".

Could the same alternative decision have been reached with appropriate preoperative investigation such as ultrasound?

INTENTION OF PROCEDURE NOT STATED

There were 110 cases where the patient had a diagnosis of cancer, and the aims of the procedure were not stated in the questionnaire. In 36/110, the procedure was undertaken in relation to the index cancer. When a patient has cancer, it is incumbent upon the treating clinician to liaise with the treating oncology team, and take account of the cancer, (including its prognosis and the effects of surgery on quality of life), even if the procedure is not being undertaken in direct relation to the index cancer. In other words, the patient must be treated as a whole, and care should not be independently compartmentalised.

Multidisciplinary teams

It is perhaps not surprising that only 17/110 (15%) of patients who underwent procedures where the intention was not stated were seen by the MDT.

Clearly, many of the procedures undertaken were likely to have been palliative, some diagnostic and some curative, but the question was not answered, by the clinicians completing the questionnaire. The majority of questionnaires were completed by the consultant. In two cases the questionnaire was completed by an SHO who did not show and agree the form with the consultant in charge. In six cases the questionnaire did not indicate what grade of clinician had completed the form.

Case Study 83

After a two month delay from referral, a 72-year-old, ASA 2 patient underwent an Ivor Lewis oesophago-gastrectomy for carcinoma of the oesophagus. The patient died of "aspiration pneumonia" 11 days after surgery. No postmortem examination was undertaken. The surgeon worked in a university teaching hospital and claimed to undertake 18 such procedures each year. Unfortunately, none of the oncology details had been completed in this questionnaire.

We cannot determine whether the standard of care was deficient or not. Compliance with NCEPOD is now mandatory under clinical governance, and it is not acceptable to return forms which have not been fully completed.

CONCLUSION

The evidence of this study demonstrates haphazard organisation of cancer services. There was poor compliance with the oncology questionnaire, and evidence of inadequate availability of data, even at a very basic level, within the cancer service.

Even where cancer units and cancer centres have been established, there is little evidence of clinical networking. A large number of cancer patients are admitted as emergencies, but they do not have equitable access to high quality cancer services.

A number of patients are undergoing complex surgical procedures with palliative intent when much simpler procedures, or non-surgical remedies, may be more appropriate.

Only a minority of patients had access to multidisciplinary oncology teams, and only a few patients were managed on wards where nursing staff had post-basic oncology qualifications.

Sadly, many of the aspirations of the Calman-Hine report are not being met.

Recommendations

- Hospitals should review the availability of sub-specialists for those patients who present as an emergency.

- Every effort should be made for all patients with a cancer to be considered by a multidisciplinary oncology team. This applies especially to those patients admitted for urgent or emergency surgery.

- All clinicians should use a recognised staging system in the management of patients.

REVIEW OF HISTOLOGY REPORTS

INTRODUCTION

MANAGEMENT OF MALIGNANCY

Key point

● A third of histology reports contained insufficient information to support tumour staging and subsequent clinical management.

Information derived from histopathological examination of tumours is essential for further clinical staging and management of patients. This has recently been acknowledged by standardisation of histopathological reporting of common tumours in all major organs using Calman Minimum Datasets, published by the Royal College of Pathologists[86], and by the need for all histopathology departments reporting tumour resection specimens to meet stringent requirements as part of nationally-established cancer service standards[87]. Commencing in July 1998, standards and minimum datasets to cover most major organ systems have now been published.

NCEPOD reviewed the content of diagnostic histology reports of patients with tumours included

in the 10% sample for 1999/00. We sought to answer the question *"Is the information in the histology reports adequate, given the type of specimen received, for further staging and management using minimum dataset-equivalent criteria"*? Although our review is only a 'snapshot', it may give an overview of the quality of pre-Calman tumour reporting and thus be a yardstick against which the quality of reports can be assessed in the future.

NCEPOD requested the diagnostic histology reports of 90 patients with malignant tumours included in the 1999/00 questionnaire returns. A total of 61 replies were received, giving a response rate of 68%. Information was abstracted from the reports using a proforma based on minimum dataset-equivalent criteria. Calman datasets for colorectal, breast, lung, oesophageal and head and neck cancers were available for the timeframe under study.

Type of specimen and anatomic site

Table 8.27	Type of specimen submitted for histology (n = 61)		
Specimen type		No	(%)
Incisional biopsy		8	(13%)
Excision biopsy		7	(11%)
Resection		42	(69%)
Not assessable from report		4	(7%)
Total		61	

Forty-two (69%) of the 61 specimens were resections (Table 8.27), 36 (59%) from the gastrointestinal tract (Table 8.28), reflecting the role of surgery as the first and optimum line of treatment for tumours at this site. Eight specimens (13%) were incisional biopsies

Table 8.28	Anatomic sites of tumours *(n=61)*		
Site		No	(%)
Colon		24	(39%)
Oesophagus / stomach		12	(20%)
Bladder		4	
Kidney		3	
Brain		2	
Larynx		2	
Lung		2	
Lymph node		2	
Metastases		3	
Other primary sites (1 each from breast, prostate, abdomen, pancreas, ovary, mouth, cervix)		7	
Total		61	

Table 8.29 Histological type of tumour (n=61)

Histological type	No	(%)
Adenocarcinoma	24	(39%)
Carcinoma, not otherwise specified	14	(23%)
Squamous cell carcinoma	7	
Clear cell carcinoma	2	
Transitional cell carcinoma	2	
Lymphoma	2	
Metastases	3	
Other (1 each of carcinosarcoma, crangiopharyngioma, glioblastoma multiforme, ductal carcinoma of breast, leiomyoma)	5	
Not known (not sampled /not found at PM)	2	
Total	**61**	

from sites such as brain, prostate, breast, larynx and bladder or excision biopsies (11%) such as lymph nodes. It was not possible to identify the site of the tumour from the report in 4 patients (7%).

Tumour origin, size, cell type and histological grade

Tumour cell type was given in 59 reports (97%) (Table 8.29). In 56 (92%), the tumours were primary to the site of biopsy/resection and 3 (5%) were metastases. In two patients (3%), both with a presumptive diagnosis of malignancy before death, the tumour was not detected at autopsy in one patient and in the other patient was seen, but, surprisingly, was not sampled for histology - a regrettable omission.

Adenocarcinoma was the predominant cell type in 24 cases (39%), reflecting the preponderance of gastrointestinal resection specimens in the study population. Disappointingly, "carcinoma, not otherwise specified" was diagnosed in 14 of cases (23%). This seems high, and whether it was the true diagnosis or related to sampling error, as might occur in incisional biopsies, inadequate sampling of resected tumours or failure to do further tests such as mucin stains, was difficult to ascertain.

Tumour size was given in 36 reports (59%) (Table

Table 8.30 Inclusion of tumour attributes in report (n=61)

Attribute	Stated	Not stated	Not applicable
Site of origin	58 (95%)	2 (3%)	1 (2%)
Size	36 (59%)	15 (25%)	10 (16%)
Type	59 (97%)	2 (3%)	-
Grade	51 (84%)	7 (11%)	3 (5%)

8.30) but, surprisingly, was omitted in 15 (25%). Histological grade was provided in 51 reports (84%) but was a notable omission in 7 (11%).

Adequacy of tumour excision

The distance of tumour from the proximal and distal margins of the resection specimen was not recorded in 42% and 28%, respectively, of reports, virtually all of colorectal resection specimens. This is probably not significant as in such specimens most pathologists measure only the 'nearest resection margin' to the tumour. The circumferential margin is important for oesophageal and rectal cancers but is not usually an issue for stomach and colon. It is of concern, therefore, that in 25% of reports, there was no comment on the circumferential margin of excision deep to the tumour, although we acknowledge that not all of these tumours were of oesophageal or rectal origin. A smaller proportion of reports omitted to comment on lymph node status or had identified fewer nodes than are regarded as adequate. The TNM staging (combined with Dukes' staging for colonic tumours) is now almost universally used to stage most solid organ tumours,

Table 8.31 Comments on tumour excision (n=61)

Comment	Yes	No	Not applicable
Proximal margin	12 (20%)	26 (42%)	23 (38%)
Distal margin	21 (34%)	17 (28%)	23 (38%)
Soft tissue margin	21 (34%)	15 (25%)	25 (41%)
Lymph node status	38 (62%)	7 (12%)	16 (26%)
Overall adequacy of excision stated?	39 (64%)	5 (8%)	17 (28%)
Staging system	28 (46%)	18 (30%)	15 (24%)

so it was surprising to note that in 30% of reports no pathological staging system at all was used.

Overall, there was sufficient information in 39 of the 44 reports (89%) on resection specimens to enable a judgement on adequacy, or otherwise, of excision to be made and pathologic staging to be done.

Adequacy of reports

Table 8.32	Does the information contained in the histology report meet accepted criteria for further staging and management?	
Answer	No.	(%)
Yes	34	(56%)
No	21	(34%)
Not applicable	6	(10%)
Total	61	

Excluding six reports (10%) which did not require further staging, the pathology advisors considered that in only 34 of the 61 reports (56%) (Table 8.32) was there sufficient information to meet accepted criteria for further staging and management. Table 8.33 summarises the reasons for the remaining 21 reports (34%) failing to meet accepted criteria, the most important being incomplete assessment of excision margins, notably the circumferential / soft tissue margin. Sampling of lymph nodes still seems to pose a problem, with failure to comment on lymph node status in six reports (29%). Comment on extramural lymphovascular invasion was absent in seven cases (33%) although it is now considered an important prognostic factor in colorectal and breast carcinoma and is included in the Minimum Dataset. No pathologic stage was given in 4 reports (19%) - the advisors considered this to be a minor omission providing there was sufficient information in the report for the clinician to work out the stage. We were unable to identify in this small study if there was specialist reporting of tumours or if the

pathologist referred to Calman dataset proformas for those tumours for which they were available.

Conclusion

In this 'one shot' review of 61 diagnostic histology reports, there was insufficient information, mainly about adequacy of excision and lymph node status, in 21 reports (34%) to meet currently accepted criteria for further staging and management. This should improve in the future with more widespread use of Calman Minimum Datasets for the standardised reporting of common cancers and the inclusion of a pathologist in the multidisciplinary team.

Recommendation

- All histology reports relating to oncology cases should match the Calman Minimum Datasets for the standardised reporting of common cancers.

Table 8.33	Advisors' reasons for considering histology reports inadequate for further staging and management (n=21, answers may be multiple)
Reasons	No. (%)
Excision margins not fully assessed	12 (57%)
No comment on vascular invasion	7 (33%)
Node status not adequately assessed/sampled	6 (29%)
Pathologic staging not given	4 (19%)
Other (No tumour size = 2, no tumour type = 1)	3 (14%)

PATHOLOGY

consented procedures were studied from the 1999/00 sample. Three hundred and twenty-eight (95%) had a full postmortem examination, but in 18 cases the examination was limited, with the most frequent exclusion being the central nervous system. All the above figures are comparable with those for 1998/99[13].

Key points

- The postmortem examination rate has remained constant at 31% in 1999/2000, a minority of these (5%) being consented (hospital) postmortem examinations.

- The majority of reports (69%) are satisfactory or better according to Royal College of Pathologists' guidelines. However, there has been a marked deterioration in the quality of postmortem reports when compared with the previous year.

- The operation is now reported in the ONS cause of death in 76% of cases, compared to 37% in 1998/1999.

- Lack of a histology report, possibly due to restrictions imposed by Coroner's Rules, detracted significantly from the quality of the postmortem report in 28% of cases.

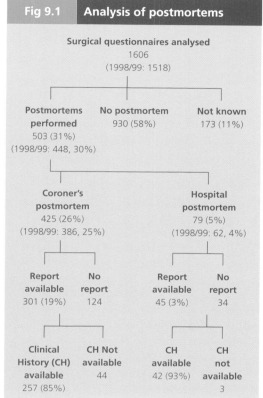

Fig 9.1 Analysis of postmortems

Postmortem rate

Of the 1606 surgical questionnaires received, 503 (31%) recorded that a postmortem examination had been performed (Figure 9.1), of which 79 (5%) were hospital (consented) procedures. Three hundred and forty-six reports were available to the pathology advisors for scrutiny, representing 69% of those cases where it was recorded that a postmortem examination had been performed. Nine hundred and ninety-three cases were recorded as having been reported to the coroner and in 425 (43%) of these, a coroner's postmortem examination was performed; in 11 of these cases it was not known whether a coroner's postmortem examination had been performed and in 39 cases the question was unanswered. In all, reports from 301 coroners' postmortem examinations and 45

Despite our predictions in the 1998/99 report, adverse media publicity has not had a significant impact on postmortem examination rates in 1999/00 nor on the number of limited examinations being undertaken. However, these figures should be monitored closely as various recommendations and guidelines on informed consent for postmortem examination and the retention of organs and tissues are fully implemented and begin to influence audit of postoperative deaths[2, 3, 23, 24].

An important question, which should be addressed in future NCEPOD reports, is the number of cases reported in which comprehensive review was hindered by the lack of a postmortem report. The reasons for this lack of a postmortem report should be investigated.

Clinical history

A clinical history was provided in 257 (85%) of coroners' postmortem reports and 42 (93%) of the hospital cases. In 274 cases (92%) the history was satisfactory or better. In the 1998/99 report NCEPOD commented that *"it is recognised that some coroners do not wish such histories included with their reports and in some cases only a brief history appears to have been available, suggesting that the notes were not scrutinised at the time of the postmortem"*[13]. The role of a 'consented' postmortem is to establish the cause of death and to provide answers to clinicians' and families' questions about the deceased's last illness and the effects of treatment. The role of a coroner's postmortem is to assist in determining whether it is a natural or unnatural death although it may also have many attributes of a 'consented' postmortem. Nevertheless, the autopsy is at the request of, and paid for by, the coroner for his purposes. Knowledge about the illness and mode of death is therefore essential to a proper 'problem-orientated' postmortem examination if such questions are to be answered. Evidence that this was so, was not available to the pathology advisors in 47 reports (21%), the clinical history being absent in 14%, or unacceptably brief, and uninformative or poor in 7%. However, as NCEPOD has stated previously[13] many coroners prefer to omit the clinical history from reports in the interest of accuracy on the basis that details may be wrong or the history may be erratic or incorrect. The introduction of these possible errors into a postmortem examination report can be very upsetting to relatives of the deceased and misleading to clinicians.

However, it should be appreciated that many postoperative deaths reported to NCEPOD have been preceded by a terminal illness characterised by multiple complications and interventions, the pathologic features of which may be masked by agonal end-organ changes. There is therefore a risk that the pathologist may issue an unsatisfactory report and a misleading cause of death if he/she interprets the postmortem findings without prior knowledge of the clinical history. Given the increasing complexity of surgical cases coming to autopsy, should there be detailed consultation, to include examination of the clinical notes between senior anaesthetists, surgeons and pathologists prior to the postmortem examination and again before the pathologist decides on the cause of death?

Description of external appearances

Most reports had an adequate description of the external appearances with 42 (12%) falling below an acceptable standard. Scars and incisions were measured in 223 (66%) cases. The height was recorded in 220 (64%) cases, but the weight was only recorded in 164 (47%). NCEPOD reiterate that in assessing the relative weight of body organs these parameters are useful, particularly the body weight in relation to the heart weight[88]. It was a concern that this was recorded in less than half the cases scrutinised. Even if facilities for weighing bodies in the mortuary are not available, the weight should have been recorded in the clinical notes in most cases, at the very least prior to induction of anaesthesia and surgery.

Gross description of internal organs and operation sites

Table 9.1	Number of organs weighed (n=346, answers may be multiple)
Organ	**Number**
Heart	329
Lungs	301
Liver	293
Brain	290
Kidneys	289
Spleen	283
Other	7
None	10

Similar to 1998/99, the descriptions of internal organs in 299 (86%) of reports were deemed satisfactory or better. In 47 reports (14%) the gross description of the internal organs was thought to be poor, inadequate, or inappropriate to the clinical problem. In 10 cases (3%) no organs at all were weighed. In many instances it was clear that despite doing a full postmortem examination, not all pathologists weighed all major organs, for no reason that was obvious to the pathology advisors. Unless the examination was stated to be limited e.g. to exclude brain or to include thoracic contents only, there should be no reason not to weigh all the major organs as a standard part of the postmortem procedure. In 33 relevant cases (10%), the operation site was not described. It is noted that most of these were orthopaedic e.g. previous hip replacements, which were less likely to be fully examined and described than sites of internal operations.

Postmortem histology

Ninety-seven (28%) of 346 cases had postmortem histology performed, i.e.74 (24%) of the 301 coroners' cases and 23 (51%) of the 45 hospital cases. In 70% of these cases a histology report was included with the postmortem report. All but one of these reports were graded satisfactory or better. In the majority of the other cases histology would have added little or nothing to the value of the postmortem and in only 64 of 278 reports with no histology (23%) was the absence of a histology report thought to detract from the value of the postmortem report. These results are similar to 1998/99. It was recognised that histology may have been undertaken on some of these cases but it was either not recorded in the anatomical report, or an additional report may have been issued at a later date that was not available for scrutiny. However, NCEPOD feel that the absence of histology more likely reflected restrictions imposed by current interpretation of Coroner's Rule 9, which states that *"the person performing a postmortem examination shall make provision, so far as is possible, for the preservation of material which in his opinion bears upon the cause of death, for such period as the coroner sees fit"*[15]. This is an unsatisfactory situation that needs addressing if proper validation of the cause of death and mortality audit of these often complex postoperative cases is to be done[17, 21].

Summary of lesions, clinicopathological correlation and ONS cause of death

Table 9.2	Cases where ONS/OPCS cause of death given	
ONS cause of death	1999/00	1998/99
Yes	332 (96%)	95%
No	14 (4%)	5%

There was a marked fall in the number of reports containing a summary of the lesions, 99 (29%) compared to 205 (76%) in 1998/99. A clinicopathological correlation was present in 62% of the 346 reports, slightly more than in 1998/99 (55%), but 21% were felt to be poor or inadequate compared to 9% in 1998/99. The majority of the reports (96%) included an ONS cause of death (Table 9.2) but in 51 (16%) of cases this did not correspond to the text report, in contrast to 9% in 1998/1999, and in 3% did not follow ONS formatting rules.

These findings of an increase in the number of reports lacking a clinically relevant summary of lesions (247, 71%), an absent, poor or inadequate clinicopathological correlation (175, 51%) and an inaccurate ONS cause of death (51, 16%) are of concern. This may reflect the highly selected patient population under study, many of whom have had coroners' autopsies done in outside mortuaries by independent pathologists, who may not necessarily have had dialogue with the clinician in charge of the patient. As already mentioned, the lack of a clinical history may hinder correlation of the postmortem findings with an often complex clinical history and documentation of a well-formulated ONS cause of death.

Table 9.3	Record of operation in ONS cause of death			
Day of death	No. of cases 1999/00	Operation in ONS cause of death 1999/00	No. of cases 1998/99	Operation in ONS cause of death 1998/99
Day of operation	44	31 (70%)	44	17 (39%)
Day 1-7	186	144 (77%)	143	54 (38%)
Day 8-30	116	88 (76%)	84	30 (36%)
Total	**346**	**263 (76%)**	**271**	**101 (37%)**

It is reassuring to note the marked increase in the number of cases in which the operation is mentioned in the ONS cause of death - 263/346 (76%) compared to 101/271 (37%) in 1998/99 (Table 9.3). There are no specific ONS guidelines on this matter, but the advisors considered that the operation was a contributory factor in the causation of death in a majority of cases and should at least be specifically recorded within part 2 of the ONS cause of death. Terminology such as 'fractured neck of left femur (operated upon)' or 'adenocarcinoma of the caecum (resected)' could be used.

We reiterate our comments in the 1998/99 survey that guidance on the formatting of ONS causes of death may be found in the front of death certificate books[89] and a training video and information pack 'Death Counts'[90] is also available. There are no lists of recommended terms issued by the ONS similar to those used for clinical and disease coding so many terms and synonyms are used. Clinicians and pathologists need to ensure that medical certification of death is accurate. It is worth noting that, as this report goes to press, a Home Office review of death certification and the coronial system is in progress[91] and may impact on this aspect of future NCEPOD reports.

Overall score for postmortem examinations

Table 9.4	Quality of postmortem examinations				
Quality of postmortem	1999/00		1998/99		
Unacceptable, laying the pathologist open to serious professional criticism	8	2%	9	3%	
Poor	96	28%	54	20%	
Satisfactory	150	43%	117	43%	
Good	73	21%	80	30%	
Excellent, (meeting all standards set by RCPath 1993 guidelines)[16]	19	5%	11	4%	
Total		346		271	

Only 8 (2%) of the 1999/00 reports were thought to be of a very low standard, often because of their brevity and lack of correlation with the clinical history. Ninety-six (28%) of the cases had a poor report, an increase of 8% over 1998/99. Two hundred and forty-two reports (70%) were graded satisfactory or better.

Table 9.5	History, antemortem clinical diagnosis and cause of death compared with postmortem findings (n=346, answers may be multiple)	
Postmortem findings	1999/00 Total	1998/99 Total
A discrepancy in the cause of death or in a major diagnosis, which if known, might have affected treatment, outcome or prognosis	29 (8%)	15 (6%)
A discrepancy in the cause of death or in a major diagnosis, which if known, would probably not have affected treatment, outcome or prognosis	52 (15%)	30 (11%)
A minor discrepancy	3 (<1%)	2 (<1%)
Confirmation of essential clinical findings	262 (76%)	221 (81%)
An interesting incidental finding	27 (8%)	15 (6%)
A failure to explain some important aspect of the clinical problem, as a result of a satisfactory autopsy	22 (6%)	9 (3%)
A failure to explain some important aspect of the clinical problem, as a result of an unsatisfactory autopsy	35 (10%)	18 (7%)

The detection of unexpected findings at postmortem examination reiterates the importance of this process in clinical mortality audit. In 81 cases (23%) there was a major discrepancy between clinical diagnosis and postmortem examination and in a further 30 cases (9%) there was a minor discrepancy or interesting incidental finding. In 57 (16%) cases there was a failure to explain some important aspect of the case, although in 22 of these the autopsy was felt to have been conducted satisfactorily.

Attendance of the surgical team at the postmortem examination

An analysis of all 503 questionnaires, indicating that a postmortem examination had taken place, showed that only 141 (29%) surgical teams reported that they had been informed of the time and place of the postmortem. Seventy-seven (56%) of these clinicians indicated attendance of a member of the team at the postmortem. Lack of attendance, when stated, was mainly due to unavailability of the surgeon, other commitments or a feeling that nothing was to be gained from the postmortem as the diagnosis was already known. Where the coroner's postmortem is performed at a public mortuary, this may be many miles away from the hospital where the death occurred. Moreover a problem may be posed by Rule 6(1) (c) Coroners' Rules 1984[15]. This provides that *"if the deceased died in a hospital, the coroner should not direct or request a pathologist on the staff of, or associated with, that hospital to make a postmortem examination if ....the conduct of any member of the hospital staff is likely to be called in question ... unless the obtaining of another pathologist with suitable qualifications and experience would cause the examination to be unduly delayed."*

Communication of the postmortem result to the surgical team

Table 9.6	Communication of postmortem results to the clinical team			
Results to clinical team	**1999/00**		**1998/99**	
Postmortem copy received	352	70%	338	75%
Postmortem copy not received	131	26%	90	20%
Not answered	16	3%	19	4%
Not known	4	<1%	1	<1%
Total	**503**		**448**	

Table 9.7	Time taken for first information to be received by clinical team		
Days after patient's death	**Coroner's 1999/00**	**Hospital 1999/00**	**Total 1999/00**
Less than 8 days	69	24	93
8 days to 30 days	40	9	49
31 days to 60 days	19	2	21
More than 60 days	30	3	33
Not answered	138	18	156
Total	**296**	**56**	**352**

In 131 (26%) of the 503 cases in which a postmortem had been done, the surgeon noted that the clinical team had not received a copy of the postmortem report. One hundred and sixty-three of the 196 who answered the question (83%) said that they received the report within 60 days - an appropriate interval given that most mortality audit meetings are likely to be held in the month following the death of the patient. The pathological information was thought by the surgeons to confirm the clinical impression in 91% of the 426 reports and in 61 (19%) they noted additional clinically unexpected findings as a result of the postmortem. These results are comparable to 1998/99.

Comment

The postmortem examination rate remains constant at 31% for 1999/00, with hospital (consented) postmortem examinations comprising 5%. The standard of the majority of postmortems continues to be satisfactory, with 69% of reports scoring as satisfactory or better according to Royal College of Pathologists' 1993 guidelines[16]. However, NCEPOD noted that previous improvement in several areas, normally contributing to the quality of the postmortem report, was not sustained.

The absence of a histology report detracted significantly from the postmortem report in 28% of cases. This may result from restrictions imposed by current interpretation of Coroner's Rule 9[15]. It may hinder refinement and validation of the cause of death[17] and thus detract from comprehensive mortality audit. Consent for retention of tissues and organs from coroners' postmortems may be forthcoming from relatives if the reasons are explained sensitively to them. We note that the Department of Health[24] recommends that systems be put in place for proper informed consenting of relatives on this issue. Their report incorporates guidance from the Royal College of Pathologists[23], the Bristol Royal Infirmary Interim Inquiry[2] and the Royal Liverpool Children's Inquiry[3].

NCEPOD noted an absent, poor, obscure or uninformative clinical history in 21% of cases, absence of a summary of lesions in 76% of cases and an absent, poor, uninformative or brief clinicopathological comment in 51% of cases. While the Pathology Advisors accept that a poor or inaccurate clinical history on the postmortem report may be misleading for clinicians and upsetting for relatives, it is in the interests of a properly-conducted 'problem-orientated' postmortem examination that there should be consultation between senior anaesthetists, surgeons and pathologists before the postmortem and also prior to issuing the medical certificate of death, especially in complex surgical cases. This will undoubtedly add to the workload of both clinician and the pathologist unless there is more careful selection of cases for coroner's postmortem examination. It is noted that in the wake of the Shipman trial in Greater Manchester, the Home Office is currently reviewing death certification[91] and the coronial system. It is anticipated that recommendations for change will follow.

The operation was mentioned in the ONS cause of death in 76% of cases, compared to 37% in 1998/99, and ONS formatting rules for the cause of death were followed in 97% of cases. However, the causes of death given in parts 1a, 1b and 1c related neither appropriately nor at all to the post mortem report in 16% of responses. We reiterate our recommendations in last year's report that the ONS should provide a standardised list of acceptable terms for causes of death and underlying conditions similar to national clinical disease coding lists and that the Royal College of Pathologists' guidelines should be updated into a minimum dataset format, with inclusion of guidance on ONS formatting for the cause of death[13].

In 20% of deaths, on average, the clinical and postmortem findings were not discussed at mortality audit. Review of cases at mortality audit has been considered best practice for many years[21]. Completed postmortem reports on straightforward cases should be made available for discussion except where a case may still be sub judice because of the need to hold an inquest or in complex cases, in which multidisciplinary discussion may provide information relevant to the terminal events, perhaps leading to modification of the postmortem report and the ONS cause of death. Such reviews would thus ensure that there is good communication across disciplines of the outcome of the postmortem examination and that information from postmortems fulfils its dual aims of ensuring accuracy in death certification and provision of answers to families and clinicians about the deceased's last illness and the effects of treatment. Families of the bereaved should be given the opportunity, should they wish, to obtain information about the final outcome of the postmortem examination.

It is worth commenting that, as in previous years, the majority (69%) of cases reported to NCEPOD did not undergo postmortem examination. While this may be appropriate in many instances, review of some of these cases may have been hindered by lack of information derived from postmortem examination. Perhaps this is an area that merits future study by NCEPOD.

Recommendations

- Recently published national recommendations for obtaining informed consent to retain tissues and organs should be applied.

- Defects in the quality of postmortem reports should be remedied by consultation between clinician and pathologist before the postmortem examination and before issuing the cause of death.

- The Royal College of Pathologists' guidelines to the postmortem examination should be updated into a minimum dataset format, with inclusion of guidance on ONS (formerly OPCS) formatting for cause of death.

- The ONS guidelines should be modified with the adoption of a restricted list of acceptable conditions similar to national clinical disease coding lists.

- Clinicians need to be informed of the time and place of the postmortem examination in order that they may attend and inform the process.

- Completed reports on hospital (consented) and coroners' postmortems should be available for review in multidisciplinary mortality audit meetings.

- Full information should be available to the families about the results of postmortem examinations.

REFERENCES

1. *Extremes of Age.* The 1999 Report of the National Confidential Enquiry into Perioperative Deaths. NCEPOD. London, 1999.

2. *Bristol Royal Infirmary Inquiry (2000). Removal and retention of human material.* Interim report of the Inquiry into the management of care of children receiving complex heart surgery at the Bristol Royal Infirmary. [Annex C of the full report of the Bristol Royal Infirmary Inquiry]. Department of Health. London, 2001.

3. *The Royal Liverpool Children's Inquiry: summary and recommendations.* Department of Health, London, 2001.

4. *The Report of the National Confidential Enquiry into Perioperative Deaths 1993/94.* NCEPOD. London, 1996.

5. Daly K, Beale R, Chang RWS. *Reduction in mortality after inappropriate early discharge from intensive care unit: logistic regression triage model.* BMJ 2001;**322**: 1274-6.

6. McPherson K. *Safer discharge from intensive care to hospital wards.* BMJ 2001;**322**:1261-2.

7. Reason J. *Human error: models and management.* BMJ 2000; **320**: 768-70.

8. Wilson RM et al. *The Quality in Australian Health Care Study.* Med J Aust, 1995; **163**: 458-471.

9. Vincent C, Neale G, Woloshynowych M. Adverse events in British hospitals: preliminary retrospective record review. BMJ 2001; **322**: 517-9.

10. Nolan TW. *System changes to improve patient safety.* BMJ 2000; **320**: 770-3.

11. Berwick DM. *Not Again!* BMJ 2001; **322**: 247-8.

12. *A Commitment to Quality, a Quest for Excellence.* Department of Health, London, 2001.

13. *Then and Now.* The 2000 Report of the National Confidential Enquiry into Perioperative Deaths. NCEPOD. London, 2000.

14. *The Report of the National Confidential Enquiry into Perioperative Deaths 1996/97.* NCEPOD. London 1998.

15. *Coroners' Rules (1984) Rule 9:Preservation of material.* HMSO, London, 1984.

16. *Guidelines for Postmortem Reports.* Royal College of Pathologists, London 1993.

17. *Evidence to the Chief Medical Officer's National Summit on the retention of organs and tissues following postmortem examination.* Royal College of Pathologists, 2001.

18. Nichols L, Aronica P, Babe C. *Are autopsies obsolete?* Am J Clin Pathol 1998; **110**:210-218.

19. Tai DY, El-Bilbeisi H, Tewari S, Mascha EJ, Wiedemann HP, Arroliga AC. *A study of consecutive autopsies in a medical ICU: a comparison of clinical cause of death and autopsy diagnosis.* Chest. 2001; **119**:530-536.

20. Rutty GN, Duerden RM, Carter N, Clark JC. *Are coroners' necropsies necessary? A prospective study examining whether a "view and grant" system of death certification could be introduced into England and Wales.* J Clin Pathol 2001; **54**:279-284.

21. *The Autopsy and Audit.* Royal College of Pathologists, London, 1991.

22. Start RD, Cross SS. *Pathological investigation of deaths following surgery, anaesthesia, and medical procedures.* J Clin Pathol 1999; **52**:640-652

23. *Guidelines for the retention of tissues and organs at postmortem examination.* Royal College of Pathologists. London 2000.

24. *The removal, retention and use of human organs and tissues from postmortem examination.* Department of Health, 2001.

25. *The Report of the National Confidential Enquiry into Perioperative Deaths 1991/92.* NCEPOD. London 1993.

26. Hoile RW. *The Pathologist's Role in the Investigation of Postoperative Deaths.* The Association of Clinical Pathologists Yearbook 1999.

27. *A First Class Service: Quality in the new NHS.* Department of Health, 1998.

28. *The National Confidential Enquiry into Perioperative Deaths (NCEPOD): An external evaluation by CASPE Research.* CASPE Research. London, 1998.

29. *Guidelines for clinicians on medical records and notes.* Royal College of Surgeons of England. London, 1994.

30. Crawford JR, Beresford TP, Lafferty KL. *The CRABEL score - a method for auditing medical records.* Ann R Coll Surg Engl, 2001; **83**: 65-8.

31. *Clinical Governance:Quality in the new NHS.* NHS Executive, 1999.

32. *Percutaneous Transluminal Coronary Angioplasty.* NCEPOD, 2000.

33. *Interventional Vascular Radiology and Interventional Neurovascular Radiology.* NCEPOD, 2000.

34. Poloniecki JD, Roxburgh JC. *Performance data and the mortuary register.* Ann R Coll Surg Engl, 2000; **82**: 401-404.

35. Lee TH, Marcantonio ER, Mangione CM, Thomas EJ, Polanczyk CA, Cook EF, Sugarbaker DJ, Donaldson MC, Poss R, Ho KKL, Ludwig LE, Pedan A, Goldman L. *Derivation and prospective validation of a simple index for prediction of cardiac risk of major noncardiac surgery.* Circulation 1999, 100: 1043-9.

36. Campling EA, Devlin HB, Hoile RW, Lunn JN. *The Report of the National Confidential Enquiry into Perioperative Deaths 1990.* London, 1992.

37. *Comprehensive Critical Care: A review of adult critical care services.* Department of Health. London, 2000.

38. *Guidelines for the Provision of Anaesthetic Services.* Royal College of Anaesthetists. London, 1999.

39. Gallimore SC, Hoile RW, Ingram GS, Sherry KM. *The Report of the National Confidential Enquiry into Perioperative Deaths 1994/95.* London, 1997.

40. Hoile RW. *Critical care beds must be increased.* NHS Trusts 2001 Commissioners' Guide. Roxby Media. London, 2001.

41. *Death registrations 2000: cause, England and Wales.* Health Statistics Quarterly, 10 (2000).

42. Campling EA, Devlin HB, Hoile RW, Ingram GS Lunn JN. *Who Operates When? A Report of the National Confidential Enquiry into Perioperative Deaths 1995/96.* London 1997.

43. *Good Surgical Practice.* The Royal College of Surgeons of England. London 2000.

44. *Reference Guide to Consent for Examination or Treatment.* Department of Health. London, 2001.

45. *Report of the Consent Working Party.* British Medical Association. London, 2001.

46. *Seeking patients' consent: the ethical considerations.* General Medical Council. London, 1999.

47. *Recommendations for standards of monitoring during anaesthesia and recovery.* Association of Anaesthetists of Great Britain and Ireland. London, 2000.

48. *Critical to Success.* Audit Commission. London, 1999.

49. *Good Practice: a Guide for Departments of Anaesthesia.* Royal College of Anaesthetists and Association of Anaesthetists of Great Britain and Ireland. London, 1998.

50. Tsui SL, Law S, Fok M, Ho E, Yang J, Wong J. *Postoperative analgesia reduces mortality and morbidity after oesophagectomy.* American Journal of Surgery 1997, **173(6)**: 472-8.

51. Liu S, Carpenter RL, Neal JM. *Epidural anaesthesia and analgesia. Their role in postoperative outcome.* Anesthesiology 1995, **82(6)**: 1474-506).

52. Goldman L, Caldera DL, Nussbaum SR, Southwick FS, Krogstad D, Murray B, Burke DS, O'Malley TA, Goroll AH, Caplan CH, Nolan J, Carabello B, Slater EE. *Multifactorial index of cardiac risk in noncardiac surgical procedures.* New England Journal of Medicine 1977, **279**: 845-50.

53. *Basic surgical training.* The Royal College of Surgeons of England London 1999.

54. *The NHS Plan.* Department of Health. London 2000.

55. Stabile BE. *Redefining the role of surgery for perforated duodenal ulcer in the helicobacter pylori era.* Annals of Surgery 2000; **231(2)** :159.

56. Donovan AJ, Berne T, Donovan JA. *Perforated duodenal ulcer: An alternative therapeutic plan.* Archives of surgery 1998;**131**: 1166-71.

57. Gul YA, Shine MF, Lennon F. *Non-operative management of perforated duodenal ulcer.* Irish Journal of Medical Science 1999;**168**: 254-6.

58. British Society of Gastroenterology. *United Kingdom guidelines for the management of acute pancreatitis.* GUT 1998; **42 Supplement** 2: S1-S13.

59. Moore EM. *The use for mnemonic for severity stratification in acute pancreatitis.* Ann R Coll Surg Engl 2000; **82**: 16-17.

60. Zeitoun G, Laurent A, Rouffet F, Hay J-M, Fingerhut A, Paquet J-C, Peillon C. *Multicentre randomised clinical trial of primary versus secondary sigmoid resection in generalised peritonitis complicating sigmoid diverticulitis.* Br J Surg 200; **87**: 1366-74.

61. Tudor RG, Farmakis N, Keighley MRB. *National Audit of complicated diverticular disease: analysis of index cases.* Br J Surg 1994; **81**: 730-2.

62. Wacha H, Linder MM, Feldman U, Wesch G, Gundlach E, Steifensand RA. *Mannheim Peritonitis Index - prediction of risk of death from peritonitis.* Theoretical Surgery 1987; **1**: 169-77.

63. Billing A, Frohlich D, Schildberg FW. *Prediction of outcome using the Mannheim Peritonitis Index in 2003 patients. Peritonitis Study Group.* Br. J. Surg 1994; **81**: 209-13.

64. Biondo S, Ramos E, Deiros M, Rague JM, De Oca J, Moreno P, Farran L, Jaurrieta E. *Prognostic factors for mortality in left colonic peritonitis: a new scoring system.* J Am Coll Surg 2000; **191**: 635-42.

65. Copeland GP, Jones D, Walters M. *POSSUM: a scoring system for surgical audit.* Br J Surg 1991; **78**: 356-60.

66. Koperna T, Schulz F. *Prognosis and treatment of peritonitis. Do we need new scoring systems?* Arch Surg 1996; **131**: 180-6.

67. Elliott TB, Yego S, Irvin TT. *Five year audit of the acute complications of diverticular disease.* Br J Surg 1997; **84**: 533 -39.

68. Williams JH, Collin J. *Surgical care of patients over eighty: a predictive crisis at hand.* Br.J.Surg 1988; **75**: 371-3.

69. *Guidelines for good practice in and audit of the management of upper gastrointestinal haemorrhage. Report of a joint working group of the BSG.* J Roy Coll Physicians of London 1992; **26**: 281-289.

70. *Upper GI haemorrhage guidelines.* British Society of Gastroenterology web site. www.bsg.org.uk

71. Kniemeyer HW, Kessler T, Reber PU et al. *Treatment of ruptured abdominal aortic aneurysm, a permanent challenge or a waste of resource?* Eur J Vasc Endovasc Surg 2000;**19**: 190-6.

72. The UK Small Aneurysm Trial Participants. *Mortality results for randomised controlled trial of early elective surgery or ultrasonographic surveillance for small abdominal aortic aneurysms.* The Lancet 1998;**352**: 1649-1655.

73. Campbell WB. *Non-intervention and palliative care in vascular patients.* Br J Surg 2000; **87**: 1601-2.

74. Naylor AR, Hayes PD, Darke S. *A prospective audit of complex wound and graft infections in Great Britain and Ireland: the emergence of MRSA.* Eur J Vasc Endovasc Surg 2001, **21**: 289-294.

75. Murphy GJ, Pararajasingamr, Nasim A, Dennis MJ, Sayers RD. *Methicillin-resistant staphylococcus aureus infection in vascular surgical patients.* Ann R Coll Surg Engl 2001; **83**: 158-163.

76. Pittet D, Hugonnet S, Harbarths, et al. *Effectiveness of a hospital-wide programme to improve compliance with hand hygiene.* The Lancet 2000; **356**: 1037-1312.

77. *Interventional Vascular Radiology and Interventional Neurovascular Radiology.* Report of the National Confidential Enquiry into Perioperative Deaths. London, 2000.

78. *A Policy Framework for Commissioning Cancer Services.* A Report by the Expert Advisory Group to the Chief Medical Officers of England and Wales. Guidance for Purchasers of Cancer Services. Department of Health, 1995.

79. Feuer DJ, Broadley KE, Shepherd JH, Barton DPJ. *Systematic review of surgery in malignant bowel obstruction in advanced gynaecological and gastrointestinal cancer.* Gynaecologic Oncology 1999; **75** (3) 312-322.

80. Hardy JR. *Medical management of bowel obstruction.* Br J Surg 2000; **87** (10), 1281-1283.

81. Baines M, Oliver DJ, Carter RL. *Medical management of intestinal obstruction in patients with advanced malignant disease.* Lancet 1985; Nov 2;2 (8462): 990-993.

82. British Association of Surgical Oncology. *Guidelines for the management of metastatic bone disease in the United Kingdom.* European Journal of Surgical Oncology. 1999:**25(1)**; 3-23.

83. *Report: Registrations of cancer diagnosed in 1994-1997, England and Wales.* Health Statistics Quarterly 07 2000.

84. *Guidelines for the management of colorectal cancer.* The Royal College of Surgeons England and Association of Coloproctology of Great Britain and Ireland, 1996.

85. *Manual of Cancer Services Assessment Standards.* NHS, 2000.

86. *Standards and Minimum Datasets for reporting common cancers.* Royal College of Pathologists. 1998 onwards.

87. *Cancer Guidance Subgroup of the Clinical Outcomes Group.* NHS Executive, 1996 onwards.

88. Kitzman D, Scholz D, Hagen P, Ilstrup D, Edwards W. *Age-related changes in normal human hearts during the first ten decades of life, part II, maturity: a quantitative anatomic study of 765 specimens from subjects 20-99 years old.* Mayo Clinic Proceedings, 1988;**63**:131-146.

89. *Medical certificates of cause of death.* Notes for doctors. ONS. Death certificate book, pages 1-4 and reverse of all death certificates.

90. *Death counts.* Training pack and video. ONS. London (Tel: 020 7396 2229).

91. *Review into Death Certification.* Home Office, 2001 (in preparation).

APPENDIX A - REPORTED DEATHS BY TRUST/HOSPITAL GROUP

The information presented here is based on data from 1st April 1999 until 31st March 2000. This is NCEPOD data supplemented by HES from the Department of Health and HIS from Northern Ireland.

HES is a database containing approximately 12 million records per year of in-patient care. Each record defines a consultant episode and includes patient-level administrative and clinical information. It should be noted that within one episode there may be more than one surgical procedure. The records are aggregated to provide statistical information and are not used to identify individuals. HES data is sourced from NHS Trusts in England through the NHS Wide Clearing Service (NWCS). Where there are fewer than five deaths for a Trust, the DoH asked us to suppress that figure for fear of identification of a particular case. These are shown by an *.

England

When reviewing these table two key issues become apparent:

- Discrepancies between NCEPOD deaths and HES deaths;

- Poor return rates of questionnaires.

Discrepancies between NCEPOD deaths and HES deaths

The deaths reported in these two columns are the number of patients who died within 30 days of a surgical procedure. Some surgical procedures (see Appendix I) have been excluded and both lists are strictly compatible in this respect. The NCEPOD data shows the number of deaths where the final procedure was performed by a surgeon or gynaecologist and the HES data shows the total number of deaths for surgical completed episodes.

However, it should be noted that it is not necessarily the case that a surgeon or gynaecologist undertook the procedures within the HES episodes, only that the patient was under the care of a surgeon or gynaecologist at the time of the procedure, and therefore the figures are not strictly comparable. Conversely, it may also be the case that NCEPOD has recorded some cases that were performed by a surgeon or gynaecologist but have been recorded in HES as a medical episode of care.

Whilst it is not surprising that there were no deaths reported to NCEPOD and HES for specialist eye hospitals for example, it is difficult to understand the reason why there were three Trusts who reported no deaths to us in this period yet reported 288 deaths to HES. Whilst NCEPOD has reluctantly accepted that fewer deaths are reported to them than are to HES, there appears to be little explanation for the Trusts where there are significantly more deaths reported to NCEPOD than to HES and it would appear that in these instances coding may be incorrect. All Trusts should review their data collection and coding systems to ensure accuracy.

Trusts currently collect the specialty of the operating doctor but this is not passed to HES at present. This should solve any discrepancies.

Poor return rates of questionnaires

Whilst it is gratifying to see response rates increasing, it is disappointing that despite the mandatory nature of this Enquiry some Trusts do not even make an 80% response rate. This was the average rate when the Enquiry was voluntary. Whilst in a small number of cases there is a valid reason for this, there are a large number of questionnaires sent and no response at all is received. For further information see the section on General Data.

Wales

It is unfortunate that the equivalent data to HES has not been published in Wales and so no comparisons can be made. The issues relating to the poor return of questionnaires are the same as England.

Northern Ireland

Whilst Northern Ireland were able to provide HIS data, they were not able to exclude those cases which NCEPOD does not consider (Appendix I). It is therefore not possible to draw any firm conclusions from this comparison but two Trusts should review their data collection systems, since the discrepancy in the figures appears to be significant. The issues relating to the poor return of questionnaires are the same as England above.

The Independent Sector, Guernsey, Jersey, Isle of Man and Ministry of Defence Hospitals

No similar data repository to HES exists in these hospitals. The response rate from the Independent Sector has shown a significant improvement compared to rates for the previous year.

Questionnaires sent and returned for 1999/00 data collection period

Trust Name	NCEPOD Deaths	HES Deaths	SQ Sent	SQ Rec'd	AQ Sent	AQ Rec'd
Addenbrooke's NHS Trust	42	163	2	2	2	2
Aintree Hospitals NHS Trust	87	131	11	8	9	8
Airedale NHS Trust	81	81	10	10	9	8
Ashford & St Peter's Hospital NHS Trust	50	95	9	9	2	1
Barking, Havering and Redbridge Hospitals NHS Trust	257	271	23	22	15	7
Barnet and Chase Farm Hospitals NHS Trust	124	180	12	12	14	14
Barnsley District General Hospitals NHS Trust	101	73	11	9	12	12
Barts and The London NHS Trust	216	235	26	17	18	9
Basildon & Thurrock General Hospitals NHS Trust	28	105	0	0	0	0
Bedford Hospital NHS Trust	88	49	10	8	9	9
Birmingham Childrens Hospital NHS Trust	11	16	2	2	1	1
Birmingham Heartlands & Solihull NHS Trust	266	223	19	16	16	16
Birmingham Women's Healthcare NHS Trust	1	0	0	0	0	0
Blackburn, Hyndburn & Ribble Valley Healthcare NHS Trust	111	97	11	10	9	6
Blackpool Victoria Hospital NHS Trust	253	146	24	15	19	14
Bolton Hospitals NHS Trust	105	131	6	5	4	4
Bradford Hospitals NHS Trust	194	174	20	16	19	19
Brighton Health Care NHS Trust	157	201	11	9	7	7
Bromley Hospitals NHS Trust	4	78	2	2	2	2
Burnley Health Care NHS Trust	2	83	0	0	0	0
Burton Hospitals NHS Trust	44	90	1	1	1	1
Bury Health Care NHS Trust	20	52	1	1	1	1
Calderdale & Huddersfield NHS Trust	172	36	15	15	11	10
Cardiothoracic Centre Liverpool NHS Trust (The)	55	61	5	4	5	5
Central Manchester & Manchester Children's University Hospitals NHS Trust	61	140	6	5	5	5
Chelsea & Westminster Healthcare NHS Trust	25	58	4	2	4	2
Chesterfield & North Derbyshire Royal Hospital NHS Trust	68	151	7	7	7	6
Chorley & South Ribble NHS Trust	included	in Preston	Acute	Trust	figures	
Christie Hospital NHS Trust	5	14	0	0	0	0
City Hospital NHS Trust (The)	166	117	15	13	13	12
City Hospitals Sunderland NHS Trust	215	129	16	14	15	14
Countess of Chester Hospital NHS Trust	92	76	8	6	4	4
Dartford & Gravesham NHS Trust	46	80	5	2	4	3
Dewsbury Health Care NHS Trust	76	54	8	7	8	8

Trust Name	NCEPOD Deaths	HES Deaths	SQ Sent	SQ Rec'd	AQ Sent	AQ Rec'd
Doncaster and Bassetlaw Hospitals NHS Trust	160	169	18	9	13	13
Dorset Community NHS Trust	1	0	0	0	0	0
Dudley Group of Hospitals	No deaths reported	122	0	0	0	0
Ealing Hospital NHS Trust	26	41	4	2	4	3
East & North Hertfordshire NHS Trust	81	125	4	4	4	4
East Cheshire NHS Trust	30	60	2	2	2	2
East Gloucestershire NHS Trust	194	111	18	18	4	3
East Kent Hospitals NHS Trust	252	254	27	20	18	16
East Somerset NHS Trust	41	69	4	2	5	5
Eastbourne Hospitals NHS Trust	126	129	7	7	7	7
Epsom and St Helier NHS Trust	106	182	11	9	9	9
Essex Rivers Healthcare NHS Trust	139	149	11	11	11	10
Frimley Park Hospitals NHS Trust	72	124	7	6	7	6
Gateshead Health NHS Trust	74	80	8	7	9	9
George Eliot Hospital NHS Trust	63	77	7	5	7	5
Gloucestershire Royal NHS Trust	190	100	17	15	16	14
Good Hope Hospital NHS Trust	95	120	12	11	12	10
Great Ormond Street Hospital for Children NHS Trust (The)	47	31	7	7	6	6
Greenwich Healthcare NHS Trust	89	52	13	13	12	12
Guy's & St Thomas' Hospital Trust	161	85	24	16	19	18
Hammersmith Hospitals NHS Trust	46	178	7	7	7	5
Harrogate Healthcare NHS Trust	72	73	4	4	4	4
Hastings & Rother NHS Trust	79	83	8	6	7	7
Heatherwood and Wexham Park Hospitals NHS Trust	60	84	4	3	4	3
Hereford Hospitals NHS Trust	15	42	1	1	1	1
Hillingdon Hospital NHS Trust	45	58	6	4	6	5
Hinchingbrooke Health Care NHS Trust	59	38	5	5	3	3
Homerton Hospital	18	40	1	1	1	1
Hull and East Yorkshire Hospitals NHS Trust	143	267	15	15	15	15
Ipswich Hospital NHS Trust	181	138	23	20	18	13
Isle of Wight Healthcare NHS Trust	68	31	1	1	1	0
James Paget Healthcare NHS Trust	120	108	13	13	13	13
Kettering General Hospital NHS Trust	135	84	9	9	9	9
King's Healthcare NHS Trust	120	98	9	6	4	3
King's Lynn & Wisbech Hospitals NHS Trust	67	71	4	3	4	4

Trust Name	NCEPOD Deaths	HES Deaths	SQ Sent	SQ Rec'd	AQ Sent	AQ Rec'd
Kingston Hospital NHS Trust	49	105	5	4	4	4
Leeds Teaching Hospitals NHS Trust (The)	521	521	44	17	38	25
Lewisham Hospital	115	28	14	12	12	11
Liverpool Women's Hospital NHS Trust	5	*	1	1	1	0
Luton & Dunstable Hospital NHS Trust	40	50	0	0	0	0
Maidstone & Tunbridge Wells NHS Trust	217	165	28	24	19	13
Mayday Healthcare NHS Trust	67	81	8	7	8	8
Medway NHS Trust	127	107	5	5	5	5
Mid Cheshire Hospitals Trust	148	123	17	16	15	9
Mid Staffordshire General Hospitals NHS Trust	56	76	3	3	2	2
Mid-Essex Hospital Services NHS Trust	100	96	10	10	10	10
Mid-Sussex NHS Trust	23	47	1	1	0	0
Milton Keynes General NHS Trust	35	70	1	1	1	1
Moorfields Eye Hospital NHS Trust	0	0	0	0	0	0
Morecambe Bay Hospitals NHS Trust	121	115	7	4	6	3
Newcastle upon Tyne Hospitals NHS Trust (The)	373	422	40	29	27	23
Newham Healthcare NHS Trust	50	57	5	3	4	4
Norfolk & Norwich Health Care NHS Trust	257	173	29	28	28	28
North Bristol NHS Trust	119	231	10	9	11	9
North Cheshire Hospitals NHS Trust	108	83	9	9	5	2
North Cumbria Acute Hospitals NHS Trust	122	107	7	6	5	4
North Durham Healthcare NHS Trust	123	109	15	13	15	15
North Hampshire Hospitals NHS Trust	48	57	3	2	2	1
North Manchester Health Care NHS Trust	54	108	5	4	5	4
North Middlesex Hospital NHS Trust	No deaths reported	38	0	0	0	0
North Staffordshire Hospital NHS Trust	117	231	12	11	11	11
North Tees and Hartlepool NHS Trust	118	94	9	9	9	9
North West London Hospitals NHS Trust	114	100	10	10	9	9
Northallerton Health Services NHS Trust	21	14	0	0	0	0
Northampton General Hospital NHS Trust	91	116	11	11	11	11
Northern Devon Healthcare NHS Trust	75	55	6	3	6	6
Northern Lincolnshire & Goole Hospitals NHS Trust	110	130	9	9	7	6
Northumbria Healthcare NHS Trust	154	138	10	10	9	9
Nottingham City Hospital NHS Trust	107	119	8	8	6	6
Nuffield Orthopaedic Centre NHS Trust	2	*	0	0	0	0
Oldham NHS Trust	106	110	12	12	12	12

Trust Name	NCEPOD Deaths	HES Deaths	SQ Sent	SQ Rec'd	AQ Sent	AQ Rec'd
Oxford Radcliffe Hospital NHS Trust	291	294	19	13	19	15
Papworth Hospital NHS Trust	94	85	9	9	9	9
Peterborough Hospitals NHS Trust	115	69	11	11	8	8
Pinderfields & Pontefract Hospitals NHS Trust	134	130	14	14	12	12
Plymouth Hospitals NHS Trust	206	180	26	25	25	25
Poole Hospital NHS Trust	No deaths reported	128	0	0	0	0
Portsmouth Hospitals NHS Trust	37	128	5	4	4	3
Preston Acute Hospitals NHS Trust	137	224	16	12	7	4
Princess Alexandra Hospital NHS Trust (The)	44	82	6	4	6	5
Princess Royal Hospital NHS Trust (The)	14	48	1	1	1	1
Queen Mary's Sidcup NHS Trust	16	60	2	2	2	2
Queen's Medical Centre Nottingham University Hospital NHS Trust	321	252	22	21	21	15
Queen Victoria Hospital NHS Trust (The)	22	13	3	3	3	3
Robert Jones/Agnes Hunt Orthopaedic Hospital NHS Trust	3	6	0	0	0	0
Rochdale Healthcare NHS Trust	52	50	6	5	6	6
Rotherham General Hospitals NHS Trust	135	71	11	11	11	11
Royal Berkshire & Battle Hospitals NHS Trust	33	132	3	3	2	2
Royal Bournemouth & Christchurch Hospitals NHS Trust	94	88	11	11	7	5
Royal Brompton & Harefield NHS Trust	145	70	9	8	9	9
Royal Cornwall Hospitals Trust	102	144	9	5	6	5
Royal Devon & Exeter Healthcare NHS Trust	271	132	25	22	20	20
Royal Free Hampstead NHS Trust	30	101	3	2	2	2
Royal Liverpool & Broadgreen University Hospitals NHS Trust	194	136	16	14	16	12
Royal Liverpool Children's NHS Trust (The)	24	61	3	3	3	3
Royal Marsden NHS Trust	24	7	4	3	3	3
Royal National Orthopaedic Hospital NHS Trust	5	*	0	0	0	0
Royal Orthopaedic Hospital NHS Trust (The)	7	7	0	0	0	0
Royal Shrewsbury Hospitals NHS Trust	14	73	2	2	2	2
Royal Surrey County Hospital NHS Trust	62	87	7	7	7	7
Royal United Hospital Bath NHS Trust	24	105	2	0	2	1
Royal West Sussex NHS Trust (The)	95	106	7	4	7	7
Royal Wolverhampton Hospitals NHS Trust (The)	155	107	14	13	14	12
Salford Royal Hospitals NHS Trust	143	144	13	13	13	13

Trust Name	NCEPOD Deaths	HES Deaths	SQ Sent	SQ Rec'd	AQ Sent	AQ Rec'd
Salisbury Health Care NHS Trust	28	*	6	5	6	5
Sandwell Healthcare NHS Trust	93	74	8	8	8	8
Scarborough & North East Yorkshire Health Care NHS Trust	96	102	11	9	11	11
Sheffield Children's Hospital NHS Trust	13	3	2	2	2	1
Sheffield Teaching Hospitals NHS Trust	319	318	35	34	33	32
Sherwood Forest Hospitals NHS Trust	118	119	6	4	5	5
South Buckinghamshire NHS Trust	51	81	4	3	4	4
South Devon Healthcare NHS Trust	106	146	9	9	9	7
South Durham Healthcare NHS Trust	60	85	5	4	5	5
South Manchester University Hospitals NHS Trust	124	205	10	7	11	11
South Tees Acute Hospitals NHS Trust	272	207	24	21	17	16
South Tyneside Healthcare Trust	68	58	6	4	6	6
South Warwickshire General Hospitals NHS Trust	57	60	3	2	3	3
Southampton University Hospitals NHS Trust	9	296	1	1	1	1
Southend Hospital NHS Trust	112	98	7	7	7	4
Southern Derbyshire Acute Hospitals NHS Trust	142	162	14	14	14	14
Southport and Ormskirk Hospital NHS Trust	81	101	4	4	4	4
St George's Healthcare NHS Trust	290	255	36	30	35	26
St Helens & Knowsley Hospitals NHS Trust	156	91	10	9	10	8
St Mary's NHS Trust	75	70	5	5	0	0
Stockport NHS Trust	68	114	6	5	6	6
Stoke Mandeville Hospital NHS Trust	49	52	5	4	0	0
Surrey & Sussex Healthcare NHS Trust	95	96	13	10	7	2
Swindon & Marlborough NHS Trust	82	93	17	16	17	17
Tameside & Glossop Acute Services NHS Trust	73	99	10	10	10	10
Taunton & Somerset NHS Trust	38	134	5	5	2	2
Trafford Healthcare NHS Trust	28	33	2	2	2	2
United Bristol Healthcare NHS Trust	89	178	8	8	6	6
United Lincolnshire Hospitals NHS Trust	276	281	33	28	32	23
University College London Hospitals NHS Trust	143	148	15	11	14	14
University Hospital Birmingham NHS Trust	185	327	20	15	19	14
University Hospitals of Leicester NHS Trust	234	416	19	9	16	14
Walsall Hospitals NHS Trust	147	65	17	17	16	15
Walsgrave Hospitals NHS Trust	217	268	23	17	22	20
Walton Centre for Neurology & Neurosurgery NHS Trust	29	51	4	4	4	4

Trust Name	NCEPOD Deaths	HES Deaths	SQ Sent	SQ Rec'd	AQ Sent	AQ Rec'd
West Dorset General Hospitals NHS Trust	113	51	7	7	6	6
West Hertfordshire Hospitals NHS Trust	144	122	11	10	11	10
West Middlesex University Hospital NHS Trust	20	42	1	1	1	1
West Suffolk Hospitals NHS Trust	98	73	5	5	5	5
Weston Area Health Trust	61	76	5	4	5	5
Whipps Cross University Hospital NHS Trust	90	97	15	12	15	12
Whittington Hospital NHS Trust	41	46	3	3	3	2
Winchester & Eastleigh Healthcare NHS Trust	63	47	9	9	8	8
Wirral Hospital NHS Trust	175	110	18	17	16	16
Worcestershire Acute Hospitals NHS Trust	169	169	16	11	15	15
Worthing & Southlands Hospitals NHS Trust	136	98	14	11	12	11
Wrightington, Wigan & Leigh NHS Trust	107	117	13	11	13	9
York Health Services NHS Trust	94	94	11	11	11	11

Total   18668   20487

Independent Hospital Groups

Trust Name	NCEPOD Deaths	SQ Sent	SQ Rec'd	AQ Sent	AQ Rec'd
Aspen Healthcare	No deaths reported	0	0	0	0
Benenden Hospital	1	0	0	0	0
BMI	87	6	4	6	5
BUPA	33	3	3	3	3
Community Hospitals Group	19	2	2	2	2
HCA International	47	6	4	6	3
Heart Hospital Ltd.	11	1	1	1	1
King Edward VII Hospital	5	2	2	2	2
King Edward VII's Hospital Sister Agnes	5	0	0	0	0
London Clinic	14	0	0	0	0
Nuffield	20	1	1	1	1

Total   242

Other Hospitals

Trust Name	NCEPOD Deaths	SQ Sent	SQ Rec'd	AQ Sent	AQ Rec'd
Guernsey	14	0	0	0	0
Isle of Man	22	6	6	6	6
Jersey	31	5	5	0	0
DSCA - The Princess Mary's Hospital	0	0	0	0	0
DCSA - Royal Hospital, Haslar	7	1	1	1	0

Total   74

Northern Ireland

Trust Name	NCEPOD Deaths	HIS Deaths	SQ Sent	SQ Rec'd	AQ Sent	AQ Rec'd
Altnagelvin Hospitals NHS Trust	12	36	2	0	2	1
Belfast City Hospital Health Trust	50	67	3	3	3	3
Causeway Health Trust	12	25	1	1	1	1
Craigavon Area Hospital Group Trust	51	73	6	5	5	4
Down Lisburn Health Trust	19	36	1	0	1	1
Green Park Healthcare Trust	3	3	0	0	0	0
Mater Hospital Belfast Health Trust	22	27	3	3	3	3
Newry & Mourne Health Trust	16	16	2	2	1	1
Royal Group of Hospitals & Dental Hospitals Health Trust	100	167	7	6	7	6
Sperrin Lakeland Health Trust	16	17	0	0	0	0
Ulster Community & Hospitals NHS Trust	35	97	4	4	4	3
United Hospitals Health Trust	24	49	2	2	1	0

Total   360   613

NB: HIS data is for all surgical procedures

APPENDICES

Wales

Trust Name	NCEPOD Deaths	SQ Sent	SQ Rec'd	AQ Sent	AQ Rec'd
Bro Morgannwg NHS Trust	6	2	2	1	1
Cardiff and Vale NHS Trust	174	19	15	3	2
Carmarthenshire NHS Trust	112	8	6	7	6
Ceredigion & Mid Wales NHS Trust	26	3	2	3	3
Conwy & Denbighshire NHS Trust	106	6	6	6	6
Gwent Healthcare NHS Trust	220	22	20	17	15
North East Wales NHS Trust	100	16	16	15	14
North Glamorgan NHS Trust	35	10	9	10	7
North West Wales NHS Trust	79	7	7	6	5
Pembrokeshire & Derwen NHS Trust	No deaths reported	0	0	0	0
Pontypridd & Rhondda NHS Trust	100	12	9	12	10
Swansea NHS Trust	215	17	16	16	14

Total   **1173**

NB: HES Data not published for Welsh Trusts

Key

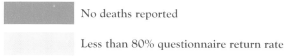

No deaths reported

Less than 80% questionnaire return rate

 * Fewer than 5 cases

SQ   Surgical Questionnaire

AQ   Anaesthetic Questionnaire

ASA 5: A moribund patient who is not expected to survive for 24 hours with or without an operation.

* The definitions are those in use during 1998/99. The wording of ASA grades 3-5 was modified and a sixth grade added in 1999, but was changed too late for inclusion in this study.

APPENDIX B
- GLOSSARY

Definition of the 1990, 1998/99 and 1999/00 sample groups

1990: A random sample of 20% of reported deaths, excluding children aged ten years or less.

1998/99: A random sample of 10% of reported deaths.

1999/00: A random sample of 10% of reported deaths.

Admission category (NCEPOD definitions)

ELECTIVE: At a time agreed between the patient and the surgical service.

URGENT: Within 48 hours of referral/consultation.

EMERGENCY: Immediately following referral/consultation, when admission is unpredictable and at short notice because of clinical need.

American Society of Anesthesiologists (ASA) classification of physical status*

ASA 1: A normal healthy patient.

ASA 2: A patient with mild systemic disease.

ASA 3: A patient with severe systemic disease that limits activity but is not incapacitating.

ASA 4: A patient with incapacitating systemic disease that is a constant threat to life

Classification of operation (NCEPOD definition)

EMERGENCY: Immediate life-saving operation, resuscitation, simultaneous with surgical treatment (e.g. Trauma, ruptured aortic aneurysm). Operation usually within one hour.

URGENT: Operation as soon as possible after resuscitation (e.g. irreducible hernia, intussusception, oesophageal atresia, intestinal obstruction, major fractures). Operation within 24 hours.

SCHEDULED: An early operation but not immediately life-saving (e.g. malignancy). Operation usually within three weeks.

ELECTIVE: Operation at a time to suit both patient and surgeon (e.g. cholecystectomy, joint replacement).

Recovery and special care areas (Association of Anaesthetists of Great Britain and Ireland definitions)

HIGH DEPENDENCY UNIT: A high dependency unit (HDU) is an area for patients who require more intensive observation, treatment and nursing care than can be provided on a general ward. It would not normally accept patients requiring mechanical ventilation, but could manage those receiving invasive monitoring.

INTENSIVE CARE UNIT: An intensive care unit (ICU) is an area to which patients are admitted for treatment of actual or impending organ failure, especially when mechanical ventilation is necessary.

RECOVERY AREA: A recovery area is an area to which patients are admitted from an operating theatre, and where they remain until consciousness has been regained, respiration and circulation are stable and postoperative analgesia is established.

APPENDIX C
- ABBREVIATIONS

A&E	Accident & Emergency
AAA	Abdominal aortic aneurysm
AF	Atrial fibrillation
APACHE	Adult Physiology and Chronic Health Evaluation
AQ	Anaesthetic questionnaire
ASA	American Society of Anesthesiologists
BMI	Body mass index
CABG	Coronary artery bypass grafts
CCF	Congestive cardiac failure
CCST	Certificate of Completion of Specialist Training
CH	Clinical history
CME	Continuous medical education
COPD	Chronic obstructive pulmonary disease
CT	Computerised tomography
CVA	Cerebrovascular accident
CVP	Central venous pressure
DA	Diploma in anaesthetics
DoH	Department of Health
ECG	Electrocardiogram
ENB	English National Board for Nursing and Midwifery
ENT	Ear, nose and throat
EPR	Electronic patient record
ERCP	Endoscopic retrograde cholangiopancreatography
FCE	Finished consultant episode
FIGO	Federation Internationale de Gynecologie et d'Obstetrique
FRCS	Fellow Royal College of Surgeons

GI	Gastrointestinal
GMC	General Medical Council
GP	General practitioner
HDU	High dependency unit
HES	Hospital episode statistics
ICU	Intensive care unit
IHD	Ischaemic heart disease
IV	Intravenous
LA	Local anaesthesia
LVF	Left ventricular failure
MDT	Multidisciplinary team
MI	Myocardial infarction
MOD	Multiple organ dysfunction
MPI	Mannheim peritonitis index
MRSA	Methyl resistent
NCCG	Non-consultant career grade
NG	Naso-gastric
NHS	National Health Service
NICE	National Institute for Clinical Excellence
NIDDM	Non-insulin dependent diabetes mellitus
OGD	Oesophagogastroduodenoscopy
ONS	Office of National Statistics
OPCS	Office of Population Census and Surveys
PCA	Patient controlled analgesia
PEG	Percutaneous endoscopic gastrostomy
PM	Postmortem
POSSUM	Physiological and operative severity score for the enumeration of morbidity and mortality
PSS	Peritonitis severity score
PTFE	Polytetra fluor ethylene
SASM	Scottish Audit of Surgical Mortality
SHO 1,2	Senior house officer, year 1 or 2
SpR 1,2,3,4	Specialist registrar, year 1, 2, 3 or 4
SQ	Surgical questionnaire
TB	Tuberculosis
THR	Total hip replacement
TIA	Transient ischaemic attack
TNM	A classification system introduced by the International Union against Cancer (UICC)
TURBT	Transurethral resection of bladder tumour

APPENDIX D - NCEPOD CORPORATE STRUCTURE

The National Confidential Enquiry into Perioperative Deaths (NCEPOD) is an independent body to which a corporate commitment has been made by the Associations, Colleges and Faculties related to its areas of activity. Each of these bodies nominates members of the Steering Group.

Steering Group (as at 30th September 2001)

Chairman

Mr J Ll Williams

Members

Dr S Bridgman   *(Faculty of Public Health Medicine)*

Dr J F Dyet   *(Royal College of Radiologists)*

Professor I T Gilmore   *(Royal College of Physicians)*

Mr B Keogh   *(Royal College of Surgeons of England)*

Mr G T Layer   *(Association of Surgeons of Great Britain and Ireland)*

Dr J M Millar   *(Royal College of Anaesthetists)*

Dr A J Mortimer   *(Royal College of Anaesthetists)*

Professor J H Shepherd   *(Royal College of Obstetricians and Gynaecologists)*

Dr P J Simpson   (Royal College of Anaesthetists)

Mr L F A Stassen   *(Faculty of Dental Surgery, Royal College of Surgeons of England)*

Mr M F Sullivan   *(Royal College of Surgeons of England)*

Professor P Toner   *(Royal College of Pathologists)*

Professor T Treasure   *(Royal College of Surgeons of England)*

Dr D J Wilkinson   *(Association of Anaesthetists of Great Britain and Ireland)*

Mrs M Wishart   *(Royal College of Opthalmologists)*

Observers

Professor P Kumar   *(National Institute for Clinical Excellence)*

Dr P A Knapman   *(Coroners' Society of England and Wales)*

Mr P Milligan   *(Institute of Healthcare Management)*

NCEPOD is a company, limited by guarantee and a registered charity, managed by Trustees.

Trustees

Chairman	Mr J Ll Williams
Treasurer	Dr J N Lunn
	Dr P J Simpson
	Mr M F Sullivan
Company Secretary	Mrs.C.M.K. Hargreaves

Clinical Coordinators

The Steering Group appoint the Principal Clinical Coordinators for a defined tenure. The Principal Clinical Coordinators lead the review of the data relating to the annual sample, advise the Steering Group and write the reports. They may also from time to time appoint Clinical Coordinators. All Coordinators must be engaged in active academic/clinical practice (in the NHS) during the full term of office.

Principal Clinical Coordinators

Anaesthesia	Dr G S Ingram
Surgery	Mr R W Hoile

Clinical Coordinators

Anaesthesia	Dr A J G Gray
	Dr K M Sherry
Surgery	Mr K G Callum
	Mr I C Martin

Funding

The total annual cost of NCEPOD is approximately £550,000 (2000/01). We are pleased to acknowledge the support of the following, who contributed to funding the Enquiry in 2000/01.

National Institute for Clinical Excellence

Welsh Office

Health and Social Services Executive (Northern Ireland)

States of Guernsey Board of Health

States of Jersey

Department of Health and Social Security, Isle of Man Government

Aspen Healthcare

Benenden Hospital

BMI Healthcare

BUPA

Community Hospitals Group

HCA International

King Edward VII Hospital, Midhurst

King Edward VII's Hospital Sister Agnes

Nuffield Hospitals

The Heart Hospital

The London Clinic

This funding covers the total cost of the Enquiry, including administrative salaries and reimbursements for Clinical Coordinators, office accommodation charges, computer and other equipment as well as travelling expenses for the Coordinators, Steering Group and advisory groups.

APPENDIX E - DATA COLLECTION AND REVIEW METHODS

The National Confidential Enquiry into Perioperative Deaths (NCEPOD) reviews clinical practice and aims to identify remediable factors in the practice of anaesthesia, all types of surgery and other invasive procedures. The Enquiry considers the quality of the delivery of care and not specifically causation of death. The commentary on the reports is based on peer review of the data, questionnaires and notes submitted; it is not a research study based on differences against a control population, and does not attempt to produce any kind of comparison between clinicians or hospitals.

Scope

All National Health Service and Defence Secondary Care Agency hospitals in England and Wales and Northern Ireland, and public hospitals in Guernsey, Jersey and the Isle of Man are included in the Enquiry, as well as many hospitals in the independent healthcare sector.

Reporting of deaths

NCEPOD collects basic details on all deaths in hospital within 30 days of a surgical procedure (with some exceptions - see Appendix I), through a system of local reporting. The Local Reporters (Appendix F) in each hospital are often consultant clinicians, but this role is increasingly being taken on by information and clinical audit departments who are able to provide the data from hospital information systems. When incomplete information is received, the NCEPOD administrative staff contact the appropriate medical records or information officer, secretarial or clinical audit staff.

Deaths of patients in hospital within 30 days of a surgical procedure (excluding maternal deaths) are included. If Local Reporters are aware of postoperative deaths at home they also report them. A surgical procedure is defined by NCEPOD as:

"any procedure carried out by a surgeon or gynaecologist, with or without an anaesthetist, involving local, regional or general anaesthesia or sedation."

Local Reporters provide the following information:

- Name of Trust/hospital
- Sex/hospital number/NHS number of patient
- Name of hospital in which the death occurred (and hospital where surgery took place, if different)
- Dates of birth, final operation and death
- Surgical procedure performed
- Name of consultant surgeon
- Name of anaesthetist

Sample for more detailed review

The data collection year runs from 1 April to 31 March. Each year, a sample of the reported deaths is reviewed in more detail. The sample selection varies for each data collection year, and is determined by the NCEPOD Steering Group (see Appendix D).

NCEPOD may, on occasion, collect data about patients who have survived more than 30 days after a procedure. These data are used for comparison with the data about deaths, or to review a specific aspect of clinical practice. Data from other sources may also be used.

The perioperative deaths, which fell within the sample group for 1999/00, were a random 10% of all deaths reported.

For each sample case, questionnaires were sent to the consultant surgeon or gynaecologist and consultant anaesthetist. These questionnaires were identified only by a number, allocated in the NCEPOD office. Copies of operation notes, anaesthetic records, fluid balance charts and postmortem reports were also requested. Surgical questionnaires were sent directly to the consultant surgeon or gynaecologist under whose care the patient was at the time of the final operation before death. When the Local Reporter had been able to identify the relevant consultant anaesthetist, the anaesthetic questionnaire was sent directly to him or her. However, in many cases this was not possible, and the local tutor of the Royal College of Anaesthetists was asked to name a consultant to whom the questionnaire should be sent. Copies of the questionnaires used in 1999/00 are available from the NCEPOD office on request.

Since the introduction of clinical governance in April 1999, participation in the confidential enquiries has become a mandatory requirement for clinicians in the NHS. Trusts/hospitals are therefore now kept informed of their participation levels on a quarterly basis.

Consultants

NCEPOD holds a database, regularly updated, of all consultant anaesthetists, gynaecologists and surgeons in England, Wales and Northern Ireland.

Analysis and review of data

The NCEPOD administrative staff manage the collection, recording and analysis of data. The data are aggregated to produce the tables and information in the reports; further unpublished aggregated data is available from the NCEPOD office on request. All data are aggregated to regional or national level only, so that individual Trusts and hospitals cannot be identified.

Advisory groups

The NCEPOD Clinical Coordinators (see Appendix D), together with the advisory groups for anaesthesia and surgery, review the completed questionnaires and the aggregated data. The members of the advisory groups are drawn from hospitals in England, Wales and Northern Ireland. The advisory group in pathology reviews postmortem data from the surgical questionnaires as well as copies of postmortem reports and for this sample reviewed the histology reports for the oncology cases.

Production of the report

The advisory groups comment on the overall quality of care within the speciality and on any particular issues or individual cases which merit attention. These comments form the basis for the published report, which is prepared by the Coordinators, with contributions from the advisors. The report is reviewed and agreed by the NCEPOD Steering Group prior to publication.

Confidentiality

NCEPOD is registered with the Data Protection Registrar and abides by the Data Protection Principles. All reporting forms, questionnaires and other paper records relating to the sample are shredded once an individual report is ready for publication. Similarly, all identifiable data are removed from the computer database.

Before review of questionnaires by the Clinical Coordinators or any of the advisors, all identification is removed from the questionnaires and accompanying papers. The source of the information is not revealed to any of the Coordinators or advisors. The Chief Executive of NCEPOD is the Caldicott Guardian for all information held.

APPENDIX F - LOCAL REPORTERS

A list of the Local Reporters as at 1 September 2001, with NHS Trusts listed according to regional divisions in place at that date.

We appreciate that there are many clinical audit and information departments involved in providing data, although we have in many cases named only the consultant clinician nominated as the Local Reporter.

EASTERN

Addenbrooke's	Dr D. Wight
Basildon & Thurrock General Hospitals	Dr A.K. Abdulla
Bedford Hospital	Mrs S. Blackley
East & North Hertfordshire	Dr A. Fattah (Queen Elizabeth II Hospital & Hertford County Hospital)
	Dr D.J. Madders (Lister Hospital)
Essex Rivers Healthcare	Mrs E. Pudney
Hinchingbrooke Health Care	Dr M.D. Harris
Ipswich Hospital	Mr I. Lennox
James Paget Hospital	Dr M.J. Wilkinson
King's Lynn & Wisbech Hospitals	Mr.D.J.Sildown

Luton & Dunstable Hospital	Dr D.A.S. Lawrence
Mid-Essex Hospital Services	Mr P. Dziewulski
Norfolk & Norwich Health Care	Dr A.J.G. Gray
Papworth Hospital	Dr M. Goddard
Peterborough Hospitals	Dr P.M. Dennis
Princess Alexandra Hospital	Dr R.G.M. Letcher
Southend Hospital	Ms W. Davis
West Hertfordshire	Dr R. Smith (Watford General Hospital & Mount Vernon Hospital)
	Dr A.P. O'Reilly (St Alban's City Hospital & Hemel Hempstead General Hospital)
West Suffolk Hospitals	Mrs V. Hamilton

LONDON

Barking, Havering and Redbridge Hospitals	Mrs D. Jago (Oldchurch Hospital & Harold Wood Hospital)
	Dr P. Tanner (King George Hospital)
Barnet and Chase Farm Hospitals	Dr W.H.S. Mohamid (Chase Farm Hospital)
	Dr J. El-Jabbour (Barnet General Hospital)
Bart's and The London	Dr K. Wark (London Chest Hospital)
	Dr D.J. Wilkinson (St Bartholomew's Hospital)
	Dr P.J. Flynn (Royal London Hospital)
Bromley Hospitals	Dr A. Turvey
Chelsea & Westminster Healthcare	Ms I. Penny

Ealing Hospital	Dr C. Schmulian	St Mary's	Ms R.A. Hittinger
Epsom and St Helier	Dr L. Temple (Epsom General Hospital)	University College London Hospitals	Ms R. Farquharson (National Hospital For Neurology & Neurosurgery)
	Dr F Anderson (St Helier Hospital)		Ms F. Johnson (University College Hospital & Middlesex Hospital)
Great Ormond Street Hospital for Children	Dr A. Mackersie		
Greenwich Healthcare	Mr S. Asher	West Middlesex University Hospital	Dr R.G. Hughes
Guy's & St Thomas'	Mr W.J. Owen (St Thomas' Hospital)	Whipps Cross University Hospital	Ms P. Hewer
	No named reporter (Guy's Hospital)	Whittington Hospital	Dr S. Ramachandra
Hammersmith Hospitals	Professor G.W.H. Stamp		

NORTH WEST

Hillingdon Hospital	Dr F.G. Barker		
Homerton Hospital	Mrs S. Kimenye	Aintree Hospitals	Dr W. Taylor
King's Healthcare	Mrs S. Bowler	Blackburn, Hyndburn & Ribble Valley Healthcare	Mr R.W. Nicholson
Kingston Hospital	Mr P. Willson	Blackpool Victoria Hospital	Dr K.S. Vasudev
Lewisham Hospital	Dr G. Phillip	Bolton Hospitals	Dr S. Wells
Mayday Health Care	Mr C. Fernandez	Burnley Health Care	Mr D.G.D. Sandilands
Moorfields Eye Hospital	Professor P. Luthert	Bury Health Care	Ms M. Ince
Newham Healthcare	Dr C. Grunwald	Cardiothoracic Centre Liverpool	Dr M. Jackson
North Middlesex Hospital	Dr K.J. Jarvis	Central Manchester & Manchester Children's University Hospitals	Dr M. Newbould
North West London Hospitals	Dr C.A. Amerasinghe (Central Middlesex Hospital)		
	Dr G. Williams (Northwick Park Hospital & St Mark's Hospital)		(Booth Hall Children's Hospital & University Hospitals Royal Manchester Children's Hospital)
Queen Mary's Sidcup	Dr E.J.A. Aps		
Royal Brompton & Harefield	Mrs S. Da Silva (Harefield Hospital)		
	Professor D. Denison (Royal Brompton Hospital)		Dr E.W. Benbow (Manchester Royal Infirmary)
Royal Free Hampstead	Dr J.E. McLaughlin	Chorley & South Ribble	Dr M. Calleja
Royal Marsden Hospital	Dr J. Williams		
		Christie Hospital	Miss S.T. O'Dwyer
Royal National Orthopaedic Hospital	Mrs K. Harris	Countess of Chester Hospital	Dr W.E. Kenyon
St George's Healthcare	Dr C.M. Corbishley	East Cheshire	Dr A.R. Williams

Liverpool Women's Hospital	Mr T. Caine
Mid Cheshire Hospitals	Miss H. Moulton
Morecambe Bay Hospitals	Dr R.W. Blewitt (Royal Lancaster Infirmary)
	Dr V.M. Joglekar (Furness General Hospital)
North Cheshire Hospitals	Dr K. Strahan (Halton General Hospital)
	Dr M.S. Al-Jafari (Warrington Hospital)
North Manchester Health Care	Dr D. Butterworth
Oldham	Mrs V. Davies
Preston Acute Hospitals	Mrs N. Leahey
Rochdale Healthcare	Dr M. Bradgate
Royal Liverpool & Broadgreen University Hospitals	Ms R. Dean
Royal Liverpool Children's	Mrs P.A. McCormack
Salford Royal Hospitals	Mrs E. Craddock
South Manchester University Hospitals	Dr J. Coyne
Southport and Ormskirk Hospitals	Dr S.A.C. Dundas
St Helens & Knowsley Hospitals	Mr M. Atherton
Stockport Acute Services	Dr M.W.J. Cutts
Tameside and Glossop Acute Services	Dr A.J. Yates
Trafford Healthcare	Ms S. Mountain
Walton Centre for Neurology & Neurosurgery	Dr J. Broome
Wirral Hospital	Dr M.B. Gillett
Wrightington, Wigan & Leigh	Mrs P. Sharkey (Royal Albert Edward Infirmary)
	Dr J.M. Frayne (Wrightington Hospital)

NORTHERN & YORKSHIRE

Airedale	Dr J.J. O'Dowd
Bradford Hospitals	Dr C.A. Sides
Calderdale & Huddersfield	Mr R.J.R. Goodall (Calderdale Royal Hospital)
	Mr A.W.F. Milling (Huddersfield Royal Infirmary)
City Hospitals Sunderland	Miss K. Ramsay
Dewsbury Health Care	Dr P. Gudgeon
Gateshead Health	Dr A. McHutchon
Harrogate Healthcare	Miss A.H. Lawson
Hull and East Yorkshire Hospitals	Mrs J. Fountain (Hull Royal Infirmary & Princess Royal Hospital)
	Mr G. Britchford (Westwood Hospital & Castle Hill Hospital)
Leeds Teaching Hospitals	Dr C. Abbott (Leeds General Infirmary)
	Mr S. Knight (St James's University Hospital)
Newcastle upon Tyne Hospitals	Miss D. Wilson (Royal Victoria Infirmary & Newcastle General Hospital)
	Dr M.K. Bennett (Freeman Hospital)
North Cumbria Acute Hospitals	Mr B. Earley (West Cumberland Hospital)
	Dr P. Stride (Cumberland Infirmary)
North Durham Healthcare	Miss S. Green

North Tees and Hartlepool	Mr I.L. Rosenberg (University Hospital of North Tees)
	Mrs A. Lister (University Hospital of Hartlepool)
Northallerton Health Services	Dr D.C. Henderson
Northumbria Healthcare	Dr A. Coleman (Hexham General Hospital)
	Dr S. Johri (North Tyneside General Hospital)
	Dr J. Rushmer (Wansbeck General Hospital)
Pinderfields & Pontefract Hospitals	Dr I.W.C. Macdonald
Scarborough & North East Yorkshire Health Care	Dr A.M. Jackson
South Durham Healthcare	Mr K. Naylor
South Tees Hospitals	Ms S. Goulding
South Tyneside Healthcare	Dr K.P. Pollard
York Health Services	Dr C. Bates

SOUTH EAST

Ashford & St Peter's Hospital	Mrs B. Driver (Ashford Hospital)
	Mrs E. Simmonds (St Peter's Hospital)
Brighton Health Care	Mr M. Renshaw
Dartford & Gravesham	Mrs R. Ballentyne
East Kent Hospitals NHS Trust	Ms M. Harvey
Eastbourne Hospitals	Mrs P. Jones
Frimley Park Hospitals	Dr G.F. Goddard
Hastings & Rother	Mr S. Ball
Heatherwood and Wexham Park Hospitals NHS Trust	Ms J. Hartley
Isle of Wight Healthcare	Ms S. Wilson

Kettering General Hospital	Dr J.A.H. Uraiby
Maidstone & Tunbridge Wells	Mr N. Munn
Medway Maritime	Mrs J.L. Smith
Mid-Sussex	Dr P.A. Berresford (Princess Royal Hospital)
	Mr P.J. Ward (Hurstwood Park Neurological Centre)
Milton Keynes General	Dr S.S. Jalloh
North Hampshire Hospitals	Ms A. Timson
Northampton General Hospital	Dr A.J. Molyneux
Nuffield Orthopaedic Centre	Dr P. Millard
Oxford Radcliffe Hospital	Dr P. Millard (John Radcliffe Hospital & Radcliffe Infirmary)
	Dr N.J. Mahy (Horton Hospital)
Portsmouth Hospitals	Dr N.J.E. Marley (St. Mary's Hospital & Queen Alexandra Hospital
	Dr.Y. Ansah Boaeteng (Royal Hospital)
Queen Victoria Hospital	Mrs D.M. Helme
Royal Berkshire & Battle Hospitals	Dr R. Menai-Williams
Royal Surrey County Hospital	Mrs G. Willner
Royal West Sussex	Mr J.N.L. Simson
South Buckinghamshire	Dr M.J. Turner
Southampton University Hospitals	Mrs S. Milne
Stoke Mandeville Hospital	Dr A.F. Padel
Surrey & Sussex Healthcare	Mrs M. Stoner
Winchester & Eastleigh Healthcare	Dr R.K. Al-Talib
Worthing & Southlands Hospitals	Mrs M. Miles

SOUTH WEST

East Gloucestershire	Dr W.J. Brampton
East Somerset	Dr J.P. Sheffield
Gloucestershire Royal	Dr P. Sanderson
North Bristol	Dr N.B.N. Ibrahim (Frenchay Hospital)
	Ms T. Lucas (Southmead Hospital)
Northern Devon Healthcare	Dr J. Davies
Plymouth Hospitals	Dr C.B.A. Lyons
Poole Hospital	Mr P. Stebbings
Royal Bournemouth & Christchurch Hospitals	Mrs E. Hinwood
Royal Cornwall Hospitals	Mrs M. Manser
Royal Devon & Exeter Healthcare	Dr R.H.W. Simpson
Royal United Hospital Bath	Ms L. Hobbs
Salisbury Health Care	Dr S. M. Khan
South Devon Healthcare	Dr N.G. Ryley
Swindon & Marlborough	Mr M.H. Galea
Taunton & Somerset	Dr B. Browne
United Bristol Healthcare	Dr M. Ashworth (Bristol Royal Hospital for Sick Children)
	Mr J. Murdoch (St Michael's Hospital)
	Mr R.A. Harrad (Bristol Eye Hospital)
	Dr E.A. Sheffield (Bristol General Hospital & Bristol Royal Infirmary)
West Dorset General Hospitals	Dr A. Anscombe
Weston Area Health	Dr M.F. Lott

TRENT

Barnsley District General Hospital	Dr M.A. Longan
Chesterfield & North Derbyshire Royal Hospital	Dr R.D. Start
Doncaster and Bassetlaw Hospital	Dr G. Kesseler (Montagu Hospital & Doncaster Royal Infirmary)
	Dr S. Beck (Bassetlaw District General Hospital)
Northern Lincolnshire & Goole Hospitals	Dr W.M. Peters (Diana Princess of Wales Hospital)
	Dr C.M. Hunt (Goole & District Hospital & Scunthorpe General Hospital)
Nottingham City Hospital	Mrs C. Wright
Queen's Medical Centre Nottingham University Hospital	Dr J.A. Jones
Rotherham General Hospitals	Ms H. Gooch
Sheffield Children's Hospital	Dr I. Barker
Sheffield Teaching Hospitals	Dr S.K. Suvarna
Sherwood Forest Hospitals	Mr P. Bend (King's Mill Hospital)
	Dr I. Ross (Newark Hospital)
Southern Derbyshire Acute Hospitals	Mr J.R. Nash
United Lincolnshire Hospitals	Dr J.A. Harvey (Lincoln County Hospital)
	Dr D. Clark (Grantham and District Hospital)
	Ms S. Sinha (Pilgrim Hospital)

University Hospitals
of Leicester

Mr M.J.S. Dennis
(Leicester General
Hospital)

Mr S. Hainsworth
(Leicester Royal
Infirmary)

Mrs S. Clarke
(Glenfield Hospital)

WEST MIDLANDS

Birmingham Childrens Hospital	Dr P. Ramani
Birmingham Heartlands & Solihull	Dr M. Taylor
Birmingham Women's Healthcare	Dr M. Mitze
Burton Hospitals	Dr N. Kasthuri
City Hospital	Dr S.Y. Chan
Dudley Group of Hospitals	Mr G. Stevens
George Eliot Hospital	Dr D. Bose
Good Hope Hospital	Dr J. Hull
Hereford Hospitals	Dr F. McGinty
Mid Staffordshire General Hospitals	Dr V. Suarez
North Staffordshire Hospital	Dr T.A. French
Princess Royal Hospital	Dr R.A. Fraser
Robert Jones & Agnes Hunt Orthopaedic Hospital	Mrs C. McPherson
Royal Orthopaedic Hospital	Mr A. Thomas
Royal Shrewsbury Hospitals	Dr R.A. Fraser
Royal Wolverhampton Hospitals	Dr J. Tomlinson
Sandwell Healthcare	Mrs I. Darnley
South Warwickshire General Hospitals	Dr R. Brown
University Hospital Birmingham	Professor E.L. Jones
University Hospitals of Coventry and Warwickshire	Dr J. Macartney
Walsall Hospitals	Dr Y.L. Hock

Worcestershire Acute
Hospitals

Ms S. Lisseman

NORTHERN IRELAND

Altnagelvin Hospitals	Dr J.N. Hamilton
Armagh & Dungannon	Mr B. Cranley
Belfast City Hospital	Mrs A. McAfee
Causeway	Dr C. Watters
Craigavon Area Hospital Group	Mr B. Cranley
Down Lisburn	Dr B. Huss (Lagan Valley Hospital)
	Dr N. Storey (Downe Maternity Hospital)
	Dr M. Milhench (Downe Hospital)
Green Park Healthcare	Dr J.D.R. Connolly
Mater Hospital Belfast	Dr P. Gormley
Newry & Mourne	Mr B. Cranley
Royal Group of Hospitals & Dental Hospitals	Mr M. McDonald
Sperrin Lakeland	Dr W. Holmes (Erne Hospital)
	Dr F. Robinson (Tyrone County Hospital)
Ulster Community & Hospitals NHS Trust	Dr T. Boyd
United Hospitals	Mr I. Garstin (Antrim Hospital)
	Mr D. Gilroy (Whiteabbey Hospital)
	Mr P.C. Pyper (Mid-Ulster Hospital)

WALES

Bro Morgannwg	Dr A. Dawson (Neath General Hospital)
	Dr A.M. Rees (Princess of Wales Hospital)
Cardiff and Vale	Dr A.G. Douglas-Jones (University Hospital of Wales)
	Dr R. Attanoos (Llandough Hosp Mrs M. Keenor (Cardiff Royal Infirmary)
Carmarthenshire	Dr R.B. Denholm (West Wales General Hospital)
	Dr L. Murray (Prince Philip Hospital)
Ceredigion & Mid Wales	Mrs C. Smith
Conwy & Denbighshire	Dr B. Rogers
Gwent Healthcare	Dr M. Rashid (Royal Gwent Hospital)
	Dr G. Evans (Nevill Hall Hospital)
North East Wales	Dr A.H. Burdge
North Glamorgan	Mrs A. Shenkorov
North West Wales	Dr A.W. Caslin
Pembrokeshire & Derwen	Dr G.R. Melville Jones
Pontypridd & Rhondda	Dr D. Stock
Swansea	Dr S. Williams (Singleton Hospital)
	Dr A. Dawson (Morriston Hospital)

DEFENCE SECONDARY CARE AGENCY

Princess Mary's Hospital	Sqdn Ldr J.M. Lewis-Russell

GUERNSEY/ISLE OF MAN/JERSEY

Guernsey	Ms J. Ellyatt
Isle of Man	Ms E. Clark
Jersey	Dr H. Goulding

ABBEY HOSPITALS LTD.

Abbey Caldew Hospital	Ms V. Holliday
Abbey Gisburne Park Hospital	Ms A. Cooke
Abbey Park Hospital	Ms J. Colyer
Abbey Sefton Hospital	Mr A. Stewart

ASPEN HEALTHCARE

Holly House Hospital	Ms J. Row
Parkside Hospital	Ms H. Bradbury

BMI HEALTHCARE

Alexandra Hospital	Mrs P. Enstone
Bath Clinic	Mrs E.M. Jones
Beardwood Hospital	Ms S. Greenwood
Beaumont Hospital	Mrs C. Power
Bishops Wood Hospital	Ms D. Dorken
Blackheath Hospital	Mrs V. Power
Chatsworth Suite, Chesterfield & N Derbyshire	Ms S. Darbyshire

Chaucer Hospital	Mrs G. Mann
Chelsfield Park Hospital	Ms C. Poll
Chiltern Hospital	Ms J. Liggitt
Clementine Churchill Hospital	Ms S. Latham
Droitwich Spa Hospital	Mrs P. Fryer
Esperance Hospital	Mrs S. Mulvey
Fawkham Manor Hospital	Miss C. Stocker
Garden Hospital	Ms J. Benson
Goring Hall Hospital	Mrs A. Bailey
Hampshire Clinic	Mrs R. Phillips
Harbour Hospital	Ms S. Prince
Highfield Hospital	Ms P. Shields
Kings Oak Hospital	Mrs C. Le May
London Independent Hospital	Mrs U. Palmer
Manor Hospital	Mrs S. Otter
Meriden Wing, Walsgrave Hospital	Ms C. Ayton
Nuneaton Private Hospital	Mrs A. Garner
Paddocks Hospital	Ms S. Hill
Park Hospital	Mrs S. Quickmire
Princess Margaret Hospital	Mrs J. Gough
Priory Hospital	Dr A.G. Jacobs
Ridgeway Hospital	Mrs R. Butler
Runnymede Hospital	Mrs P. Hill
Sandringham Hospital	Mr S. Harris
Sarum Road Hospital	Ms Y.A. Stoneham
Saxon Clinic	Mrs V. Shiner
Shelburne Hospital	Mrs M. Jones
Shirley Oaks Hospital	Mrs S. White
Sloane Hospital	Miss J. Matthews
Somerfield Hospital	Mrs M. Lewis
South Cheshire Private Hospital	Mrs A. Peake
Thornbury Hospital	Mrs J. Cooper
Three Shires Hospital	Mrs C. Beaney
Werndale Hospital	Mrs A. Morgan
Winterbourne Hospital	Mrs S. Clark

BUPA

BUPA Alexandra Hospital	Mrs J. Witherington
BUPA Belvedere Hospital	Mrs E. Vincent
BUPA Cambridge Lea Hospital	Miss M. Vognsen
BUPA Chalybeate Hospital	Miss M. Falconer
BUPA Dunedin Hospital	Ms E. Prior
BUPA Fylde Coast Hospital	Mrs D. Hodgkins
BUPA Gatwick Park Hospital	Mrs A-M. Hanley
BUPA Hartswood Hospital	Ms S. Fraser-Betts
BUPA Hastings Hospital	Mrs S. Parsons
BUPA Hospital Bristol	Miss M. O'Toole
BUPA Hospital Bushey	Mrs J. Salmon
BUPA Hospital Cardiff	Dr A. Gibbs
BUPA Hospital Clare Park	Ms M. Wood
BUPA Hospital Elland	Ms V. Cryer
BUPA Hospital Harpenden	Ms S. Ryan
BUPA Hospital Hull & East Riding	Mrs K. Newton
BUPA Hospital Leeds	Mr D. Farrell
BUPA Hospital Leicester	Mrs C.A. Jones
BUPA Hospital Little Aston	Mrs J. Moore
BUPA Hospital Manchester	Ms A. McArdle
BUPA Hospital Norwich	Ms J. Middows
BUPA Hospital Portsmouth	Mrs J. Ward
BUPA Methley Park Hospital	Mrs J. Shaw
BUPA Murrayfield Hospital	Miss J.C. Bott
BUPA North Cheshire Hospital	Mrs A. Parry
BUPA Parkway Hospital	Mrs M.T. Hall
BUPA Redwood Hospital	Miss A.M. Hanley
BUPA Regency Hospital	Ms D. Davies
BUPA Roding Hospital	Mrs D. Britt
BUPA South Bank Hospital	Ms C. Stubbs
BUPA St Saviour's Hospital	Mr N. Bradley
BUPA Tunbridge Wells Hospital	Mrs B. Thorp

BUPA Washington Hospital	Ms J. Davis
BUPA Wellesley Hospital	Mrs P. Stellon
BUPA Yale Hospital	Mrs J. Bidmead

COMMUNITY HOSPITALS GROUP

Ashtead Hospital	Ms R. Hackett
Berkshire Independent Hospital	Ms J. McCrum
Duchy Hospital	Ms D. Martin
Euxton Hall Hospital	Ms B. Dickinson
Fitzwilliam Hospital	Ms S. Needham
Fotheringhay Suite	Ms G. Jones
Fulwood Hall Hospital	Ms C. Aucott
Mount Stuart Hospital	Ms J. Abdelrahman
New Hall Hospital	Ms H.L. Cole
North Downs Hospital	Mrs M. Middleton
Oaklands Hospital	Mrs I. Russell
Oaks Hospital	Ms M. Gallifent
Park Hill Hospital	Ms D. Abbott
Pinehill Hospital	Ms K. Elliott
Renacres Hall Hospital	Ms A. Shannon
Rivers Hospital	Ms K. Handel
Rowley Hall Hospital	Ms L. Serginson
Springfield Hospital	Ms J. Inggs
West Midlands Hospital	Ms F. Allinson
Winfield Hospital	Ms M. Greaves
Woodland Hospital	Ms L. Hutchings
Yorkshire Clinic	Ms J. Sands

HCA INTERNATIONAL

Harley Street Clinic	Ms S. Thomas
Lister Hospital	Mrs J. Norman
London Bridge Hospital	Ms Y. Terry
Portland Hospital for Women and Children	Miss A.D. Sayburn

Princess Grace Hospital	Mrs D. Hutton
Wellington Hospital	Mr R. Hoff

NUFFIELD HOSPITALS

Acland Hospital	Miss C. Gilbert
Birmingham Nuffield Hospital	Ms E. Loftus
Bournemouth Nuffield Hospital	Mrs E. Cornelius
Cheltenham & Gloucester Nuffield Hospital	Ms J.T. Cassidy
Chesterfield Nuffield Hospital	Mr P. Garrett
Cleveland Nuffield Hospital	Ms V. Lacey
Duchy Nuffield Hospital	Mrs T. Hampson
East Midlands Nuffield Hospital	Mrs C. Williams
Essex Nuffield Hospital	Mrs P. Turner
Exeter Nuffield Hospital	Mrs T. Starling
Grosvenor Nuffield Hospital	Mrs J.L. Whitmore
Guildford Nuffield Hospital	Mrs I. Houghton
HRH Princess Christian's Hospital	Ms S. Fisher
Huddersfield Nuffield Hospital	Ms B. Woodrow
Hull Nuffield Hospital	Mrs B. Menham
Lancaster & Lakeland Nuffield Hospital	Mrs K. McKay
Leicester Nuffield Hospital	Ms M. Damant
Lincoln Nuffield Hospital	Mrs E. Ashpole
Mid Yorkshire Nuffield Hospital	Miss M. Falconer
Newcastle Nuffield Hospital	Mrs D. Thornton
North London Nuffield Hospital	Ms B. Harrison
North Staffordshire Nuffield Hospital	Mrs S. Gowers
Nottingham Nuffield Hospital	Ms R. Bradbury
Plymouth Nuffield Hospital	Ms G. Mansfield

Purey Cust Nuffield Hospital	Mrs S.A. Brown
Shropshire Nuffield Hospital	Mrs S. Crossland
Somerset Nuffield Hospital	Mrs J.A. Dyer
Suffolk Nuffield Hospital	Ms S. Verow
Sussex Nuffield Hospital	Mrs F. Booty
Thames Valley Nuffield Hospital	Ms H. Dob
Tunbridge Wells Nuffield Hospital	Ms R. Stephens
Warwickshire Nuffield Hospital	Mrs J. Worth
Wessex Nuffield Hospital	Mrs V. Heckford
Woking Nuffield Hospital	Ms K. Barham
Wolverhampton Nuffield Hospital	Mr B. Lee
Wye Valley Nuffield Hospital	Mrs W.P. Mawdesley

OTHER INDEPENDENT HOSPITALS

Benenden Hospital	Mr D. Hibler
Foscote Private Hospital	Mrs L. Tuzzio
Heart Hospital	Ms A. Harvey
King Edward VII Hospital	Dr J. Halfacre
King Edward VII's Hospital Sister Agnes	Mrs J. Jordan-Moss
London Clinic	Mrs K. Perkins
St Anthony's Hospital	Ms C. Hagan
St Joseph's Hospital	Sister Bernadette Marie

APPENDIX G - PARTICIPANTS

CONSULTANT ANAESTHETISTS

These consultant anaesthetists returned at least one questionnaire relating to the period 1 April 1999 to 31 March 2000. We are not able to name all of the consultants who have done so, as their names are not known to us.

Abbott P.	Appadu B.	Barker G.L.	Bhaskaran N.C.
Ackers J.W.L.	Appleby J.N.	Barker I.	Bhatti T.H.
Adams T.J.	Aps C.	Barker J.P.	Bhishma R.
Adley R.	Archer P.L.	Barnard M.	Bingham R.
Adly-Habib N.	Armstrong R.F.	Barrera-Groba C.	Birks R.J.S.
Aglan M.	Arrowsmith A.E.	Barrett R.F.	Bishton I.
Ainley T.C.	Arrowsmith J.	Barrow P.	Biswas A.
Ainsworth Q.	Arthurs G.	Bastiaenen H.L.R.	Biswas M.
Akhtar M.	Ashurst N.H.	Baxandall M.	Blossfeldt P.
Akinpelu O.E.	Astley B.A.	Bayley P.	Blundell M.D.
Al Quisi N.K.S.	Atayi M.	Baynham P.R.W.	Boaden R.W.
Al-Shaikh B.Z.	Atherton A. M. J.	Beck G.P.	Board P.
Alexander R.	Aveling W.	Bedford T.	Bogod D.G.
Alexander-Williams M.	Babatola O.	Beeby C.P.	Bolton D.T.
Ali M.A.	Bachra P.	Bell J.	Bonner S.
Allan M.W.B.	Bailey C.R.	Bellamy M.C.	Boobyer M.D.
Allison N.	Bailie R.	Bellin J.M.	Boralessa H.
Allman K.G.	Bainton A.B.	Bem J.	Borman E.
Allt-Graham J.	Baker C.	Benham M.	Boscoe M.J.
Ammar T.A.A.	Baker J.R.	Beniston M.	Botha R.A.
Anathhanam J.J.	Balachandra K.	Berridge J.C.	Bousfield J.D.
Anderson J.	Balakrishnan P.H.	Berry C.	Bowden T.
Andrew L.	Ballard P.K.	Berthoud M.C.	Bowry A.
Andrews C.J.H.	Balmer H.G.R.	Bexton M.	Boyd I.M.
Andrews J.I.	Banks I.C.	Bhar D.	Boyd M.
Ankutse M.	Bapat P.	Bhasin N.	Boyd T.
Antrobus J.H.L.	Bardgett D.M.M.	Bhaskar H.K.	Boyd V.

Boys J.E.	Campbell D.N.	Collingborn M.	Dawson A.D.G.
Bracey B.J.	Campbell I.T.	Collins C.	Day C.
Bradburn B.G.	Campkin N.	Collis R.	Daya H.
Bradshaw E.	Caranza R.	Collyer J.	De Silva P.
Braithwaite P.	Carling A.B.	Columb M.	De Zoysa S.L.
Bramwell R.G.B.	Carnie J.C.	Colville L.J.	Deacock S.
Brandner B.	Carr B.	Conacher I.D.	Dearden N.M.
Braude N.	Carr C.M.E.	Coniam S.W.	Denny N.M.
Breen D.P.	Carter J.A.	Conn D.	Dent H.
Bremner W.G.	Carter J.H.	Cook L.B.	Desborough R.C.
Brim V.B.	Cartwright D.P.	Cooper A.E.	Desmond M.J.
Broadley J.	Cashman J.N.	Cooper D.	Deulkar U.V.
Broadway J.W.	Cattermole R.	Cooper J.	Devine A.
Broadway P.	Cave W.P.	Cooper P.D.	Devlin J.C.
Brocklehurst I.C.	Cavill G.	Cooper R.	Dexter T.
Brocklesby S.	Chaffe A.G.	Cooze P.H.	Dhariwal N.K.
Bromley P.	Challiner A.	Copp M.	Dhillon A.
Brooks A.M.	Chalmers E.P.D.	Craig R.	Diba A.
Brooks N.C.	Chamberlain M.E.	Criswell J.C.	Dichmont E.V.
Brooks R.J.	Chandradeva K.	Cross R.	Digby S.J.
Broomhead C.	Chapman J.M.	Cruickshank R.H.	Dinsmore J.
Brosnan C.	Charway C.L.	Cudworth P.	Dixon A.M.
Brown M.	Cheema S.	Culbert B.	Dixon J.
Brown R.	Chitkara N.	Cundill G.	Dobson A.
Brown R.M.	Choksi M.A.	Da Costa F.	Dobson P.M.S.
Browne G.	Christmas D.	Daniels M.	Doshi R.M.
Browning M	Chung R.A.	Dark A.	Dow A.
Brownlie G.	Chung S.K.N.	Dasey N.	Dowdall J.W.
Brunner H.	Church J.J.	Dash A.	Dowling C.
Bryan G.	Ciccone G.	Dashfield A.	Drake S.
Buckley P.M.	Clark R.	Daugherty M.O.	Drewery H.
Bulmer J.N.	Clarke T.N.S.	Daum R.E.O.	Dua R.
Burgess A.J.	Clements E.A.F.	Davies I.	Duffy C.
Burke S.	Clowes N.W.B.	Davies J.R.	Duggal K.
Burlingham A.N.	Coates M.B.	Davies M.	Duncan N.H.
Burnley S.	Cobner P.G.	Davies M.	Dunkley C.
Burns A.	Coe A.J.	Davies M.H.	Dunn S.R.
Burt D.	Coghill J.C.	Davies P.R.F.	Dunnill R.P.H.
Byrne A.J.	Coghlan S.	Davies R.	Durcan T.
Bywater N.J.	Cohen D.G.	Davies S.	Dutton D.
Caddy J.M.	Collier I.F.	Davis M.	Dwyer N.

Dwyer S.	Fielden J.	Gilliland H.	Hargrave S.A.
Dye D.J.	Filby H.J.	Girling K.	Harling D.H.
Eadsforth P.	Findlow D.	Glover D.J.	Harper J.
Earlam C.	Fitz-Henry J.	Goodall J.R.	Harpin R.
Eastwood D.	Fitzgerald P.	Gormley W.P.	Harris D.N.F.
Eccersley P.S.	Fletcher I.R.	Gothard J.W.W.	Harris J.W.
Edbrooke D.L.	Forrest E.	Gough M.B.	Harris R.W.
Edmends S.	Forrest M.	Goulden M.	Harris T.J.B.
Edmondson L.	Forster D.M.	Gouldson R.	Harrison N.
Edwards A.E.	Forster S.	Grant I.C.	Harvey A.
Edwards N.D.	Foster R.N.	Gray A.J.G.	Harvey D.C.
Edwards R.	Foxell R.M.	Gray C.	Hasan M.A.
Elliot J.M.	Fozard J.R.	Grayling G.G.	Hatcher I.
Elsworth C.	Francis G.A.	Green J.D.	Hawkins D.J.
Elton R.J	Fraser A.	Gregory M.A.	Hearn M.
Enani S.	Freeman J.	Greiff J.	Heath P.J.
Entwistle M.D.	Freeman J.	Greig D.G.	Hemming A.E.
Erwin D.C.	Friend J.	Grewal M.S.	Henderson K.
Eskander A.	Froese S.	Griffin R.	Henderson P.A.L.
Evans C.S.	Gabrielczyk M.R.	Griffiths D.E.	Heneghan C.P.H.
Evans F.E.	Gallagher M.	Griffiths H.B.A.	Hett D.
Evans G.	Gamlin F.	Griffiths R.	Hewlett A.M.
Evans K.	Ganado A.	Griffiths R.B.	Hicks I.R.
Evans M.L.	Gardner M.	Groom R.	Hill A.
Evans P.	Garrett C.P.O.	Grummitt R.	Hill S.
Evans R.J.C.	Gass C.W.J.	Grundy E.M.	Hille I.
Ewart I.A.	Gavin N.J.	Gupta S.	Hilton P.J.
Fairbrass M.J.	Gay M.P.	Guratsky B.P.	Hinds C.J.
Fairfield J.E.	Gaynor P.A.	Hadaway E.G.	Hitchings G.M.
Fairfield M.	Gell I.R.	Haigh A.	Hoad D.J.
Fale A.	Gemmell L.W.	Haines D.R.	Hobbiger H.
Farling P.A.	George S.	Hall G.M.	Hobbs A.
Faroqui M.H.	Ghaly R.G.	Hall J.	Hodgson C.A.
Farquharson D.	Ghobrial E.	Hambly P.	Hodgson R.M.H.
Farrell M.C.	Ghosh S.	Hamer M.S.F.	Hodzovic I.
Fawcett W.	Ghurye M.	Hamilton-Davies C.	Hoffler D.E.
Fazackerley E.J.	Gibson J.S.	Hamlin G.W.	Hogarth I.
Fearnley S. J.	Gill K.J.	Hampson J.M.	Hollis J.N.
Fell L.	Gill N.	Haq A.	Hollister G.R.
Fenner S.	Gill S.S.	Hardwick M.	Hollywood P.G.
Ferguson M.R.	Gillighan S.	Hardy I.	Holmes J.W.L.

Hopkinson J.M.	Jarvis A.P.	Kettern M.A.	Lewis P.
Horton W.	Jayarajah M.	Khanna V.K.	Lilburn J.K.
Hough M. B.	Jayaratnasingam S.	Kilner A.J.	Lilburn K.
Housam G.D.	Jefferies G.	Kilpatrick S.M.	Lillywhite N.
Howard E.C.	Jena N.M.	King T.A.	Lim G.H.
Howell S.	Jenkins B.J.	Kingsbury Q.D.	Lim M.
Howes D.	Jenkins C.	Kini K.J.	Lintin D.J.
Howes L.J.	Jennings F.O.	Kirby I.J.	Liu D.
Hughes A.	Jeyapalan I.	Kirk P.	Loader B.W.
Hughes J.	Johnson G.	Kneeshaw J.	Lockhart A.S.
Hughes J.	Johnson M.	Koehli N.	Logan S.W.
Hughes J.A.	Johnson R.W.	Kong K.L.	Longan M.A.
Hughes K.R.	Johnson T.W.	Koussa F.	Loveland R.
Hughes T.J.	Johnston C.G.	Kraayenbrink M.A.	Lowry D.W.
Hugo S.	Johnston P.	Kruchek D.	Loyden C.F.
Hull J.	Jones A.G.	Krupe I.	Luney S.
Hulse M.G.	Jones D.F.	Kulkarni A.	Lynch L.
Hunsley J.E.	Jones G.N.	Kusurkar A.	Lytle J.
Hunt P.C.W.	Jones H.E.	Kutarski A.A.	Macaulay D.
Hunt T.M.	Jones I.W.	Kyriakides K.	MacIntosh K.C.
Hunter S.J.	Jones K.E.	Lahoud G.	Mackaness C.
Hurst J.	Jones P.I.E.	Lake A.P.J.	Mackay J.H.
Hutchinson G.	Jones R.A.	Lam F.Y.	MacKenzie A.A.
Hutchinson S.E.	Jooste C.	Lamb F. J.	MacKenzie S.I.P.
Ince C.S.	Joshi P.	Lamberty J.	MacKinnon J.C.
Ingram G.S.	Justins D.M.	Landes A.	Macleod J.
Ingram K.S.	Kanagasundaram S.	Langham B.T.	Macleod K.G.A.
Irving C.	Kandasamy R.	Langton J.A.	MacLeod K.R.
Isaac J.L.	Kapoor S.C.	Latimer R.D.	Macmillan R.R.
Iskander L.N.	Kay P.M.	Laurenson J.	Madden A.P.
Jackson I.J.B.	Keeler J.	Lavies N.G.	Madej T.H.
Jackson R.M.	Keep P.J.	Lawton G.	Madhavan G.
Jagadeesh S.V.	Kelleher A.	Leach A.B.	Maher O.A.
Jaidev V.C.	Kelly C.	Leadbeater M.J.	Mahmood N.
Jaitly V.	Kelly D.	Lear G.	Maile C.J.D.
James D.	Kelsall P.	Lee K.G.	Makkison I.
James J.	Kendall A.P.	Lehane J.	Mallick A.
James R.H.	Kennedy A.	Leigh J.M.	Manam V.R.
James W.	Kent A.P.	Leng C.	Mannakara C.
Jamieson J.R.	Kerr K.	Levy D.M	Mannar R.
Jappie A.G.	Kesseler G.	Lewis D.G.	Mansfield M.

Manson E.	Mead M.	Mundy J.V.B.	O'Donoghue B.
Marsh R.H.K.	Meadows D.P.	Muralitharan V.	O'Donovan N.P.
Marshall A.G.	Mehta A.	Murphy J.	O'Kelly S.
Marshall F.P.F.	Meikle R.J.	Murphy P.	O'Riordan J.A.
Marshall P.	Mellor J.	Murphy P.G.	O'Sullivan G.M.
Martin A.J.	Mendham J.	Murray A.	Okell R.W.
Martin M.	Mensah J.A.	Murthy B.	Old S.
Masey S.A.	Messant M.	Myatt J.K.	Olivelle A.
Mason D.G.	Messer C.	Nagar M.	Olver J.J.
Mason J.S.	Metias V.F.	Nalliah R.S.C.	Onugha C.O.
Mather S.P.	Michael R.	Nancekievill M.L.	Oosthuysen S.A.R.
Matheson K.H.	Milaszkiewicz R.M.	Nandi K.	Orr D.A.
Matta B.	Millar J.M.	Nash J.	Page J.
Matthews P.J.	Millican D.L.	Nash P.J.	Page R.J.E.
Matthews R.F.J.	Mills G.H.	Nathanson M.H.	Page V.
Mayne D.J.	Milne B.R.	Nathwani D.	Pannell M.
Mazumder J.K.	Milne I.S.	Neasham J.	Pappin J.C.
McAndrew P.	Mitchell J.	Nejad Y.	Park J.
McAnulty G.R.	Mobley K.A.	Nel M.	Park W.G.
McAra D.	Moloney D.	Newby D.M.	Parker C.J.R.
McAteer M.P.	Monks P.S.	Newson C.	Parker J.R.
McAuley F.	Moore C.A.	Newton N.I.	Parkin G.
McConachie I.W.	Moore K.C.	Niblett D.J.	Parry H.M.
McCoy E.	Moores C.	Nicholl A.D.J.	Patel A.
McCrirrick A.	Morgan C.J.	Nicholls B.J.	Patel N.
McCrory J.W.	Morgan R.	Nickalls R.	Pateman J.A.
McCulloch W.J.D.	Morley A.	Nicol A.	Paterson I.
McDonald P.	Morris A.	Nithianandan S.	Pathy G.V.
McDowell D.P.	Morris K.	Norley I.	Patient P S
McEwan A.	Morrison A.	Norman B.	Paton H.
McGeachie J.F.	Morrow B.	Normandale J.P.	Payne N.E.S.
McGinty M.	Mosieri C.	Norris A.	Peacock J.E.
McGregor R.R.	Moss E.	Northwood D.	Pearson R.M.G.
McHutchon A.	Mottart K.	Norton A.C.	Pennefather S.H.
McIndoe A.	Moulla F.	Norton P.M.	Pepall T.
McLellan I.	Mousdale S.	Notcutt W.G.	Peters C.G.
McLeod T.J.	Moxon M.A.	Nunez J.	Phillips A.
McLoughlin C.	Mudie L.L.	O'Beirne H.A.	Phillips B.J.
McLure H.A.	Mukasa F.J.	O'Brien D.	Phillips K.A.
McMurray T.J.	Mulvey D.	O'Connor B.	Pick M.J.
McPherson J.J.	Mumtaz T.	O'Connor M.	Pierce J.M.T.

Pillow K.	Ratcliffe F.	Russell G.	Shribman A.J.
Pinnock C.	Ravalia A.	Ruston J.	Sides C.A.
Platt N.	Ravindran R.	Ryall D.M.	Sigston P.
Plumley M.H.	Rawle P.R.	Ryder W.	Simpson P.J.
Pocklington A.G.	Rawlings E.	Saad R.	Sinclair M.
Pollock C.G.	Rayner P.R.	Sabar M.	Sinden M.
Ponte J.C.	Razis P.A.	Saddler J.M.	Singh S.
Poole D.	Redfern N.	Saha D.	Sinha P.
Porter G.E.	Redman D.R.O.	Sainsbury M.	Sizer J.
Porter J.S.	Reeder M.	Saleh A.	Skilton R.
Potter F.A.	Rhodes A.	Sammut M.	Skinner A.C.
Poulton B.	Rich P.	Sanchez A.	Skinner J.B.
Powell D.R.	Richards A.	Sanders G.	Skoyles J.R.
Powell R.	Richards E.	Sanderson P.	Smith B.A.
Powles A.B.	Richards M.J.	Sanehi O.	Smith C.
Powroznyk A.V.V.	Richmond D.J.H.	Sanikop S.	Smith D.
Prasad B.	Rickford W.J.K.	Sarma V.	Smith H.S.
Pridie A.K.	Riddington S.	Saunders D.A.	Smith M.
Proctor E.A.	Riedel B.	Scawn N.	Smith M.
Prosser J.A.	Rigg C.	Schwarz P.A.	Smith P.
Pryle B.	Ritchie P.	Scott M.	Smith P.D.
Purcell G.	Robbins P.	Scott P.V.	Smith S.
Purday J.P.	Roberts F.L.	Scott R.	Smyth P.R.F.
Purdy G.	Robertson S.M.	Scott R.B.	Snape J.
Puttick N.	Robinson K.N.	Scull T.	Snape S.
Quader M.A.	Robinson P.N.	Scullion D.	Somanathan S.
Radford P.	Rogers C.M.	Scuplak S.	Soni N.C.
Radhakrishnan D.	Rogers J.	Searle A.E.	Southern D.
Rafferty M.P.	Romer H.	Sekar M.	Spanswick C.C.
Raftery S.M.	Rooney M.J.	Seymour A.H.	Speedy H.M.S.
Rajasekaran T.	Rose D.J.A.	Shah J.L.	Spencer E.M.
Rajendram R.	Rose N.	Shaikh R.	Spencer I.
Ralph S.	Ross M.T.	Shannon P.	Spittal M.
Ralston S.	Roulson C.	Sharpe R.	Sprigge J.S.
Rampton A.J.	Royle P.	Shaw I.H.	Spring C.
Ramsay T.M.	Roysam C.	Shaw T.C.	Squires S.J.
Ranasinghe D.	Ruff S.J.	Shaw T.J.I.	Stakes A.F.
Randall P.J.	Ruggier R.	Shawket S.	Stanton J.M.
Rao J.J.	Ruiz K.	Shearer E.	Staunton M.
Raphael G.	Rush E.	Sherwood N.	Steven C.M.
Rasanayagam R.	Rushmer J.	Shetty R.N.	Stevens A.J.

Stevens J.W.M.
Stevens K.D.
Stewart H.
Stoddart A.P.
Stokes M.
Stone P.G.
Stoneham M.
Stratford N.
Sudunagunta S.
Sumner E.
Sury M.
Swaine C.
Sweeney J.E.
Sweet P.T.
Swinhoe C.F.
Szafranski J.S.
Tandon B.
Taylor A.
Teasdale A.
Tehan B.
Tham L.
Thiagarajan J.
Thind G.S.
Thind J.
Thomas D.A.
Thomas D.I.
Thomas D.L.
Thomas D.W.
Thomas W.A.
Thompson H.
Thompson J.F.W.
Thornberry A.
Thorniley A.
Thornton R.J.
Timmins A.C.
Tofte B.C.
Tolhurst-Cleaver C.L.
Tomlinson P.
Tring I.C.
Trotter T.
Turner M.A.

Turner R.J.N.
Turtle M.J.
Twohey L.C.
Twohig M.M.
Tzabar Y.
Uddin S.M.K.
Umo-Etuk J.
Uncles D.R.
Vaidya A.
Valentine J.
Van Hamel J. C.
van Miert M.
Vater M.
Vaughan S.T.A.
Veall G.
Vella A.
Veness A.M.
Venkat N.
Venkataraman P.
Verghese C.
Vickers A.P.
Vijay V.
Vine P.R.
Vohra A.
Vuylsteke A.
Wade M.J.
Wagle A.
Waite K.E.
Walder A.
Waldmann C.S.
Walker G.
Walker H.A.C.
Wall T.
Walters F.
Walton D.P.
Ward R.M.
Ward S.
Wark K.J.
Warnell I.H.
Warwick J.
Waterland J.

Waters H.R.
Waters J.H.
Watkins T.G.
Watson D.
Watson D.M.
Watson D.M.
Watt J.M.
Watt S.
Weatherill D.
Weaver M.K.
Webb A.
Webb L.J.
Wedley J.R.
Wee L.
Weir P.
Weisz M.
Welchew E.A.
Wheatley E.
Whelan E.
Whibley H.K.
White J.B.
White S.
White W.D.
Wielogorski A.K.
Wijetilleka A.
Wilkey A.D.
Wilkins C.J.
Wilkinson K.
Will R.
Williams C.
Williams E.
Williams N.
Williams N.J.
Williams S.H.
Williamson A.
Wilson A.J.
Wilson A.T.
Wilson I.
Wilson S.
Windsor J.P.W.
Withington P.S.

Wolff A.
Wolverson A.S.
Wood D.W.
Wood P.J.
Woodall N.M.
Woodhouse M.
Woods I.
Woodsford P.V.
Wooldridge W.
Woollam C.H.M.
Wright E.
Wright J.
Wright M.M.
Wrigley S.
Wyse M.
Xifaras G.P.
Yanny W.A.
Yaqoob M.
Yate B.
Yates D.W.
Yetton R.
Young J.D.
Youssef H.
Youssef M.S.

APPENDIX H - PARTICIPANTS

CONSULTANT SURGEONS AND GYNAECOLOGISTS

These consultant surgeons and gynaecologists returned at least one questionnaire relating to the period 1 April 1999 to 31 March 2000.

Abercrombie J.F.	Andrews N.	Badger I.	Baxter J.N.
Abeyewickreme N.	Andrews S.	Badiuddin F.	Beacon J.P.
Ackroyd J.S.	Anson K.	Bailey M.E.	Beard J.D.
Adair H.M.	Antrum R.M.	Bain I.	Bearn P.
Adamson A.	Appleyard I.	Baird R.N.	Bearn P.
Adiseshiah M.	Apthorpe H.	Bajekal R.	Beck R.
Afify S.E.	Archer D.J.	Baker A.R.	Beckingham I.J.
Agunwa W.	Archibald D.	Baker W.N.W.	Bedford A.F.
Ahmad S.M.	Arkell D.G.	Bamford D.	Bedford N.A.
Ainscow D.A.P.	Armitage N.C.	Banks A.J.	Beggs F.D.
Ajulo S.O.	Armstrong C.P.	Bannister C.M.	Belcher H.
Al-Dadah Q.	Arnstein P.M.	Bannister G.C.	Bell B.A.
Al-Sabti A.	Ashour H.	Bannister J.J.	Bell K.M.
Albert J.S.	Ashworth M.	Bardsley D.	Bell M.S.
Alexander D.J.	Aspoas R.	Barham C.P.	Bellini M.J.
Ali D.	Atkinson S.	Barker J.R.	Benjamin J.C.
Allardice J.	Attwood S.E.A.	Barlow A.P.	Benke G.J.
Allen D.R.	Au J.	Barnes D.G.	Bennett S.
Allen M.	August A.	Barr H.	Bentley P.G.
Allen S.	Aukland A.	Barrie J.L.	Berry A.R.
Amrani M.	Aukland P.	Barrington R.L.	Berstock D.A.
Anderson D.R.	Ausobsky J.R.	Barsoum G.	Bett N.J.
Anderson I.D.	Austin C.	Basheer G.M.	Betts C.D.
Anderson J.T.	Avery B.S.	Bashir M.	Bevis C.R.A.
Andrew D.R.	Awad R.	Bassili F.S.	Bhattacharya S.
Andrews C.M.	Babajews A.V.	Battersby R.D.E.	Billings P.J.
Andrews C.T.	Backhouse C.M.	Bawarish A.	Bintcliffe I.W.L.

Birch N.	Brough S.J.	Carey J.	Coen L.D.
Bircher M.D.	Browell D.	Carlson G.L.	Cohen B.
Biswas S.P.	Brown A.A.	Carter C.J.	Cohen C. R.
Black R.J.	Brown C.	Carter J.L.	Cohen G.L.
Blackburn N.	Brown J.G.	Carty N.J.	Coleman N.
Blackburne J.S.	Brown J.N.	Case W.G.	Colin J.F.
Blackett R.L.	Brown M.J.K.	Cawdell G.M.	Collins F.J.
Blackford H.N.	Brown R.J.	Chadwick D.R.	Collins R.E.C.
Blacklock A.R.E.	Brown S.	Chakrabarty G.	Conybeare M.E.
Blair S.D.	Brown T.H.	Chan H.Y.	Cooke R.S.
Bloomfield M.D.	Browne A.O.J.	Chana G.	Cooke T.J.C.
Blower A.	Browne T.	Chandler C.	Cooke W.M.
Boardman K.P.	Browning N.	Chandrasekaran V.	Cooper G.J.
Bolger B.	Browse D.	Channon G.M.	Cooper J.C.
Bollen S.	Brunskill P.J.	Chapman M.A.S.	Cooper M.J.
Bolton-Maggs B.G.	Bryan A.	Chare M.J.B.	Cooper Wilson M.
Bonnici A.V.	Bryant P.A.	Charnley R.M.	Copeland G.P.
Bonser R.	Budhoo M.R.	Chatterji S.	Corbett W.A.
Booth C.M.	Buick R.G.	Cheatle T.R.	Corless D.J.
Borowsky K.	Bull P.D.	Cheshire N.	Corner N.
Botha A.	Bullen B.R.	Chilvers A.S.	Corson J.
Bourke J.B.	Burgess P.	Choksey M.S.	Cowen M.E.
Bradley J.	Burkitt D.	Choudhari K.A.	Cox P.J.
Bradley P.J.	Burnand K.G.	Chougle A.	Crabbe D.C.G.
Braithwaite P.A.	Butchart E.G.	Chumas P.D.	Crabtree S.D.
Brar A.	Byrne P.O.	Churchill M.A.	Crate I.D.
Brearley S.	Cade D.	Citron N.D.	Crawford D.J.
Brett M.	Cahill C.J.	Clague M.B.	Crawford R.
Brewster N.	Cairns D.W.	Clark D.W.	Crerand J.
Bridges J.	Calder D.A.	Clark G.W.B.	Crighton I.L.
Bridle S.H.	Cale A.R.J.	Clark J.	Cruickshank H.
Briffa N.	Callam M.J.	Clarke A.M.	Crumplin M.K.H.
Brigg J.K.	Callum K.G.	Clarke D.	Cullen P.J.
Britton B.J.	Calthorpe D.	Clarke J.	Cunliffe W.J.
Britton J.P.	Calvert P.T.	Clarke J.M.F.	Curley P.J.
Brockbank M.J.	Cameron A.E.P.	Clarkson P.K.	Currie I.
Brodribb A.J.M.	Campbell J.K.	Clason A.E.	Curtis M.
Bromage J.D.	Campbell P.	Clothier P.R.	Curwen C.
Brooke N.	Campbell W.B.	Coakham H.	Cuschieri R.J.
Brooks M.	Campbell W.J.	Cobb J.P.	D'Arcy J.C.
Brooks S.G.	Carey D.	Cobb R.A.	Da Silva A.

Dahar N.A.

Darke S.G.

Darzi A.

Das S.

Das Gupta A.R.

Davies A.H.

Davies C.J.

Davies H.G.

Davies J.

Davies J.N.

Davies N.

Davies R.M.

Davies-Humphreys J.

Davis C.H.G.

Davison O.W.

Dawson J.W.

Day A.C.

De Bolla A.R.

de Cossart L.M.

de Leval M.

Deacon P.B.

Deane A.M.

Deans G.

Dehn T.C.B.

Delicata R.J.

Deliss L.J.

Denton G.W.L.

Derodra J.

Derry C.D.

Desai J.B.

Desai K.M.

Dewar E.P.

Dhebar M.I.

Dias P.S.

Dickson W.A.

Dingle A.F.

Dixon A.R.

Dixon J.H.

Donaldson P.J.

Donnell S.

Donovan I.A.

Dormandy J.A.

Douglas D.L.

Dowell J.K.

Downing R.

Drabu K.J.

Drakeley M.J.

Duffy T.J.

Dunn J.

Dunn M.

Dunning J.

Dunning P.G.

Durham L.

Durning P.

Durrans D.

Dussek J.E.

Duthie J.S.

Dutta P.

Dykes E.

Dyson P.H.P.

Earnshaw J.J.

Earnshaw P.

Ebbs S.R.

Edmondson R.

Edmondson S.

Edwards J.L.

Edwards P. R.

El-Barghouti N.

El-Fakhri T.

Ellenbogen S.

Elliott M.J.

Ellis B.W.

Ellis D.J.

Ellis S.

Elsworth C.F.

Emmerson K.

Evans A.S.

Evans D.A.

Evans G.H.

Eyre-Brook I.A.

Fairbank A.C.

Fairbrother B.J.

Farhan M.J.

Farouk M.

Farouk R.

Farquharson-Roberts M.A.

Farrington W.T.

Fayaz M.

Ferguson C.J.

Ferro M.

Fielding J.W.L.

Finan P.J.

Finch D.R.A.

Firmin R.K.

Flannery M.

Fleetcroft J.P.

Fligelstone L.

Flook D.

Flowerdew A.F.

Foley R.

Forrest L.

Forrester-Wood C.

Forsyth A.A.

Fortes Mayer K.D.

Forty J.

Fowler C.G.

Fox A.D.

Fox H.

Fox J.N.

Foy M.A.

Foy P.

Fozard J.B.J.

Friend P.J.

Gale D.

Galea M.

Gallagher P.

Gartell P.C.

Garvan N.

Gatzen C.

George B.D.

George N.J.R.

Geroulakos G.

Ghali N.N.

Ghosh S.

Gibb P.

Gibbons C.P.

Gibbs A.N.

Gibbs S.

Gibson R.J.

Gilbert H.W.

Gilbert P.

Gilling-Smith G.L.

Glasgow M.M.S.

Glass R.E.

Glazer G.

Goldie B.S.

Goodall R.J.R.

Goodman A.J.

Goring C.C.

Gosling D.C.

Gough A.L.

Gough M.J.

Gourevitch D.

Gowar J.P.

Grace D.L.

Graham K.

Graham T.R.

Grant A.J.

Greaney M.G.

Greatorex R.A.

Greiss M.E.

Griffin S.M.

Griffiths A.B.

Griffiths N.J.

Gryf-Lowczowski J.

Guest J.

Guy A.J.

Haggie S.J.

Haines J.F.

Hale J.E.

Hall C.

Hall J.H.

Hall R.I.

Halliday A.G.

Ham R.J.	Hendrickse C.	Iftikhar S.Y	Jones M.
Hamer D.B.	Hendry W.F.	Imman I.	Jones N.A.G.
Hammer A.J.	Hennessey C.	Imray C.H.E.	Jones P.A.
Hammonds J.C.	Hennigan T.W.	Ingham-Clark C.	Jones R.B.
Hancock B.D.	Henry A.D.	Ingram N.P.	Jones S.M.
Handley C.	Heras L	Ions G.K.	Joseph J.V.
Hands L.J.	Herring D.W.	Irvin T.T.	Jourdan M.H.
Hannon R.J.	Hershman M.	Irwin A.	Journeaux S.
Haray P.N.	Hewitt G.R.	Isgar B.	Joyce P.W.
Hardy S.C.	Hickey M.S.J.	Iskander I.S.	Kambouroglou G
Hariharan K.	Higman D.J.	Ismaiel A.H.	Kane P.J.
Harland R.N.L.	Hill J.T.	Ismail W.	Kanse P.
Harper P.H.	Hind R.	Ivory J.P.	Kapadia C.R.
Harper W.M.	Hinton C.P.	Iyer S.V.	Kar A.K.
Harris D.R.	Hitchcock R.	Izzidien A.Y.	Karanjia N.
Harris P.L.	Hocken D.B.	Jackson A.M.	Karat D.
Harrison B.J.	Hoile R.W.	Jackson D.	Karim O.
Harrison G.S.M.	Holden D.	Jacob J.S.	Kaye J.C.
Harrison J.D.	Holdsworth J.D.	Jadhav A.	Keenan D.J.M.
Harrison R.A.	Holdsworth P.J.	Jaffe V.	Keighley M.R.B.
Harrison S.C.W.	Holford C.P.	Jain S.	Kellerman A.J.
Harrison T.A.	Holland E.F.N.	Jakeways M. S.	Kennedy C.L.
Hart J.C.D.	Holland J.P.	Jakubowski J.	Kennedy R.H.
Hart R.O.	Holt M.	Jamdar J. K.	Kenney A
Hartfall W.G.	Hope D.T.	James E.T.R.	Kent S.J.S.
Hartley M.	Hopkinson B.R.	James M.I.	Keogh B.
Harvey C.F.	Horner J.	Jarvis A.C.	Kerr G.
Harvey D.R.	Hosie K.B.	Javle P.	Kerr R.S.C.
Harvey R.A.	Houghton P.W.J.	Jeffery I.T.A.	Kerrigan D.
Hasan A.	Hoyle M.	Jeffery P.J.	Kerry R.M.K.
Hassan A.I.	Huddy S.P.J.	Jeffery R.S.	Ketzer B.
Havard T.J.	Hulton N.R.	Jenkinson L.R.	Keys R.
Hawe M.J.G.	Humphreys W.V.	Jibril J.A.	Khaira H.S.
Hawthorn I.E.	Hunter D.C.	John T.G.	Khan A.H.
Hay D.J.	Hunter J.B.	Johnson D.	Khan F.
Haynes I.G.	Hunter S.	Johnson J.N.	Khan M.
Haynes S.	Hurley P.	Johnstone D.	Khan M.A.A.
Heath D.V.	Hurst P.A.	Jones C.	Khan M.Z.G.
Heather B.P.	Hutchins P.M.	Jones D.J.	Khan O.
Heddle R.M.	Hutchinson G.H.	Jones D.R.	Khoo D.
Helm R.H.	Hutchinson I.F.	Jones D.R.B.	Khoury G.A.

APPENDIX H - PARTICIPANTS

Kilby D.	Lee J.O.	Mackle E.J.	McLean N.R.
Kinder R.B.	Lee P.W.R.	MacSweeney S.	McNally M.
King A.	Lees T.A.	Madan M.	Mearns A.J.
Kings G.L.M.	Leese T.	Mady S.M.	Mellon J.K.
Kingsnorth A.N.	Leeson S.C.	Mahendran V.	Mellor S.
Kingston R.E.	Leicester R.J.	Maheson M.V.S.	Menzies D.
Kirby R.M.	Leitch J.	Majeed A.W.	Menzies-Gow N.
Kirwan P.	Lennard T.W.J.	Makar A.	Metcalfe-Gibson C.
Kitchen N.D.	Leveson S.H.	Mal R.K.	Meyer C.H.A.
Klimach O.	Lewis C.T.	Mallucci C.	Mfinanga R.E.
Kmiot W.A.	Lewis J.L.	Mannas D.	Miles A.J.G.
Knight M.J.	Lewis K.	Manning M.	Milewski P.J.
Knox A.J.S.	Lewis M.H.	Mansfield A.O.	Miller G.V.
Knox R.	Lewis M.P.N.	Manur K.	Milling A.W.F.
Kocialkowski A.K.	Lewis P.	Marsh G.	Millner J.
Kolar K.M.	Lewis W.	Marshall J.	Mills S.J.
Korsgen S.	Linsell J.C.	Martin J.L.	Mirza D.
Kourah M.A.	Lipton J.R.	Marzouk D.	Misra D.
Kramer D.G.	Little G.	Mason P.F.	Mitchell I.C.
Krishnamurthy G.	Littler B.	Mason R.C.	Mitchenere P.
Krishnan R.G.	Livesley P.J.	Matheson D.M.	Mohan J.
Kulatilake E.N.P.	Livingstone J.	Mathew B.G.	Mohsen A.
Kurdy N.	Lloyd D.A.	Mathias D.B.	Monk D.
Lagattolla N.	Lock M.	Matthews S.J.E.	Monson J.R.T.
Lahoti O.	Lock M.R.	Maxwell W.A.	Montgomery A.C.V.
Lam F.T.	Locker A.	Maybury N.K.	Moody A.
Lambert D.	Loh A.	Mayer A.D.	Moore A.J.
Lambert W.G.	Lonsdale R.J.	Maynard N.D.	Moore P.J.
Lamerton A.J.	Loosemore T.	Mbubaegbu C.	Morrell M.T.
Lane I.F.	Lopes A.	McAuliffe T.B.	Morris K.
Langkamer G.	Lord M.G.	McCollum C.N.	Mosieri J.
Lansdown M.	Lucarotti M.E.	McCollum P.T.	Mosley J.G.
Large S.R.	Luke I.	McCormick M.S.	Motson R.W.
Lau J.O.	Lyndon P.J.	McCutchan J.D.S.	Mowbray M.A.S.
Law N.	Lyttle J.A.	McDonald P.	Moyes S.
Lawrance R.J.	Macdonald D.A.	McGlashan J.A.	Mudan S.
Lawrence R.N.	MacEachern A.G.	McIlroy B.S.	Mudd D.G.
Lawson A.H.	MacFarlane R.	McIntosh I.H.	Mullan F.
Lawton F.	MacFie J.	McIrvine A.J.	Munsch C.M.
Lawton F.G.	MacGowan S.	McKie L.	Munson K.W.
Leather A.	Mackie C.R.	McKinley A.	Murali S.

Murday A.	Ormiston M.C.	Phillips N.	Rather G.
Murdoch J.B.	Osman F.A.	Phillips S.	Raut V.
Murphy D.J.	Osman I.S.	Philp T.	Ravi S.
Murray A.	Owen T.D.	Phipps R.S.	Rayter Z.
Murray A.	Owen W.J.	Pike J.	Read L.
Murray K.H.	Packer G.	Pillai R.	Reasbeck P.G.
Murray S.A.	Padgham N.	Pillay T.M.	Reddy P.
Muscroft T.	Paes T.	Piper I.H.	Redfern D.R.M.
Nada A.N.	Page R.D.	Plaha H.S.	Redmond E.
Nadkarni J.B.	Palmer B.V.	Pobereskin L.H.	Redwood N.
Nair U.	Palmer J.D.	Pollard R.	Reece-Smith H.
Nanu A.	Panayiotopoulos Y.	Ponting G.A.	Rees A.J.S.
Nargund V.	Papagrigoriadis S.	Poston G.J.	Rees B.I.
Nash A.G.	Papastefanou S.L.	Powell J.M.	Rees G.M.
Nash J.R.	Pape S.A.	Powis S.J.A.	Reid D.
Nashef S.A.M.	Pardy B.J.	Powles D.P.	Reilly D.
Nasra S.	Parekh S.	Pozzi M.	Reinbach D.
Naylor A.R.	Parker R.W.	Price A.J.	Reissis N.
Neal D.E.	Parkinson R.	Pritchett C.J.	Rela M.
Nelson I.W.	Parmar H.V.	Pryor G.A.	Rennie J.A.
Neoptolemos J.P.	Parr D.C.	Psaila J.V.	Renton S.
Neumann L.	Parr N.J.	Pullan R.	Reynolds J.R.
Newey M.L.	Parry G.W.	Puntis M.C.A.	Rhind J.R.
Newman J.H.	Parsons D.C.S.	Purkiss S.F.	Rhodes B.
Nicholas R.M.	Parvin S.	Pye J.K.	Rice R.
Nicholl J.	Patel A.	Querci Delle Rovere G.	Rich A.J.
Nicholson M.L.	Patel R.L.	Qureshi A.R.	Richardson D.
Nicholson R.W.	Paton R.W.	Radcliffe A.G.	Richardson P.
Nicholson S.	Patterson J.E.	Radford W.	Rickford C.R.K.
Nolan J.F.	Pattison C.W.	Rae D.M.	Ridge J.A.F.
Norris J.	Payne J.G.	Raftery A.T.	Rigg K.M.
North A.D.	Pearse M.F.	Raimes S.A.	Roberts L.J.
Norton E.R.	Pearson H.J.	Raines M.F.	Roberts P.N.
Nuseibeh I.	Pearson R.C.	Raj D.	Robertson C.
O'Donoghue D.	Pemberton R. M.	Raju K.S.	Robinson L.
O'Reilly G.	Pepper J.R.	Ramus N.I.	Robinson M.H.
O'Riordan B.	Pereira J.H.	Ranaboldo C.	Robson M.J.
O'Riordan J.	Perkins C.	Rangan A.	Rochester J.R.
Oates S.	Petri J.	Rao G.S.	Rooney P.S.
Obeid M.L.	Phelan P.S.	Rao S.	Rosenberg I.L.
Ohri S.	Phillips H.	Rate A.	Rosin M.D.

Ross E.R.S.	Selvakumar S.	Singhal H.	Stonelake P.
Ross S.A.	Selvan T.	Sivapragasam S.	Stoodley B.J.
Rossouw D.J.	Sengupta R.P.	Skidmore F.D.	Strachan C.J.L.
Rothwell N.	Sergeant I.D.	Skipper D.	Strachan J.R.
Roushdi H.	Sethia B.	Slater N.	Stuart A.E.
Rowe P.H.	Sethia K.K.	Slater R.N.S.	Sturzaker H.G.
Rowles J.	Shafqat S.O.	Slibi M.	Sulaiman S.K.
Rowley S.	Shah T.	Small P.	Super P.
Rowntree M.	Shaikh N.A.	Smith A.T.	Swift R.I.
Roxburgh J.C.	Shakespeare D.T.	Smith E.E.J.	Tabaqchali M.A.
Royle C.	Shandall A.	Smith S.R.G.	Tacconi L.
Royston C.M.S.	Shanker J.	Snooks S.J.	Tait W.F.
Rundle J.S.H.	Sharif H.I.	Somasundran G.	Talati V.R.
Rutter P.C.	Sharif M.A.	Soni R.K.	Tang D.
Ryan P.G.	Sharma A.K.	Soomro N.A.	Tasker T.P.B.
Sabin H.I.	Sharma R.K.	Souka H.	Taylor A.R.
Sadler G.	Sharr M.M.	South L.M.	Taylor B.A.
Sagar P.M.	Shaw D.L.	Speakman C.T.	Taylor L.
Sagar S.	Shaw J.	Springall R.G.	Taylor M.
Salem A.	Shaw N.J.	Spychal R.T.	Taylor R.S.
Salman A.	Shaw S.J.	Spyt T.	Taylor S.A.
Salter M.C.P.	Shea J.G.	Stacey-Clear A.	Teanby D.N.
Samuel A.W.	Shehata M.	Standfield N.J.	Templeton P.
Sanderson C.J.	Shenolikar A.	Staniforth P.	Thacker C.R.
Sansom J.R.	Shepperd J.A.N.	Stanley D.	Thomas D.G.T.
Sant Cassia L.J.	Sher J.L.	Stapleton S.	Thomas D.M.
Saran D.	Sherlock D.J.	Stebbing M.A.	Thomas D.R.
Sarang K.	Shieff C.L.	Stebbings W.S.L.	Thomas P.A.
Sarin S.	Shinkfield M.	Steingold R.F.	Thomas P.R.S.
Scammell B.	Shore D.F.	Stephen I.B.M.	Thomas R.J.
Schilders E.	Shorthouse A.J.	Stephen J.G.	Thomas T.L.
Schizas C.	Shrivastava M.	Stephenson G.C.	Thomas W.E.G.
Scholefield J.H.	Shute K.	Stephenson R.N.	Thompson D.
Scott I.H.K.	Silverman S.H.	Stewart D.J.	Thompson J.F.
Scott M.H.	Simms J.M.	Stewart J.	Thompson M.H.
Scott N.	Simo R.	Stewart R.D.	Thomson G.J.L.
Scott S.D.	Simson J.N.	Stirling W.J.I.	Thomson H.J.
Scriven M.	Singh D.	Stoddard C.J.	Thomson W.H.F.
Sefton G.K.	Singh G.	Stoker T.A.M.	Thorneloe M.H.
Sells R.A.	Singh J.	Stokes M.	Todd N.V.
Sellu D.	Singh S.	Stone C.D.P.	Todd R.C.

Tomouk M.W.	Walsh A.K.M.	Williams R.J.
Toon P.G.	Walsh C.J.	Williams R.J.
Treasure T.	Walsh M.	Williams W.
Tresadern J.C.	Walters A.M.	Williamson D.
Trevett M.	Wand J.S.	Williamson E.P.M.
Trotter G.	Ward R.G.	Williamson P.
Tsang T.T.	Wasserberg J.	Wilson B.G.
Tsang V.	Waterworth T.A.	Wilson N.V.
Tsui S.	Watkins L.	Wilson P.
Tubbs O.N.	Watkins R.M.	Wilson Y.G.
Tulloch C.J.	Watson D.C.T.	Windsor A.C.J.
Turnbull T.J.	Webster K.	Winslet M.C.
Turner A.G.	Wedgwood K.R.	Wise D.I.
Turner P.G.	Weir D.J.	Withanage A.S.
Tweedle D.E.F.	Welbourn R,	Wolverson R.L.
Twiston-Davies C.W.	Welch A.R.	Womack N.
Unsworth-White M.J.	Welch N.T.	Wood A.
Vaizey C.J.	Wells F.C.	Wood C.P.L.
Vale J.	Wellwood J.M.	Woodhouse C.R.J.
Varma T.	Wemyss-Holden G.	Woods D.
Vashisht R.	Wenham P.W.	Woods W.
Vaughan R.	Westaby S.	Woodward A.
Vaughan-Lane T.	Westwood C.A.	Woodyer A.B.
Veitch P.S.	Wheatley K.E.	Wootton J.
Velineni V.	Whiston R.	Worlock P.H.
Venn G.E.	White C.M.	Wray C.C.
Vennam R.B.	Whitehead S.M.	Wright K.U.
Vetrivel S.M.	Whiteley M.	Wyatt M.G.
Vine S.	Whyman M.R.	Wyman A.
Virdi J.	Wilkins D.C.	Wynne K.S.
Vohra R.K.	Wilkins J.L.	Yacoub M.H.
Waddington R.T.	Wilkinson D.	Yeo R.
Waldram M.A.	Wilkinson J.M.	Yeung C.K.
Walesby R.K.	Wilkinson M.J.S.	Young H.L.
Walker C.	Willett K.	Zafiropoulos G.
Walker D.I.	Williams C.	Zaidi A.Z.
Walker J.	Williams C.R.	Zaman M.M.
Walker M.A.	Williams G.	Zeraati M.
Walker R.T.	Williams G.T.	
Wallace R.G.H.	Williams H.	
Wallis J.	Williams J.G.	

APPENDIX I - EXCLUSIONS

OPCS Code	Description
A52	Therapeutic lumbar epidural injection
A53	Drainage of spinal canal
A54	Therepeutic spinal puncture
A55	Diagnostic spinal puncture
A70	Neurostimulation of peripheral nerve
A76	Chemical destruction of sympathetic nerve
A77	Cryotherapy to sympathetic nerve
A78	Radiofrequency controlled thermal destruction of sympathetic nerve
A79	Other destruction of sympathetic nerve
A83	Electroconvulsive therapy
A84	Neurophysiological operations
B37	Other operations on breast
C39.5	Radiotherapy to lesion of conjuctiva
C45.5	Radiotherapy to lesion of cornea
C82.3	Radiotherapy to lesion of retina
F14	Orthodontic operations
G21	Other operations on oesophagus
G47	Intubation of stomach
G57	Other operations on duodenum
G67	Other operations on jejunum
G82	Other operations on ileum
H30	Other operations on colon
H46	Other operations on rectum
K51	Diagnostic transluminal operations on coronary artery
K55	Other open operations on heart
K57	Other therapeutic transluminal operations on heart
K58	Diagnostic transluminal operations on heart
K60	Cardiac pacemaker system introduced through vein
K61	Other cardiac pacemaker system

OPCS Code	Description
K63	Contrast radiology of heart
K65	Catheterisation of heart
K66	Other operations on heart
L72	Diagositic transluminal operations on other artery
L95	Diagnostic transluminal operations on vein
M47	Urethral catheterisation of bladder
N34	Other operations on male genital tract
P06.4	Extirpation of lesion of vulva - Implantation of radioactive substance into vulva
P20.5	Extirpation of lesion of vulva - Implantation of radioactive substance into vagina
Q12	Intrauterine contraception device
Q13	Introduction of gemete into uterine cavity
Q14	Introduction of abortifacient into uterine cavity
Q15	Introduction of other substance into uterine cavity
Q55	Other examination of female genital tract
Q56	Other operations on female genital tract
R01	Therapeutic endoscopic operations on fetus
R02	Diagnostic endoscopic examination of fetus
R03	Selective destruction of fetus
R04	Therapeutic percutaneous operations on fetus
R05	Diagnostic percutaneous examination of fetus
R10	Other operations on amniotic cavity
R12	Operations on gravid uterus
R14	Surgical induction of labour
R15	Other induction of labour
R17	Elective caesarean delivery
R18	Other caesaraen delivery
R19	Breech extraction delivery
R20	Other breech delivery
R21	Forceps cephalic delivery
R22	Vacuum delivery
R23	Cephalic vaginal delivery with abnormal presentation of head at delivery without instrument
R24	Normal delivery
R25	Other methods of delivery
R27	Other operations to facilitate delivery
R28	Instrumental removal of products of conception from delivered uterus
R29	Manual removal of products of conceptions from delivered uterus
R30	Other operations on delivered uterus
R32	Immediate repair of obstetric laceration
R34	Other obstetric operations

OPCS Code	Description
T48	Other operations on peritoneum
T90	Contrast radiology of lymphatic tissue
V48	Denervation of spinal facet joint of vertebra
X17	Separation of conjoined twins
X29	Continuous infusion of therapeutic substance
X30	Injection of therapeutic substance
X31	Injection of radiocontrast material
X32	Exchange blood transfusion
X33	Other blood transfusion
X34	Other intravenous transfusion
X35	Other intravenous injection
X36	Blood withdrawal
X37	Intramuscular injection
X38	Subcutaneous injection
X40	Compensation for renal failure
X41	Placement of ambulatory apparatus for compensation for renal failure
X42	Placement of other apparatus for compensation for renal failure
X45	Donation of organ
X46	Donation of other tissue
X48	Immobilisation using plaster cast
X49	Other immobilisation
X50	External resuscitation
X51	Change of body temperature
X59.9	Unspecified anaesthetic without surgery
Y09	Chemical destruction of organ noc
Y12	Chemical destruction of lesion of organ noc
Y21	Cytology of organ noc
Y33	Puncture of organ noc
Y35	Introduction of removable radioactive material into organ noc
Y36	Introduction of non removable radioactive material into organ noc
Y38	Injection of therapeutic inclusion substance into organ noc
Y39	Injection of other substance into organ noc
Y53	Percutaneous approach to organ under image control
Y90	Other non-operations

APPENDIX J - CASE STUDIES BY SPECIALTY

Case Study	Procedure	Page
General Surgery		
2	Laparotomy	16, 71
4	Hemicolectomy	17
9	Hartmann's procedure	47
10	Whipples resection	47
11	Open drainage of abscess	47
12	Colectomy and cholecystectomy	48
15	Drainage of perineal abscess	55
16	Closure of colostomy	55
17	Partial proctocolectomy	55
18	Laparotomy	55, 104
19	Closure of perforated duodenal ulcer	55
21	Bronchoscopy	57
22	Closure of anastomosis of ileum	57
23	Extended hemicolectomy	57
24	OGD, laparotomy and gastrectomy	58
25	Abdominal washout	58
26	Cholecystectomy	58
27	Laparotomy	62
28	Oversew perforated gastric ulcer	63
29	Closure of perforated ulcer of duodenum	63
30	Hartmann's procedure	63
31	Abdominoperineal excision of rectum	64
35	Sigmoid colectomy	66
39	Sigmoid colectomy	68
40	Right hemicolectomy	68, 74
41	Repair of strangulated inguinal hernia	68

Case Study	Procedure	Page
42	Anterior resection of rectum	68
43	Subtotal colectomy	69
44	Repair of perforated transverse colon	71
47	Repair and reduction of femoral hernia	72
48	Cystocopy and TURT	72
49	Debridement of gluteal ulcer	72
50	Ileectomy and anastomosis of ileum to ileum	73
51	Closure of perforation of duodenum	73
52	Laparotomy - under running of bleeding duodenal ulcer	73
53	Sigmoid colon resection	73
54	Hemicolectomy	74
56	Abdoperineal resection	74
57	Laparotomy, biliary decompression (cholecystectomy)	80
58	Laparotomy	80
59	Laparotomy	80
60	Laparotomy, cholecystectomy	80
61	Partial gastrectomy	81
62	Closure of perforated ulcer of duodenum	81
63	Laparotomy and oversewing of duodenal ulcer	81
71	Sigmoid colectomy	97
72	Laparotomy	100
73	Laparotomy	103
74	Hemicolectomy	104
75	Appendicectomy following oesophagectomy	105
78	Nephrectomy	108
82	Laparotomy	111
83	Oesophagectomy	112

Gynaecology

8	Diagnostic laparoscopy	19
76	Laparotomy-	107
77	Hysterectomy	107
80	Hysterectomy	110

Neurology

81	Burrhole for biopsy	110

Case Study	Procedure	Page
Orthopaedics		
1	Closed reduction of fracture of long bone	15
5	Dynamic hip screw	17
6	Hemiarthroplasty	18
7	Open reduction of perforated ulcer of duodenum	18
13	Hemiarthroplasty	48
32	Sliding hip screw	64
33	Thompson's hip replacement	64
34	Shoulder replacement	66
36	Thompson's hip replacement	67
37	Hemiarthroplasty	67
38	Dynamic hip screw	67
46	Hemiarthroplasty	71
Vascular		
3	Below knee amputation	16
14	Repair of AAA	51
20	Embolectomy of femoral artery	56
45	Amputation of toe	71
55	Arterial bypass	74
64	Repair of AAA	86
65	Repair of AAA	87
66	Aortobifemoral graft	87
67	Femerotibial bypass	87
68	Repair of AAA	89
69	Repair of AAA	89
70	Repair of AAA	89
Otorhionolaryngology		
79	Tracheostomy	109